AF522607

# WHAT CONGRESS, GANDHI AND NEHRU HAVE DONE TO DR AMBEDKAR

## ALSO BY THE SAME AUTHOR

**Dr Ambedkar**
*The Man Who Shaped India's Democratic Republic* (English, Hindi, and Marathi) (2025)
**The Reserve Bank of India** (2023)
**Volume 5 (1997–2007)**
(Chairman, RBI History Advisory Committee)
**Future of the Indian Education System**
*How Relevant is the National Education Policy, 2020?* (2020)
**New-Age Technology and Industrial Revolution 4.0**
*Global Public Policy Issues in Economy, Democracy, National Security and World Peace* (2019)
**Bharat Ratna Dr Babasaheb Ambedkar**
*An Intellectual Colossus, Great National Leader and Universal Champion of Human Rights (Photo-Biography in English and Marathi)* (2016)
**Ambedkar:** *An Economist Extraordinaire* (2015)
**Ambedkar:** *Awakening India's Social Conscience* (An Intellectual Biography) (English and Marathi) (2014)
**Ambedkar Writes**
*Completed Writings of Dr Ambedkar* (Edited) (English, Marathi and Hindi) (2014)
Vol. I: Political Writings, Vol. II: Scholarly Writings
**Ambedkar Speaks** (2013)
*Seminal Speeches* Edited: Vol. I, II and III (English 300, Marathi 500)
**Trilogy on Ravindranath Tagore** (Marathi) (2011)
*Ravindranath Tagore: Yuga Nirmata Vishvamanav*
*Ravindranath Tagore: Samagra Sahitya Darshan*
*Bhaya Shoonya Chitta Jeth: 151 Pratinidhik Kavita*
**Untouchables** (2005, 2007)
*My Family's Triumphant Journey Out of the Caste System in Modern India*
(International Bestseller – in 15 languages)
**Monetary Policy, Financial Stability and Central Banking in India** (2006)
**Re-emerging India – A Global Perspective** (2005)
**Challenges to Indian Banking: Competition, Globalization and Financial Markets** (Edited) (1996)
**Monetary Economics for India** (1994)
**Aamcha Baap Aan Amhi** (Marathi, Family Autobiography) (1993)
***The first international bestseller in Marathi**, the book achieved its 200th edition milestone in April 2024. It has sold nearly a million copies in 15 languages, including English, French, Spanish, Korean and Thai.*

# WHAT CONGRESS, GANDHI AND NEHRU HAVE DONE TO DR AMBEDKAR

NARENDRA JADHAV

**Konark Publishers Pvt. Ltd**
206, First Floor
Peacock Lane, Shahpur Jat
New Delhi - 110 049
+91-11-4105 5065
india@konarkpublishers.com, us@konarkpublishers.com
www.konarkpublishers.com



ISBN: 978-81-963629-3-5

Edited by Preeta Priyamvada
Jacket design by Sourish Mitra
Typeset by Saanvi Graphics, Noida
Printed and bound in India by Thomson Press India Ltd

*Dedicated humbly and admiringly to:*

*The Four National Leaders*

*Dr Manmohan Singh*
*Smt Sonia Gandhi*
*Dr Mohan Bhagwat and*
*Shri Narendra Modi*

*with whom I have had the great privilege of working closely (in that order)*

# Contents

# Foreword

## by Professor Kevin Brown

It is a singular honor to have the privilege of writing this Foreword to Dr Jadhav's insightful book, *What Congress, Gandhi and Nehru Have Done to Dr Ambedkar*, about the relationship of Dr Ambedkar and Mohandas K. Gandhi. I first met Dr Jadhav in April 2010 at a Conference in celebration of the Fiftieth Anniversary of the Law Faculty of the University of Mumbai, where he delivered a brilliant keynote address. We met again two years later at a Conference entitled *Diversity, Discrimination and Social Exclusion in India and the USA*, sponsored by the Jindal Global Law School, where once again Dr Jadhav delivered the Keynote Address.

While sitting in the audience and listening to his informative talks, I was filled with a special pride because Dr Jadhav had received his PhD in Economics from Indiana University-Bloomington in 1986, the year before I started to teach at the Maurer School of Law at Indiana University. Thus, he was one of my university's own distinguished alums.

Dr Jadhav came to Indiana University in November 2016 to deliver the sixth annual Patrick O'Meara International Lecture. This is the most prestigious international lecture held every year on the Bloomington campus. Others who had delivered an O'Meara lecture included a Chairman of the US Senate Committee on Foreign Relations, the Executive Director of UNICEF, and a former US Presidential candidate who also served as the US Ambassador to both Russia and China.

During Dr Jadhav's visit to Bloomington, I had the distinct privilege of hosting a dinner for him at my home, attended by university dignitaries. As I was going to lead a group of Indiana University students on a 17-day trip to India in the summer, Dr Jadhav graciously offered to host my students for a dinner when we were in New Delhi. Not only did he and his gracious wife make good on that offer, but he also hosted another group of Indiana University students that I led to India in the summer of 2019.

Both groups of students expressed great admiration for the insights and knowledge Dr Jadhav imparted to them and considered his dinner one of the highlights of their trip.

The strength of *What Congress, Gandhi and Nehru Have Done to Dr Ambedkar* lies in the way Dr Jadhav discusses Gandhi's relationship with the Dalit struggle by focusing on Gandhi's conflicts with Ambedkar. In doing so, Dr Jadhav shows how Ambedkar's vision of Dalit liberation conflicted with that of Gandhi. And it crystallizes the shortcomings of Gandhi's vision for overcoming the historic discrimination visited upon Dalits by caste Hindus.

For anyone seeking to understand those shortcomings, which continue to limit India's ability to rectify its past and ongoing discrimination against Dalits, this book is a necessary read. As an African-American scholar steeped in the struggles of both Dalits and African-Americans, the most effective Foreword I could write is one that shows how *What Congress, Gandhi and Nehru Have*

*Done to Dr Ambedkar* plays into a fundamental reassessment of the relationship of the African-American Community to issues of oppression on the Indian subcontinent.

By the mid-1930s, Gandhi's reputation in the African-American Community as someone deeply committed to both Indian independence and abolishing untouchability was firmly established. So much so that during 1936, several prominent African-American leaders came to India and interacted with Gandhi. Their journeys to India occurred at the same time that Ambedkar was composing his masterpiece, *Annihilation of Caste*, and Gandhi was responding to the criticisms in it.

Dr Jadhav's book is extraordinarily helpful in this regard. Given the high esteem that the African-American Community has for Gandhi, any meaningful reappraisal of the African-American relationship with Dalits has to start by revisiting the relationship of Gandhi to the Dalit struggle. For African-Americans, Gandhi was the focal point of the dual victory of the Indian independence movement that drew so many African-Americans to the cause of the Indian Freedom Fighters.

While the African-American Community knew Gandhi well, it did not know Ambedkar. Thus, there is no better way for African-Americans to revisit the relationship of Gandhi to the Dalit struggle than by discussing Gandhi's conflicts with Ambedkar. In providing Ambedkar's alternative perspective and arguments on the struggle of Dalits, Dr Jadhav is spelling out the limits of Gandhi's vision for abolishing untouchability.

African-American leaders will certainly pay close attention to Ambedkar's insights as the primary historical spokesperson for the Dalits because African-Americans have long experienced whites who speak about us on our behalf. We already know that it is impossible for whites to tell our story the way we can.

In closing, I want to refer to an old African proverb, "Until lions have their historians, tales of the hunt shall always glorify the hunter".

**Kevin Brown**
Mitchell S. Willoughby Distinguished Professor,
Joseph F. Rice School of Law, University of South Carolina;
Richard S. Melvin Professor Emeritus,
Indiana University Maurer School of Law
Bloomington, Indiana, USA

# Prologue

## Gandhi–Ambedkar: Clash of Titans Begins

Date: 14 August 1931
Place: Mani Bhavan, Mumbai

Two great minds were going to come face-to-face for the first time that day. The contrast between their personalities could not have been sharper. One was a lean figure, half clad in traditional Indian garb while the other one was a stocky figure, elegantly dressed in Western attire. One was resolute, yet soft-spoken while the other was an emerging firebrand. One was born in an affluent family—the son of the *Diwan* of Porbandar state in Gujarat, while the other was born in a poor family—the son of a school teacher in the British Army. One was brought up in an Upper Caste conservative Hindu family, whereas the other was raised in a family of Untouchables—whose mere touch would cause pollution and even shadow meant irreverence.

Divergent upbringings between the two had played an important role in their public personalities. While one had assimilated the essential influences of the *Vaishnavite* tradition, including vegetarianism, fasting for self-purification and compassion for all living beings; the other had come up against all odds, suffering from Caste-based discrimination and humiliation which made him strong-willed and combative. One was already called *Mahatma* (Great Soul) while the other was going to be called *Mahamanav* (Great Human Being). The two great leaders meeting on that momentous day were Mohandas Karamchand Gandhi (i.e., Mahatma Gandhi) and Dr Bhimrao Ramji Ambedkar (i.e., Dr Babasaheb Ambedkar).

Gandhiji was 22 years older than Dr Ambedkar. In fact, he had already become a barrister in England around the time Bhimrao was born (1891). Coincidentally, by the time Dr Ambedkar himself became a barrister in 1922, Gandhiji had already emerged as a prominent national leader in India's struggle for freedom.

Dr Ambedkar had known of Gandhiji for quite some time, but had not had the opportunity for one-on-one interaction. He was aware of Gandhiji's accomplishments—his return to India in 1915 after successfully leading the non-violent movement for civil rights of the Indian community in South Africa and his efforts to organize peasants, farmers and labourers in India at Champaran (Bihar) and Kheda (Gujarat) in 1918. By December 1921, Gandhiji had become a national leader in India.

Dr Ambedkar also knew that under Gandhiji's leadership, the Indian National Congress was reorganized to become a mass movement aimed at winning *Swaraj* (i.e., Home Rule). Dr Ambedkar referred to Gandhiji as a "Great Man" and, in fact, had acknowledged once: "Before Mahatma Gandhi, no politician in this country maintained that it was necessary to remove social injustices in order to do away with tensions and conflicts."[1]

---

1 Joseph Lelyveld, *Great Soul: Mahatma Gandhi and His Struggle with India* (NY: Knopf, 2011), p. 212.

On the other hand, Gandhiji, at least till then, did not seem to know Dr Ambedkar. Whatever little he did know of Dr Ambedkar was seemingly inadequate and even incorrect. Gandhiji, it appears, did not know that Dr Ambedkar was not only a foreign-trained barrister like himself, but also had a PhD in Economics from Columbia University, USA, in addition to a DSc degree in Economics from the London School of Economics. What is more, Gandhiji did not know that Dr Ambedkar was an Untouchable. As Gandhiji once confessed to his Secretary Mahadev Desai, "I did not know he [Ambedkar] was a *Harijan.*[2] I thought he was some benevolent Brahmin who took a deep interest in *Harijans* and, therefore, talked intemperately."[3]

Gandhiji and Dr Ambedkar had socio-economic visions which were distinctly dissimilar. In fact, they had deeply contrasting conceptions of India as a nation. While Gandhiji was essentially a traditionalist leader of the Congress Party, one who sought to identify with India's poor, he was also a social reformer in his own unique way. However, Dr Ambedkar believed that Gandhiji's reformism did not go far enough. In contrast to the radical writings of saints such as Kabir, Ravidas and Tukaram, Gandhiji's Vaishnavism lacked the passion for equality. As a corollary, this meant that Gandhiji did not find it necessary to condemn the most

---

2 A term coined by Gandhiji to refer to Untouchables. Literally, it meant "Children of God". It is now resented by the former Untouchables.

3 Mahadev Desai, *The Diary of Mahadev Desai* (Mumbai: Navajivan Publishing House, 1953), Vol. I, p. 52, quoted in Dhananjay Keer; *Dr Ambedkar: Life and Mission* (Mumbai: Popular Prakashan, First published 1954, 2005 Reprint), p. 168. Many scholars, notably Gail Omvedt, call this reaction "revelatory of the stereotypes about Untouchables that Gandhiji held" (Gail Omvedt, *Ambedkar: Towards an Enlightened India* [Delhi: Penguin, 2004], p. 43).

extreme expressions of Caste-based inequality. To the contrary, Gandhiji wrote in *Young India* in December 1920: "I believe that Caste has saved Hinduism from disintegration [...] I consider the four divisions [*Chaturvarna*] alone to be fundamental, natural and essential. [...] I am certainly against any attempt at destroying the fundamental divisions [of *Chaturvarna*]. The Caste system is not based on inequality, there is no question of inferiority."[4]

Gandhiji steadfastly believed in children following their ancestral professions. He only added a caveat that all occupations should be equally respected. True to his *Vaishnavaite* upbringing, Gandhiji was inclined to romanticize the village life in India where people had limited needs and happily worked in their traditional Caste-based occupations. He symbolized this vision with the concept of the age-old notion of *Ram Rajya*, making it easy to understand for even the illiterate.[5] Gandhiji firmly believed that the traditional *Chaturvarna* was an ideal model of organization which assigns to each individual a social and occupational vocation, thereby ensuring that society as a whole functions harmoniously. Within this framework of a "conflict-free" society, Gandhiji held that the prevalence of various Castes contributed towards social harmony besides economic stability.[6]

Dr Ambedkar could not have disagreed more. He looked upon the Caste system as a "system of graded inequality". It had an "ascending scale of reverence and descending scale of contempt", which had done an irrevocable damage to the Indian society. Unlike Gandhiji, he did not accept the law of *karma* and was strongly opposed to the *Chaturvarna,* which, he argued, had

---

4 Christophe Jaffrelot, *Dr Ambedkar and Untouchability: Analyzing and Fighting Caste* (New Delhi: Permanent Black, 2005), p. 61.

5 Omvedt, *Ambedkar.*

6 As argued in Jaffrelot, *Dr Ambedkar and Untouchability.*

turned the Indian society into a multi-storey building with no vertical movement allowed; one must die on the floor on which one was born. Dr Ambedkar also immensely disliked Gandhiji's glorification of villages. He called villages "cesspools" that fostered Caste-based oppression and socio-economic backwardness. Moreover, what Gandhiji called *Ram Rajya* reminded Dr Ambedkar of Untouchables like Eklavya and Shambuka who were penalized harshly for stepping out of their place in the *Chaturvarna*. He, therefore, believed in a "complete overhauling" of Hindu society. His freedom struggle was not confined merely to the transfer of power to Indians, but also envisioned as an opportunity to rebuild the nation as a socio-economic democracy embodied in the trinity of liberty, equality and fraternity.

It was against this backdrop that the historic meeting between Gandhiji and Dr Ambedkar was going to take place. Given the sharp differences in their views, the meeting was likely to be awkward and stormy, and it did turn out to be worse than expected.

* * *

Dr Ambedkar arrived at Mani Bhavan at 2 p.m. along with a few colleagues. They were shown in to the third floor where Gandhiji was busy talking with his party men and some visiting newspaper reporters. Dr Ambedkar and colleagues bowed to Gandhiji and sat on a rug. For some time, Gandhiji ignored Dr Ambedkar and kept chatting with the foreign journalists. Dr Ambedkar was getting impatient and just when his colleagues feared that he would explode any moment, Gandhiji finally turned to Dr Ambedkar and asked:[7] "Well, Doctor, what do you have to say in the matter?"

---

7 The only detailed account of this historic meeting is available in Keer, *Dr Ambedkar*, from where the conversation has been drawn (pp. 165-67). Keer, in turn, quoted a magazine *Navayug* (Ambedkar Special Number) 13 April 1947.

"You have called me to hear your views. Please tell me what you have to say. Or you may please ask me some questions and I shall answer," said Dr Ambedkar.

With a sharp look at Dr Ambedkar, Gandhiji said: "I understand that you have got some grievances against me and the Congress. …I have been thinking over the problem of Untouchables ever since my school days—when you were not even born."

Gandhiji explained that he had put in "enormous amount of effort" so as to "incorporate this problem in the programme of the Congress". As a result of which "the Congress has spent not less than Rupees 20 lakhs[8] on the upliftment of the Untouchables." And, then he remarked sharply: "It is really surprising that men like you should offer opposition to me and to the Congress. If you have to say anything to justify your stand, you are free to do so."

To the complete disbelief of Gandhiji, Dr Ambedkar retorted: "It is true *Mahatmaji* that you started to think about the problem of Untouchables before I was born. All old and elderly persons always like to emphasize the point of their age."

Gandhiji had met many Untouchables before. But he never had a face-off with an Untouchable intellectual. Perhaps, till that point of time, no Indian leader had.

Dr Ambedkar admitted that it was because of Gandhiji that the Congress Party had recognized the problem. But he lamented that the "Congress did nothing beyond giving formal recognition to this problem." Regarding the Congress spending more than Rs 20 lakhs on the upliftment of the Untouchables, Dr Ambedkar said that "it was all waste".

Dr Ambedkar was unstoppable now. He continued: "…the Congress is not sincere… Had it been sincere, it would have surely

8 Rs 20 lakhs = Rs 2 million.

made the removal of Untouchability a condition, like the wearing of *khaddar,* for becoming a member of the Congress."

He added: "No person who did not employ Untouchable women or men in his house, or rear up an Untouchable student or eat food at home with an Untouchable student at least once a week should have been allowed to be a member of the Congress…"

At this point, Dr Ambedkar made a direct charge: "You might say that the Congress wanted strength and, therefore, it was unwise to lay down such a condition. Then my point is that the Congress cares more for strength than for principles. This is my charge against you and the Congress."

Dr Ambedkar emphatically said: "We believe in self-help and self-respect. We are not prepared to have faith in great leaders and *Mahatmas*. Let me be brutally frank about it. History tells that *Mahatmas*, like fleeting phantoms, raise dust, but raise no level. Why should the Congressmen oppose our movement and dub me as a traitor?"[9]

Dr Ambedkar paused for a moment and then continued in a bitter, resentful tone: "Gandhiji, I have no homeland."

Taken aback, Gandhiji cut him short yet again and said: "You have got a homeland and from the reports that have reached me of your work at the Round Table Conference, I know you are a patriot of sterling worth."

Dr Ambedkar, however, persisted, saying: "How can I call this land my own homeland and this religion my own where we are treated worse than cats and dogs, where we cannot get water to drink? No self-respecting Untouchable worth his name will be proud of this land."

---

9 The Congress had boycotted the first session of the Round Table Conference (RTC) convened by the British Government while Dr Ambedkar did not. That is why some Congress leaders labelled him as a traitor.

About being dubbed as a traitor by the Congress Party, Dr Ambedkar pointed out that “the injustices and sufferings inflicted upon us by this land are…enormous.” He added, “I do not feel sorry for being branded as a traitor; for the responsibilities of our action lie with the land that dubs me a traitor.”

Dr Ambedkar clarified further that it was his “endeavour to secure human rights for … [the] people, who have been trampled upon in this country for ages… It is owing to the promptings of my conscience that I have been striving to win human rights for my people without … doing any harm to this country.”

The atmosphere was charged. Gandhiji was getting increasingly restless. Dr Ambedkar then raised the most pertinent issue, which indeed was the main purpose for the meeting. Referring to the recognition of the political safeguards to the Muslims and Sikhs, Dr Ambedkar asked: “The First Session (of the Round Table Conference) has given recognition to the political rights of the Depressed Classes and has recommended for them political safeguards and adequate representation. According to us, that is beneficial to the Depressed Classes. What is your opinion?”

By then the veteran leader had recovered from the initial shock. Having regained his composure, Gandhiji”s reply was firm and forthright. He said, “I am against the political separation of the Untouchables from the Hindus. That would be absolutely suicidal.”

Angry and agitated, Dr Ambedkar rose from where he was seated and curtly said: “I thank you for your frank opinion. It is good that I know where we stand as regards this vital problem. I take leave of you.”

The meeting ended on a dismal note, not entirely unexpected. Both Gandhiji and Dr Ambedkar must have astonished each other. Gandhiji was the topmost leader of the Indian masses. Given his age and authority, nobody could have dared to hit back at Gandhiji as fearlessly as Dr Ambedkar had. To talk to Gandhiji intemperately was sure to invite permanent annoyance and wrath. Nevertheless, Dr Ambedkar brazenly did it because of his bold and raging resolve to fight out the human rights for the downtrodden masses. On his own part, Dr Ambedkar himself must have also been surprised to see Gandhiji being equally adamant on his own point of view.

* * *

The spark of confrontation was ignited. It was only the beginning of a series of direct and indirect confrontations. It is in these repeated battles between these two iconic leaders that one can witness the unique conflict between (political) "independence" and (socio-economic) "freedom", and through these public debates unfolds the story of the emergence of modern India as a Sovereign, Democratic Republic.

And, in this process of historical evolution, while Mahatma Gandhi came to be regarded as the Father of the Indian Nation, and indeed rightly so, Dr Babasaheb Ambedkar ought to have been recognized as the Man who shaped the Republic of India.

Regrettably, that has not happened so far.

**Dr Narendra Jadhav**

# Acknowledgements

**Foreword and Afterword:**

Professor Kevin Brown
*Richard S. Melvin Professor of Law Emeritus*
*Indiana University Maurer School of Law Bloomington, Indiana, USA*

**Thoughtful Suggestions:**

A.K.D. Jadhav IAS (Retd)

**Editorial Assistance:**

Preeta Priyamvada, Jiza Joy, and Lekshmi Parameswaran

**Plagiarism Check:**

Kazim Rizvi & Konark Editorial Team

**Technical Assistance:**

Sruti Kalyanikar and Prabhakar Gaikwad

**Other Assistance:**

Samir Arora

**Family Support:**

Vasundhara Jadhav (Wife)
Tanmoy (Son) and Kejal (Daughter-in-law)
Dr Apoorva (Daughter) and Dr Ekim Muyan (Son-in-law)
Agastya, Eymir, Kimaya and Keyan (Grandchildren)

# PART I

# Making of Dr Ambedkar

CHAPTER ONE

# Emergence of Dr Ambedkar

Dr Bhimrao Ramji Ambedkar was born on 14 April 1891 in Mhow, which is the popular name of Military Headquarters of War, a small town in Central India (in the State of Madhya Pradesh today) to an Untouchable family with military service background. The family hailed from the coastal region of the State of Maharashtra and belonged to the *Mahar* Caste—numerically, the largest Untouchable Caste in the State.[1]

Bhimrao's grandfather Maloji had served in the British Army, as had his father Ramji. His father had served in the British Army since 1866 and was promoted to the rank of the subedar. He was later appointed as Headmaster of an army school in Mhow. Bhimrao's mother also came from a *Mahar* family with significant military tradition. Since education was compulsory for children of army personnel, even women in her family were literate, which was highly unusual at that time. Ramji and his wife Bhimabai had 14 children of which only five survived. It was the 14th child named

---

1 As per the 1931 Census, *Mahars* comprised nearly 69 per cent of the then Untouchables in the Bombay Presidency compared with 16.2 per cent *Chamars* and 14.9 per cent *Mangs,* the other two major Untouchable Castes.

Bhim (also called Bhiva) who was to emerge later as Dr Babasaheb Ambedkar.

Initially, living in a military cantonment, Bhim had little contact with the outside world, and in the early years he was protected from the discrimination generally faced by Untouchables. This, however, did not last long. While Bhim was still very young, the family moved to Ratnagiri district and then to Satara (both in today's Maharashtra State) where his father took up a job as a storekeeper in the Public Works Department.

## Early Experiences of Untouchability

It was in Satara, in 1900, that young Bhim was admitted in the first standard of the English-medium Government High School, as Bhimrao Ramji Ambavadekar. Since the family surname "Sankpal" was indicative of a so-called lowly Caste, Bhim's father decided to use the name of their native village, Ambavade. Hence, the family name was changed to Ambavadekar. Incidentally, one of Bhim's teachers in Satara was a Brahmin named Ambedkar, which sounded like Ambavadekar. The bright and charming Bhim became a favourite student of this teacher. In order to spare Bhim from walking the long distance back to his house, the kind teacher provided him daily lunches. It was in the honour of this teacher that Bhim's family name was later re-registered as Ambedkar, instead of Ambavadekar.

Once Bhim was outside the protected environment of the cantonment, in Satara, he soon had to face the stark realties of an Untouchable's life. Dr Ambedkar himself narrated several incidents in his writings and speeches.[2] These incidents, no doubt, instilled

2 *Dr Babasaheb Ambedkar: Writings and Speeches* (BAWS). The BAWS Volumes were first published by the Government of Maharashtra in 1979. To date, 22 volumes have been published.

the spirit of defiance and rebellion which later became a distinctive feature of his personality.

Dr Ambedkar recollects the humiliating experience of his journey with his brother to meet their father where they could not even get drinking water. Dr Ambedkar bares his heart out:[3]

> This incident has a very important place in my life. I was a boy of nine when it happened. But it has left an indelible impression on my mind. Before this incident occurred, I knew that I was an Untouchable and that Untouchables were subjected to certain indignities and discriminations. For instance, I knew that in the school I could not sit in the midst of my class students according to my rank but that I was to sit in a corner by myself. I knew that in the school I was to have a separate piece of gunny cloth for me to squat on in the classroom and the servant employed to clean the school would not touch the gunny cloth used by me and I was required to carry the gunny cloth home in the evening and bring it back the next day.
>
> While in the school I knew that children of the Touchable Classes could go out to the water tap, open it and quench their thirst. I could not touch the tap and unless a Touchable person opened it, I could not quench my thirst. The permission of the teacher was not enough; the presence of the school peon was necessary, for he was the only person whom the class teacher could use for such a purpose. The situation can be summed up in the statement—no peon, no water.
>
> At home I know that the working of washing clothes was done by my sisters. Not that there was (*sic*) no washermen in Satara. Not that we could not afford to pay the washermen. Washing was done by my sisters because we were Untouchables and no washerman would wash the clothes of an Untouchable.

---

3 From incomplete and "unpublished" autobiography titled 'Waiting for a Visa', later published in BAWS, Vol. 12, pp. 665–71.

The work of cutting the hair or shaving the boys including myself was done by our elder sister who had become quite an expert barber by practicing the art on us, not that there were no barbers in Satara, not that we could not afford to pay the barber. It was because we were Untouchables and no barber would consent to shave an Untouchable.

All this I knew. But this incident (of not even getting drinking water) gave me a shock such as I never received before, and it made me think about Untouchability, which before this incident happened, was with me as a matter of course, as it is with many Touchables as well as the Untouchables.

## Love for Studying

When Bhim was barely five years old, his mother passed away in December 1896. When the family moved to Satara, his father married a second time. Bhim immensely disliked the idea of another woman taking his mother's place. He decided to run away to Mumbai (known as Bombay then) and find a job in the textile mills. But he needed cash to be able to travel to Mumbai. He then planned to steal money from his aunt but failed because there was no money in her purse.

This incident, however, turned out to be a blessing in disguise and a critical turning point in the life of Bhim. This little boy, who till then had little or no interest in studies, suddenly grew up overnight! As he indicated in a public speech later (on 20 January 1942):

> For three successive nights I tried to remove the purse tucked up at the waist of my aunt, but without any success. On the fourth night, I did get hold of the purse, but to my disappointment I found only half an *anna* in it. And in half of an *anna*, of course,

> I could not go to Bombay. The three nights' experience was so nerve-racking that I gave up the idea of collecting money in this shameful manner and I came to another decision—a decision that gave an entirely different turn to my life. I decided that I must give up my truant habits that I must study hard and get through my examinations as fast as possible, so that I might earn my own livelihood and be independent of my father.[4]

In a dramatic irony, the little boy who had dreamt of becoming a mill worker in Mumbai rose, many years later, to become the Labour Minister of India in the Viceroy's Executive Council (1942–46).

It was Bhim's father who was responsible for his early education. Ramji was a follower of the Kabir *Panth*. Devotional singing or *Bhajans* and recitation of holy texts took place in the family frequently. Ramji was also an admirer of Mahatma Jyotiba Phule who had pioneered major reforms among the non-Brahmins in the latter part of the 19th century. Not surprisingly, many years later, Dr Ambedkar referred to Buddha, Kabir and Phule as his three Gurus.

Father Ramji was also responsible for Bhim's love for books. His father's strong desire was that his son should not study only to clear his examinations but rather pass them with distinction.

In 1904, Ramji lost his job and had to shift to Mumbai with his family. Bhim was enrolled at Elphinstone High School and his education continued. Ramji encouraged him and even used his monthly pension to buy almost any book that Bhim demanded.

---

4 As quoted in Dhananjay Keer's *Dr Ambedkar: Life and Mission* (Mumbai: Popular Prakashan, 2005), p. 15. This biography first appeared in 1954 when Dr Ambedkar was alive. Therefore, it is often claimed as an official or approved biography of Dr Ambedkar.

When that small amount was over, Ramji would persuade his two married daughters to give him their jewellery and pawn it to buy more books until the next instalment of his pension arrived. In spite of his meagre income, Ramji never hesitated to provide new books for Bhim. The love for books became a permanent hallmark of Bhim's personality.

During his time in school, Bhim was once called by the teacher to solve an arithmetic problem on the blackboard. A commotion ensued in the classroom as children from the so-called Upper Caste Hindus rushed to retrieve their tiffin boxes placed behind the blackboard for fear of "pollution". When Bhim expressed interest in studying Sanskrit, he was told that, being the sacred language of the *Vedas*, it was prohibited for Untouchables; his only options were English or Persian. These experiences of Untouchability undoubtedly made a profound impact on young Bhim's mind.

As a young lad, Bhim did not have many friends and had a reputation for frequent fights with his schoolmates. He spent much of his time reading in a garden near his school. It was during this period that he was noticed by social activist Krishnaji Arjun Keluskar, the then Principal of Wilson High School. He took a liking for this hardworking studious boy. Keluskar introduced himself, and for long thereafter remained an important well-wisher and supporter of Bhim.

While Bhim was still a high school student, he married Ramabai, who was nine years old, in 1905. It was an arranged marriage. Bhim was only 14 when he got married.[5] The venue for the marriage ceremony was also rather unconventional; it took place in the open market shed of the Byculla Vegetable Market in Mumbai after business hours.

---

5 While child marriages are now forbidden by law, they were quite common in early 20th-century India.

Seven years later, Bhimrao became a father when his son Yashwant was born. Yashwant was the only one of Bhimrao's children to survive, despite four more children being born subsequently.

In 1907, Bhimrao passed his Matriculation examination from Elphinstone High School. This was surely an unusual accomplishment for an Untouchable and called for celebrations in his community. After the public ceremony, Principal Keluskar presented Bhim with a biography of the Buddha titled *Life of Gautam Buddha*. Neither of them could have imagined that in the years to come, Dr Ambedkar would become a great champion of Buddhism, leading millions of his followers to the path of Buddha.

After completing his initial schooling, Bhimrao was encouraged by his father to join the Elphinstone College in Mumbai. Even here, Bhimrao could not escape the pangs of Untouchability—the Brahmin canteen-owner at the college would not give him tea or water. Mercifully again, some teachers lent him a helping hand. A European teacher—Professor Muller—lent him books and gave him clothes.

Bhimrao began his studies in right earnest, but due to ill-health, lost one year. When Bhimrao passed the Intermediate examination, his father ran out of money and Principal Keluskar stepped forward to help. He arranged a scholarship for Bhim from the Princely State of Baroda. With this opportunity, Bhimrao joined Elphinstone College on a scholarship of Rs 25 a month.

Bhimrao resumed his college education and started working very hard. Around that time, the family moved their residence to another place in Parel—Bombay Improvement Trust (BIT) *Chawl* Number 1. Dr Ambedkar mentioned many years later that in those two rooms lived ten family members (parents, brothers and sisters' children) and one she-goat. He studied, sometimes up to 21 hours of the day, under a dim light of kerosene lamp at night.[6] In 1912 he obtained his BA degree from Bombay University in Economics and Political Science. It was only after overcoming innumerable social and financial obstacles that Bhimrao became one of the first Untouchables in India to obtain a college degree.

Young Bhimrao, a college graduate at 22, had to take up a job to honour the Scholarship Agreement. He became a Probationer in the Accountant General Office of the State of Baroda with a monthly salary of Rs 75. His decision caused a major disagreement with his father, who was concerned that Bhimrao would be subjected to more discrimination in Baroda and, hence, wanted Bhimrao to continue his stay in the liberal and cosmopolitan atmosphere of Mumbai.

On reaching Baroda, Bhimrao realized that his father could not have been more right in his fears. He could not find any residence except for sleeping quarters in the Arya Samaj office. Further, he was forced to dine in the distant Untouchable neighbourhood of the city. Caste discrimination was very evident on the professional front as well. Bhimrao was tossed across departments without being given any meaningful work. Still, he persisted with his stay for about fifteen days. It was only on getting the news of his father's illness that Bhimrao returned to Mumbai to see his ailing father, who died on 2 February 1913.

Thanks again to Principal Keluskar, subsequently, Bhimrao had an opportunity to present his case before the Maharaja of Baroda in Mumbai. The kind-hearted Maharaja Sayajirao Gaekwad offered him a scholarship (£11.50 a month for two years) to study

---

6 Marathi Speech at the Pune Untouchables Students' Conference, Pune (11 September 1928). For the full text, see *Ambedkar Speaks,* edited by Narendra Jadhav (New Delhi: Konark Publishers, 2013), Vol. I. pp. 443-48. This is a collection of thematically edited 300 speeches in English and 500 speeches in Marathi in three volumes.

at Columbia University in New York city. As per the agreement, Bhimrao was required to serve the State of Baroda for ten years on completion of his education abroad.

This was an unprecedented opportunity for young Bhimrao, or for any Untouchable for that matter.

***

Opportunity for higher studies in the US was, of course, a major turning point in the life of young Bhimrao Ambedkar. Potentially, it could transform the bright and hardworking Untouchable Bhimrao's life and mission forever and it did.

## MA and PhD at Columbia University, USA

A completely new and stimulating phase in the life of Bhimrao Ambedkar began in 1913, when he was admitted for Post-Graduate Studies at Columbia University, New York. He was among the first group of Indians who went to the USA in the first quarter of the 20th century to receive advanced training in economics.

At Columbia University, Bhimrao came under the influence of several great thinkers, including Philosopher John Dewey, Anthropologist A.A. Goldenweiser and Economist Edwin Seligman who were his teachers at the University. Under the guidance of Professor Seligman—a leading authority in Public Finance and History of Economic Thought at that time—Bhimrao was awarded his MA in 1915. He was 24 then. His thesis for the MA degree was titled 'Administration and Finance of the East India Company'.

Within two more years, at the age of 26, Bhimrao submitted his Dissertation for PhD which was accepted for the Doctorate in 1917. His PhD Dissertation was titled "National Dividend: A Historical and Analytical Study". Several years later in 1925, the Dissertation was published in a book form with the title *The*

*Evolution of Provincial Finance in British India,* whereupon Bhimrao was formally awarded his PhD degree by Columbia University (June 1927).[7]

Interestingly, the book has been dedicated to His Highness Shri Sayajirao Gaekwad, Maharaja of Baroda. The dedication reads: "As a token of gratitude for his help in the matter of my education."

## DSc and Bar-at-Law in Britain

After finishing his MA and PhD from the US, Dr Ambedkar was keen on earning another Doctorate from the London School of Economics and also on becoming a Barrister, so that after serving the Baroda government as per the Scholarship Agreement, he could earn his livelihood as a practicing lawyer and devote himself to social work and writing books.

There was, however, an administrative hitch. His scholarship was expiring in June 1916, and as such he needed a two-year extension to the scholarship for completing his studies. His request for a two-year extension was turned down. Disappointed and desperate, Dr Ambedkar consulted his PhD guide Professor Seligman, who advised him to re-apply for an extension along with his strong letter of recommendation. Eventually, the Maharaja of Baroda gave an extension, but only for a year for the time being.

In the meantime, an "unstoppable" Dr Ambedkar set out for London in May 1916 without waiting for the approval of the request for extension of the scholarship. He carried with him a letter of recommendation from Professor Seligman to Professor

---

7 According to the University rules at that time, the students were required to publish their dissertations in the book form and to submit the copies to the University for a formal award of the PhD degree.

Sydney Webb, who was himself a great Economist and Thinker holding a key position in the London School of Economics.

As the story goes, Dr Ambedkar left without any money in his pocket. On reaching Liverpool by ship, his person, clothes, shoes and luggage were meticulously searched by the British Police authorities on the suspicion that he may be connected with Indian Revolutionary Army. He was released with great reluctance upon the verification of his recommendation letters. Dr Ambedkar then travelled to London by train without ticket and managed to escape without being caught. Fortunately, two days later, a letter from the Government of Baroda arrived awarding Dr Ambedkar a one-year extension for his scholarship.

Dr Ambedkar was admitted to the London School of Economics (11 October 1916) and for Bar-at-Law at the Gray's Inn (11 November 1916). He was all set now working very hard in the right earnest. A few months later, Dr Ambedkar sent another appeal to the State of Baroda to grant another extension. This time, however, his request for extension of scholarship was firmly declined by the Maharaja of Baroda and he was instructed to return to India to serve the Baroda State as per the Scholarship Agreement.

Dr Ambedkar was left with no choice but to return to India. Utterly disturbed, he applied to the London School of Economics for condoning his unanticipated discontinuity in studies and allowing him some time. The University of London "excused the interruption of his course of study for a period not exceeding four years from October 1917". Similar permission was also obtained from the Gray's Inn.

***

## Serving the Baroda State: Humiliations Abound

As a part of the Scholarship Agreement with the Baroda State, Dr Ambedkar had signed a bond for serving the Princely State for ten years in return for the scholarship to study abroad. The Maharaja wanted to appoint Dr Ambedkar as the Finance Minister of the Baroda State. However, to begin with, the Maharaja appointed Bhimrao as his Military Secretary on his return to Baroda in 1917, on a salary Rs 150 per month.

Even after earning exceptionally strong academic credentials, coming back to India for Dr Ambedkar was a return to Caste-ridden system. Despite his advanced degrees and senior rank in the Service, Dr Ambedkar was once again subjected to discrimination. He could not find housing in Baroda owing to his lowly Caste. He finally found quarters in a Parsi Boarding Home but only under an assumed Parsi name.

There was no comfort at his workplace either. Brahmin clerks and subordinates were rude. They kept a distance, literally throwing papers and files at his desk to avoid any physical contact.[8] When he tried to join a club where officers met in their leisure time, he was seated in a corner and told not to participate in any games. In the hostile and conservative Baroda, Dr Ambedkar could not find any friends and was forced to withdraw himself in solitude.

The inhuman treatment reached its climax when an angry group of Parsis besieged the Boarding House that Dr Ambedkar was staying in, determined to beat him up. And thus, utterly disappointed, humiliated and frustrated, Dr Ambedkar tendered his resignation and returned to Mumbai on 31 August 1917.

---

8 This was "social distancing" possibly, at its worst form.

## Back to Mumbai: Struggles for a Decent Career

Back in Mumbai, Dr Ambedkar tried to find ways to make a living for his growing family. His elder brother Anandrao who had supported his family died in November 1917. Dr Ambedkar was desperate. He worked as a private tutor and accountant for a Parsi businessman earning Rs 50 per month. He even set up a small firm for stock-broking and worked as an investment consultant, which failed when his clients found out that he was an Untouchable.

For the want of a better alternative, Dr Ambedkar started teaching Economics, Banking and Mercantile Law at Davar's College of Commerce, earning Rs 50 per month. With his limited monthly earning, it was barely possible to make the two ends meet. There was no scope for saving money for financing his incomplete education abroad. As was described by Blake Clarke later,[9] "one of India's best educated men lived in Bombay for the next year and a half unemployed, poverty-stricken and miserable."

After a lot of struggle and frustrating efforts, Dr Ambedkar got a one-year position as Professor of Political Economy at Sydenham College, Mumbai, on a salary of Rs 450 per month, which he held from 11 November 1918 to 11 March 1920. Even there, while he was popular with the students, fellow teachers constantly harassed him by practicing Untouchability in the college.

In 1920, Dr Ambedkar took an important social initiative—the publication of a fortnightly titled *Mook Nayak* (Leader of the Silent) in Mumbai with the help of a visionary ruler, Maharaja Shahu Chhatrapati of the Kolhapur Princely State. Dr Ambedkar was not the official editor of the *Mook Nayak* (since he was working as Professor in a Government College) but the fortnightly became his

---

9 Blake Clarke, "Ambedkar: The Untouchable", *Christian Herald*, March 1950, p. 80.

mouthpiece. He used this journal to criticize the Indian political community for their reluctance to fight Caste-based discrimination.

In the first issue of *Mook Nayak* (31 January 1920), Dr Ambedkar advocated the need for a forum "to deliberate on the injustices let loose or likely to be imposed on us and other Depressed people and to think of their future development and appropriate strategies towards it critically." Comparing the Hindu Society to a tower which has several storeys but no ladder or an entrance, he said, one must die in the storey in which one was born. For saving the Depressed Classes from perpetual slavery, poverty and ignorance, formidable efforts must be made, he argued, to awaken them to their disabilities.[10]

Six months thereafter, with financial help from Maharaja Shahu Chhatrapati of Kolhapur, a personal loan of Rs 5,000 from an old Parsi friend Naval Bhathena and his own savings of Rs 7,000, Dr Ambedkar could finally return to London on 5 July 1920 to complete his advanced studies.

***

## Resuming Higher Studies in London

On his return to London in August 1920, Dr Ambedkar resumed his studies, from September 1920, both at the London School of Economics and at the Bar at the Gray's Inn.

With the meagre amount of money at his disposal, it was a life of extreme abstinence and hardship for the young scholar. Staying at a boarding house, he would rise at 6 a.m. With a frugal breakfast consisting of a cup of tea, a piece of bread with little bit of jam and a piece of fish, he would rush to the library and would always be the first one to enter. Then he would commence his intense reading and making copious notes for hours together without any break

---

10 Keer, *Dr Ambedkar: Life and Mission*, p. 41.

even for lunch. He would be fully engrossed in his readings till the closing of the library, and would always be the last person to leave, which he did only after a friendly reminder by the security guards. The second session of the study would begin soon, after a brief walk and an early dinner at the boarding house. After the short break, the reading would start again till the early morning hours. When his Indian roommate pleaded him to get some rest, he would say: No money, no food; and no time, no sleep!

Days rolled by. Dr Ambedkar's back-breaking research was coming to fruition. He was awarded the degree of Master of Science (MSc) for his Thesis "Provincial Decentralization of Imperial Finance in British India" in June 1921. It was a prerequisite for the degree of Doctor of Science (DSc). In early 1922, he submitted his Dissertation entitled "The Problem of the Rupee" for his DSc degree. His supervisor this time was another eminent Economist, Professor Edwin Cannon. In the meantime, on 28 June 1922, Dr Ambedkar was called to the Bar, to become a Barrister.

At this point, Dr Ambedkar decided to pursue further studies in Germany. He began to study both German and French. On getting the necessary clearance from Bonn University, he left for Germany. Subsequently, however, his supervisor in London informed Dr Ambedkar that his London examiners had refused to approve his Doctoral Dissertation. He agreed to rewrite his Dissertation without changing his conclusions.

Since Bhimrao was running out of financial resources, there was no choice for him but to return to Mumbai, which he did in April 1923. In the following five months, Dr Ambedkar revised his Dissertation and forwarded it to London. In November 1923, he was informed by telegram that he was awarded the degree of Doctor of Science (DSc) in Economics. This Dissertation was published in the form of a book in the same year with the title *The Problem of the Rupee: Its Origin and Its Solution.*

The book represents a highly significant contribution by Dr Ambedkar to the field of Monetary Economics. The book has been dedicated to the memory of his parents, in his abiding "gratitude for the sacrifices they made and the enlightenment they showed in the matter of his education."

Dr Ambedkar was now a Barrister with two Doctoral Degrees in Economics, PhD from Columbia University in the USA, and DSc from London School of Economics, a feat that was exceedingly difficult for anybody, and simply unbelievable for an Untouchable!

## CHAPTER TWO

# Genesis of Dr Ambedkar's World View

At the onset of the 20th century, England was the default choice for Indian students to pursue higher studies. England boasted of being the hub of academic institutions that were centuries old. However, getting an opportunity to study in the US was a welcome change for young Bhimrao. As opposed to the Colonial power that England was, America was a flourishing democracy. The values of liberty, equality and fraternity were espoused in the Constitution of the country. It was in the US that young Bhimrao formed his world view by assimilating the liberal Republicanism.[1]

Life in the US was Bhimrao's first exposure to a "free world". For the first time in his life, he could feel and appreciate what it

---

1 Liberalism is defined here as a political and moral philosophy based on individual liberty and equality before the law. Republicanism, on the other hand, is believed to be a political ideology centred on citizenship in a nation organized as a Republic. The essence of classical Republicanism lies in uncompromising commitment to liberty and in abiding faith in natural rights of individuals.

meant to be truly free. He could move as per his will and could mingle with all others with a status of equality, something he had never experienced before. His day-to-day existence had a new purpose, a new meaning. It rekindled in him an insatiable quest for knowledge, which was going to be his hallmark for the rest of his life.

Young Bhimrao Ambedkar's arrival in the US (in 1913) coincided with a period of major change in the American history. It had been 50 years since the Emancipation Proclamation was signed by President Abraham Lincoln (1863). The Proclamation had declared "that all persons held as slaves" within the rebellious states "are, and hence forward shall be, free." Following the Emancipation Declaration, there were three supportive amendments to the US Constitution called the Reformation Amendments (1865, 1868 and 1870).

Regrettably, within seven years thereafter, discrimination against African Americans re-emerged (1877) in the form of "Black Codes" (preventing African Americans from entering occupations other than menial labour) and "Jim Crow Laws" (forcing African Americans to live in segregated neighbourhoods and restricting their access to public utilities).

When Bhimrao reached the US in the year 1913, the country was witnessing movements against racial and gender inequalities. The cause of African American citizens was then led by Booker T. Washington (1856–1918) and William Du Bois (1868–1963), who were fighting for equality in their own distinct ways. During Ambedkar's time in the US, Booker T. Washington was fading out while William Du Bois was gaining prominence. In fact, just three years before Bhimrao's arrival in New York, in 1910, the National Association for Advancement of the Coloured People (NAACP), the largest and most pre-eminent civil rights organization in the US, was founded with Du Bois as a co-founder. Du Bois, by then, had emerged as the leading voice against the "Black Codes" and "Jim Crow Laws".

Around the same time, the US also foresaw the rise of another historic movement—the Women's Suffrage Movement. In this regard, two developments marked 1913, the year of Bhimrao's arrival in the US. First, Alice Paul organized the Women's Suffrage Procession—a parade in Washington D.C.—the largest one till then. The parade was attacked, but no arrests were made. Secondly, the US Senate voted on a Women's Suffrage amendment, but it could not go through.[2]

Young Bhimrao must have watched these developments closely and with keen interest. But he did not seem to have been actively involved in any way. There is no record of his thoughts on the issue at that time, nor of his experience of living in the close proximity of Harlem,[3] which is in the vicinity of Columbia University where he was studying.

A few years later (probably in 1918) when Dr Bhimrao was studying in London, Lala Lajpat Rai, a great national leader who played a pivotal role in the Indian Independence movement, tried hard to persuade him to "join the political if not the revolutionary movement for the freedom of India". Apparently, Dr Bhimrao "told the great leader of India that he was a student and he must complete his studies without betraying the sacred trust of the Maharaja who had given him an opportunity in his life."[4]

Evidently, it was very important for young Bhimrao to stay focused on his studies. The same consideration might be a valid

---

2 It took seven more years for women in the US to finally get the right to vote. This happened when the 19th Amendment to the US Constitution was ratified in 1920.

3 Harlem is generally believed to be the "Black Mecca of the world".

4 Keer, *Dr Ambedkar: Life and Mission*, Third Edition, Reprint 2005, p. 27.

explanation for Bhimrao not getting actively involved in the social movements in the US during the period of his stay there (i.e., 1913–1917), despite the fact that they were so close to his heart.

***

While studying at Columbia University, Bhimrao had opted for Moral Philosophy, Anthropology, Sociology and Economics for his academic pursuits. His "coursework" during the three years (including summers) consisted of maximum number of course credits in Economics, 11 in History, 6 in Sociology, 5 in Philosophy, 4 in Anthropology, 3 in Politics, and 1 each in Elementary French and German. These courses and the back-breaking hard work that Bhimrao put in were going to serve him well in leading the Untouchables of India on to the path of equality, self-dignity and empowerment.

## Dr Ambedkar, Professor Dewey and Thomas Paine

At Columbia University, his favourite teacher was Professor John Dewey. Prof. Dewey was the one "whom I owe so much", Dr Ambedkar recalled much later. Prof. Dewey (1859–1952) was a Professor of Philosophy.

Professor Dewey, as a social and political philosopher, focused on helping resolve the problems that plagued mankind. These included common problems such as bad sanitation, poor working conditions, inequalities of income distribution and the exclusion of some strata of the society. Prof. Dewey's "Philosophy of Pragmatism" was refreshingly different from the traditional philosophies that concerned themselves with abstractions such as: "Being", "Essence" and "Truth".[5] Prof. Dewey's philosophy gave

5 Lane W. Lancaster, *Masters of Political Thought: Hegel to Dewey*, Vol. 3 (London: George G. Harrap and Co Ltd, 1959), p. 332.

social status and dignity to everyone in society irrespective of their profession, i.e., whether it was dignified or menial. That is precisely what must have greatly appealed to young Bhimrao.

Bhimrao's favourite quotation of Prof. Dewey was: "Every society gets encumbered with what is trivial, with deadwood from the past and with what is positively perverse… As a society becomes more enlightened, it realises that it is responsible not to conserve and transmit the whole of its existing achievements, but only such as make for a better future society."

Dr Ambedkar used this quote later in his classic essay, "Annihilation of Caste" (1936), to criticize the orthodox Hindus living in and reviving the so-called glorious past of India. Dr Ambedkar advocated moral regeneration of the Hindu society, which needed intellectual regeneration, and he felt that basking in the past glory was coming in the way.

Another great American Philosopher and Political Theorist who made a deep impression on young Bhimrao was Thomas Paine (1737–1809). Professor Jagdish Shivpuri[6] indicated on several occasions that Dr Ambedkar spoke very fondly of Thomas Paine's book *Rights of Man* (first published in 1791).

Dr Ambedkar, according to Prof. Shivpuri, was never tired of quoting Thomas Paine from his book *Rights of Man*. His most favourite ones included the following:

- The world is my country, all mankind are my brethren, and to do good is my religion.
- Man did not enter into society to become worse than he was before, nor to have fewer rights than he had before, but to have those rights better secured.

---

6 Prof. Jagdish Shivpuri was a colleague of Dr Ambedkar who taught English at Siddharth College (Mumbai), founded by Dr Ambedkar. The author has had the privilege of being a close friend of Prof. Shivpuri.

- Whatever is my right as a man is also the right of another; and it becomes my duty to guarantee as well as possess.

The egalitarian individualism of Thomas Paine had a profound influence on him. These were the kind of thoughts that shaped the liberal and Republican mindset of young Bhimrao.

***

While in New York at Columbia University (for MA and PhD) and in London (at London School of Economics for DSc and Gray's Inn for Bar-at-Law) and even later after returning to India, Dr Ambedkar studied a very wide range of Western Thinkers, Philosophers and Historians who wrote about the well-being of humanity.

These included Greek Philosophers such as Socrates (470–399 BC), Thucydides (460–400 BC), Thrasymachus (459–400 BC), Plato (424–347 BC) and Aristotle (384–322 BC), and later European scholars such as Prof. Martin Luther (1483–1546), Voltaire (1694–1778), Edmund Burke (1729–1797), Daniel O' Connell (1775–1847), John Stuart Mill (1806–1873), Bertrand Russel (1872–1970) and Harold Laski (1893–1950).

In the United States, besides Prof. John Dewey and Thomas Paine, Dr Ambedkar closely studied Thomas Jefferson (1743–1826), William Garrison (1805–1879), Fredrick Douglass (1818–1895), Abraham Lincoln (1809–1865), Booker T. Washington (1856–1918) and William Du Bois (1868–1963). All these great scholars left deep imprints on young Bhimrao's mind. In fact, Dr Ambedkar quoted several of these Philosophers and Historians in many of his speeches[7] as well as in his prolific scholarly writings.[8]

---

7 Narendra Jadhav (ed), *Ambedkar Speaks,* Vol I,II & III (New Delhi: Konark Publishers 2013).

8 Narendra Jadhav (ed), *Ambedkar Writes,* Vol I & II (New Delhi: Konark Publishers, 2013).

Indeed, it is possible to get insights into the intellectual impact of these scholars on Dr Ambedkar by analysing their quotes used by him. An interesting attempt in that direction has already been made.[9]

## Dr Ambedkar, Lincoln, Booker T. Washington and William Du Bois

Dr Ambedkar's "approved" biographer Dhananjay Keer has claimed[10] that while in the US, Dr Ambedkar's mind "must have been deeply impressed with two things: First, the fourteenth Amendment to the US Constitution which declared the 'freedom of Negroes'. Second, the life of Booker T. Washington…'whose work…broke the shackles of bondage which had crushed the Negroes for ages physically, mentally and spiritually'."

The first claim is factually misleading whereas the second claim is patently false, as would be evident from the discussion that follows.

Given his Untouchable background and the social disabilities that he had seen and experienced, it goes without saying that the racial problems in the US were very close to Dr Ambedkar's heart.

At one point Dr Ambedkar, in fact, compared the two inhuman institutions—Slavery and Caste System—and called the Untouchables in India the children of India's ghetto.[11] He said:

---

9 See D.T. Khabde, PhD Dissertation submitted to Dr Babasaheb Ambedkar Marathwada University in 1985. This chapter, to an extent, draws from this Dissertation which is available on https://shodhganga.inflibnet.ac.in

10 Keer, *Dr Ambedkar: Life and Mission*, p. 31.

11 Dr Ambedkar, *Untouchables or the Children of India's Ghetto,* unpublished manuscript, published by the Government of Maharashtra after Dr Ambedkar's death. See BAWS, Vol. 5, p. 15.

"Slavery was never obligatory. But Untouchability is obligatory. The law of slavery permitted emancipation. Once a slave always a slave was *not* the fate of the slave. In Untouchability there is no escape. Once an Untouchable, always an Untouchable."

Dr Ambedkar also argued that "Untouchability is an indirect form of slavery". Depriving a man's freedom directly and openly is a "preferable form of enslavement" because it "makes the slave conscious of his enslavement" and that is the "first and most important step in the battle for freedom". On the other hand, "if a man is deprived of his liberty indirectly, he has no consciousness of his enslavement" and that is what Untouchability is.

Dr Ambedkar was very impressed by the American Declaration of Independence of 1776, with Thomas Jefferson stating: "We hold these truths to be self-evident, that all men are created equal; that they are endowed by their Creator with certain unalienable Rights; that among these are Life, Liberty and the pursuit of Happiness. That to secure these rights, Governments are instituted among Men, deriving their just powers from the consent of the governed."[12]

Dr Ambedkar, however, lamented that the implementation of this Declaration has been a "tragic episode" in the history of the United States. "...this charter of human Liberty was not applied to the Negroes. ...There is certainly no doubt about the faith of Jefferson," for he wrote, "I am sorry for my countrymen."[13]

Dr Ambedkar was greatly influenced by William Lloyd Garrison (1805–1879), a white social reformer and journalist who founded an anti-slavery newspaper called *The Liberator* in 1831. Dr Ambedkar quoted him in a number of his speeches and

---

12 B.R. Ambedkar, *Mr Gandhi and the Emancipation of the Untouchables*, Monograph, first published in 1943. BAWS, Vol. 9. For Summary, see Jadhav (ed), *Ambedkar Writes*, Vol. I, p. 256.

13 Ibid.

writings. What Garrison wrote in the first issue of *The Liberator* seems to be the most favourite of Dr Ambedkar:

> I shall strenuously contend for the immediate enforcement of our slave population ... On this subject, I do not wish to write, or speak or think, with moderation. No. No. Tell a man whose house is on fire, to give a moderate alarm. Tell him to moderately rescue his wife from the hands of the ravisher. Tell the mother to gradually extricate her babe from the fire into which she has fallen, but urge me not into moderation in a cause like the present. I am in earnest—I will not excuse—I will not retreat a single inch and I will be heard.[14]

In his interview to British Broadcasting Corporation (BBC) in 1955, while criticizing Gandhiji, Dr Ambedkar said: Gandhiji "was not like Garrison in the US who, despite being white, fought for the Negroes."[15]

***

When President Abraham Lincoln signed the Emancipation Proclamation (1 January 1863), it no doubt paved the way for the abolition of slavery in the US. Dr Ambedkar, who studied the life and mission of Abraham Lincoln, was certainly impressed by his sincerity in wishing the slaves to be free. Dr Ambedkar was also moved by President Lincoln's appeal during the American Civil War that the nation shall not survive half slave and half free.

Dr Ambedkar must have been deeply moved by one of the earliest African-American social reformers—Frederick Douglass (1818–1895). Douglass was a great orator, who said in a speech in New York (3 August 1857)—i.e., nearly five years *before* the

---

14 Khabde, PhD Dissertation.

15 Khabde has missed this point. Further details in Chapter 16.

Emancipation Proclamation, that: "If there is no struggle, there is no progress. Those who profess to favour freedom and yet deprecate agitation are men who want crops without ploughing up the ground ... The limits of tyrants are prescribed by the endurance of those who they oppress."[16]

Dr Ambedkar was well aware that after the Emancipation Declaration of 1863, there was a brief period of "Reconstruction". During this period, three important amendments were made to the US Constitution:

| | |
|---|---|
| 13th Amendment: | Former slaves ceased to be slaves (1865) |
| 14th Amendment: | Former slaves given citizenship rights and equal protection under law (1868) |
| 15th Amendment: | Right to vote given irrespective of "race, colour or previous condition of servitude" (1870). |

All three "Reconstruction" Amendments were laudable indeed. Dr Ambedkar knew, however, that they remained only on paper. Illustratively, the 14th Amendment conferred citizenship on all persons including the African Americans born or naturalized in the US. However, as he pointed out, "the Southern States had no intention to respect the 14th Amendment. All except Tennessee had rejected the amendment and had set up governments of the white inhabitants."[17] Discrimination against African Americans re-emerged around 1877 in the form of "Black Codes" (forcing African Americans to work only as menial labour) and "Jim Crow Laws" (forcing African Americans to live in segregated

16 Khabde, PhD Dissertation.

17 Ibid, p. 73.

neighbourhoods). And this was very much prevalent during Dr Ambedkar's stay in the US and continued even thereafter. Why would then Dr Ambedkar be "impressed" by the 14th Amendment of the US Constitution?

***

Dr Ambedkar was undoubtedly impressed by the fact that Booker T. Washington who, born a slave, struggled to acquire education for himself and then dedicated his life to educating others. But his admiration for Washington ends there. Dr Ambedkar could not have supported Washington's "accommodative" stance towards the racial problems in the US. Washington's Atlanta Compromise (1895) was widely seen as his endorsement of segregation and accommodative stance of social policy. "We can be separate as fingers, yet one as the hand, in all things essential to mutual progress," he had said.[18] There is just no way that Dr Ambedkar would have approved of this approach of Booker T. Washington and the person himself.

Intellectually, Dr Ambedkar was closer to the stance adopted by William Du Bois. Du Bois was the first African American to earn a doctorate just as Dr Ambedkar was the first Untouchable to get a PhD in America. Unlike Booker T. Washington, Du Bois insisted on full civil rights and increased political participation. Du Bois wanted the African Americans to educate themselves in the best possible manner—not just for mechanical work, as suggested by Washington—so that they could not only compete with the white on equal footing but also could bring about the much-needed social change.

---

18 See Narendra Jadhav, *India and the US: Caste, Race and Economic Growth,* Sixth Annual Patrick O'Meara International Lecture (Nov 2016), Indiana University, Bloomington, USA.

In fact, there was an exchange of letters between the two—Dr Ambedkar and Dr Du Bois—in their common pursuit of equality and justice. In 1945, Du Bois was a member of a three-person delegation from the NAACP that attended the Conference at which the United Nations (UN) was established. The NAACP delegation wanted the UN to endorse racial equality. On 2 July 1946, Dr Ambedkar sent a letter to Du Bois exploring the possibility of taking up the question of Untouchability to the newly formed United Nations. He had also requested for a copy of the representation that had been submitted at that time to the United Nations.

In his reply dated 31 July 1946, Du Bois did send the desired document to Dr Ambedkar. It is not clear what happened next. While Du Bois was getting frustrated "because his efforts to report racist practices in the US as human rights abuses to the newly formed UN were being completely blocked," Dr Ambedkar was fully engrossed in the political turmoil leading to the Independence of India. This could possibly be one reason why Dr Ambedkar does not seem to have pursued the issue of Untouchables at the UN.[19]

* **

## Dr Ambedkar and European Thinkers

As indicated before, Dr Ambedkar studied the entire evolution of liberal and humanitarian thought, right from the Greek thinkers and philosophers up to the liberal political philosophy in the 18th and 19th century England. The running theme of these thoughts was "a sense of importance of human individuality, a liberation of the individual from complete subservience to [any] group and a

19 A. M. Rajasekhariah, *B.R. Ambedkar: The Politics of Emancipation* (Bombay: Sindhu Publications, 1971), p. 11. Both letters are also available in a feature authored by P. Dayanandan on roundtable.co.in.

relaxation of the tight hold of the custom, law and authority ..."[20] In other words, "the emergence of liberalism, in the broadest sense, seeks to protect the individual from arbitrary external restraints that prevent the full realization of his potentialities."[21] And, in his prolific writings and numerous speeches, Dr Ambedkar quoted them, time and again.

Dr Ambedkar quoted the Greek Historian Thucydides (460–400 BC) on the opening page of his book *What Congress and Gandhi Have Done to the Untouchables,* first published in 1945. In the so-called "Melian Dialogue" reported by Thucydides, Melians said to Athenians before the siege of Melos: "It may be your interest to be our masters, but how can it be ours to be your slaves?" Dr Ambedkar used this quote, directly and indirectly, to impress upon his Untouchable followers to rise and fight for their human rights.

Another Greek dialogue that seemingly had a lot of appeal to Dr Ambedkar was the discussion between the two great Greek Philosophers, Socrates (470–399 BC) and Thrasymachus (459–400 BC).[22] In this discussion, in response to a question by Socrates, Thrasymachus responded:

> I proclaim that might is right and justice is the interest of the stronger ... The different forms of government make laws—democratic, aristocratic, or autocratic—with a view to their respective interests; and these laws, so made by them to serve their interests, they deliver to their subjects as 'justice' and punish as 'unjust' anyone who transgresses them ...

---

20 As quoted by Khabde, PhD Dissertation, from Encyclopaedia Britannica, Vol. X, p. 848

21 Ibid.

22 Will Durant, *The Story of Philosophy* (NY: Simon & Schuster, 1926). This quote is from the 1957 edition, p. 16.

In this definition of justice, given by Thrasymachus, one can certainly find compassion for the oppressed and depressed classes in any society. As such, this discussion, arguably, may have planted the seedling of Republicanism in the mind of Dr Ambedkar.

***

Dr Ambedkar had also studied the European history thoroughly—from the Renaissance (1300–1600) which saw the transition of Europe from the Middle Ages to Modernity on to the Protestant Reformation (1517–1648) which challenged the Roman Catholic Church and Pope's authority, and further on to the French Revolution (1789–1799).

In all these studies, Dr Ambedkar's interest unfailingly centred upon the suppressed and oppressed people, everywhere in the world. No wonder, while writing or speaking about the downtrodden in India, he often referred to Romans and their slaves, Spartans and their helots (a class of serfs with a status between slaves and citizens), British and their villeins (serfs tied to the land in the feudal system).[23]

During the post-Protestant Reformation period, Dr Ambedkar's favourite thinker seems to have been the French Philosopher and Historian, Voltaire (1694–1778). All his life, Voltaire struggled against the Popes and Catholic orthodoxy. He wrote quite sarcastically, "Christianity must be divine, since it has lasted 1700 years despite the fact that it is so full of villainy and nonsense. All ancient people had myths and they are invented by priests."[24]

Will Durant has quoted Voltaire saying to common masses: "Men fed by your labours in a comfortable idleness, enriched by your sweat and your misery, struggled for partisans and slaves. They

23 Ambedkar, *Mr. Gandhi and the Emancipation of the Untouchables*, p. 12.

24 Khabde, PhD Dissertation, p. 121.

inspired you with a destructive fanaticism that they might be your masters. They made you superstitious, not that you might fear God, but that you might fear them."[25]

Dr Ambedkar questioned as to why no Brahmin scholar came forward to play the part of Voltaire. He said:

> Today all scholarship is confined to the Brahmins. But unfortunately, no Brahmin scholar has so far come forward to play the part of a Voltaire who had the intellectual honesty to rise against the doctrines of the Catholic Church in which he was brought up … It is a grave reflection on the scholarship of the Brahmins that they should not have produced a Voltaire.[26]

Dr Ambedkar argued on similar lines as Voltaire when he said: "The Hindu civilization, gauged in the light of these social products (i.e., Casteism and Untouchability), could hardly be called a civilization. It is a diabolical contrivance to suppress and enslave humanity. Its proper name would be infamy."[27]

Another thinker that Dr Ambedkar often quoted in his speeches and writings in support of his point of view was Edmund Burke, an Irish Statesman and Philosopher (1729–1797).

Dr Ambedkar regarded Edmund Burke as a great teacher of political philosophy. Not surprisingly there are several parallels in their beliefs and expression. Both Burke and Ambedkar stood for the humanity, justice and moral order. Both always championed the cause of the suppressed people. Both emphasized the spirit and principles of morality into the conduct of public affairs. Both

25 Durant, *The Story of Philosophy*, p. 215.

26 B.R. Ambedkar, *The Untouchables: Who were they and why they become untouchables*, BAWS, Vol. 7, Preface (first published in 1948).

27 Ibid. The Preface has been reproduced in Jadhav (ed), *Ambedkar Writes*, Vol. II, pp. 128-29.

strongly advocated moral regeneration of society through educating the public opinion.

Burke had said:

> The use of force alone is but temporary. It may endure for a moment; but does not remove the necessity of subduing again, and a nation is not governed which is perpetually to be conquered ... A further objection to force is that you impair the object by your very endeavours to preserve it. The thing you fought for is not the thing which you recover, but depreciated, sunk, wasted and consumed in the context.[28]

Dr Ambedkar used this quote from Burke at least twice: first, at the Round Table Conference in London in 1931, appealing to the British authorities not to use force in turning down the demands of the Depressed Classes in India and, secondly, in the Constituent Assembly debates, in the context of addressing the Hindu-Muslim problem.

Dr Ambedkar was also under a great intellectual influence of John Stuart Mill (1806–1873) who was a British Philosopher, Political Economist and Civil Servant. With his monumental book *On Liberty*, first published in 1859, Mill became an acknowledged philosophical leader of the British liberalism.

Mill's *On Liberty* is a philosophical essay which lays out standards for the relationship between the authority (such as Government) and individual liberty. J.S. Mill maintains that democratic ideals may lead to the "tyranny of the majority."

In the essay, Mill argues, *inter alia*: "...there needs to be protection also against the tyranny of the prevailing opinion and feeling; against the tendency of society to impose, by other means

---

28 Edmund Burke, *Reflections on the Revolution in France* (London: James Dodsley, 1790).

than civil penalties, its own ideas and practices as rules of conduct on those who dissent from them; …"

According to Mill, there is "a limit to the legitimate interference of collective opinion with individual independence, and to find that limit and maintain it against encroachment, is as dispensable to a good condition of human affairs as protection against political despotism."

Building on Mill's argument of the "tyranny of the majority", Dr Ambedkar pointed out:

> In India, the majority is not a political majority. In India, majority is born, it is not made [as in European democracies]. There is a difference between a communal majority and a political majority. A political majority is not a fixed or a permanent majority. It is a majority which is always made, unmade and remade. [On the other hand] a communal majority is a permanent majority fixed in its attitude … If there is so much objection [in terms of the tyranny] to a political majority, how very fatal must be the objection to a communal majority.[29]

Again, while addressing the Constituent Assembly, Dr Ambedkar said: "…in the name of democracy, there must be no tyranny of the majority over minority. The minority must always feel safe although the majority is carrying on the government, the minority is not being hurt or the minority is not being hit below the belt."

In order to avoid the danger of tyranny by communal majority against the Depressed Classes, Dr Ambedkar recommended that the Indian Constitution must contain checks and balances. He forcefully argued that there should be provisions of safeguards that

---

29 B.R. Ambedkar, "Annihilation of Caste", first published in 1936, BAWS Vol. 1.

will prevent the majority from indulging into tyrannical acts against the interests of the minorities.

Yet again, while addressing the Constituent Assembly, Dr Ambedkar quoted John Stuart Mill. In order to maintain democracy not merely in form but also in fact, among other things, Dr Ambedkar maintained that: "…we must do is to observe the caution which John Stuart Mill has given to all who are interested in the maintenance of democracy, namely, not to lay their liberties at the feet of even a great man, or to trust him with powers which enable him to subvert their institutions."[30]

When it came to patriotism, Dr Ambedkar would often quote the Irish political leader Daniel O'Connell (1775–1847) who famously said, "No man can be grateful at the cost of his honour, no woman can be grateful at the cost of her chastity and no nation can be grateful at the cost of its liberty."[31]

Amongst the then contemporary thinkers who influenced Dr Ambedkar, one name that stands out[32] is Professor Harold Laski (1893–1950), who was a British Political Theorist and Economist.

Dr Ambedkar was very much influenced by Harold Laski's view: "The moral order is always taken for granted in democracy. If there was no moral order, democracy will go to pieces."[33]

Dr Ambedkar argued in a similar vein on more than one occasion. According to him the majority of the people are left to

---

30 Historic Speech in the Constituent Assembly while presenting the final draft of the Indian Constitution (25 November 1949). Reproduced in Jadhav (ed), *Ambedkar Speaks*, Vol. II, pp. 533-34.

31 Ibid. p. 534.

32 According to Keer, Prof. Harold Laski was actually present when Dr Ambedkar read a paper at the London School of Economics. However, there is no independent confirmation.

33 H. Laski, *A Grammar of Politics* (London: George Allen and Unwin, Ltd, 1925). Also quoted by Khabde in his PhD Dissertation.

be governed not so much by the law as by morality. Law plays a small part in human activity, where there is dispute and disorder.

* **

In a public speech in 1954, Dr Ambedkar indicated that he has had three *Gurus*. He said, "I am a devotee of Gautam Buddha, Kabir and Mahatma Phule, and a worshipper of learning, self-respect and character."[34]

Dr Ambedkar remained a keen student all his life. A great book lover, collector and, of course, an exceptionally sharp reader, he was probably the only person in the world who built a house only for storing his huge book collection.[35]

As a lifelong worshipper of learning, Dr Ambedkar studied a very wide range of Western thinkers from Socrates (470–399 BC) to Harold Laski (1893–1950), especially the evolution of liberal and humanitarian thought.

In this process, Dr Ambedkar emerged as an intellectual colossus, great thought leader and a universal champion of human rights whose political philosophy centred on liberal thinking and the spirit of Republicanism.

---

34 Marathi Speech. For English translation, see Jadhav (ed), *Ambedkar Speaks,* Vol. I, p. 58.

35 "Raj Gruha", his personal residence in Mumbai, built around 1934.

CHAPTER THREE

# Scholar in Mass Movement

Back home in India, Dr Babasaheb Ambedkar faced problems in setting up a household with his wife, child, and several relatives dependent on him. To start his law practice, he had registered at the Mumbai High Court (on the Appellate side) in June 1923. Unable to afford an office near the High Court in South Mumbai, Dr Ambedkar set up an office at Damodar Hall in Parel (Central Mumbai) with the help of some friends. It took several months for him to secure his first case, as the so-called High-Caste Hindus were hesitant to entrust him with legal matters. Much later, in 1925, he managed to get a part-time job teaching Mercantile Law on a salary of Rs 200 per month, and supplemented his income by serving as an examiner for Bombay University.

## Bahishkrit Hitakarini Sabha

On 9 March 1924, Dr Ambedkar took the first step towards initiating a mass movement by forming a social organization for the Depressed Classes which he called *Bahishkrit Hitakarini Sabha,* with himself as the Chairman of its Managing Committee.[1] The motto of the organization: "Educate, Organize and Agitate" was going to resonate in India for decades.

The objectives of this organization were to promote the spread of education and culture, *inter alia,* by opening hostels, libraries, social centres or study circles; to improve economic conditions by starting Industrial and Agricultural Schools;[2] and to represent the grievances of the Depressed Classes. The *Sabha* initially started a small library in Parel, Mumbai, and a hostel for students of the Depressed Class in Solapur (in January 1925). It also began holding rallies and meetings throughout the Bombay Presidency.

In his early speeches, Dr Ambedkar clearly set out his mission and explicitly carved out a role for himself. In a speech in Mumbai (on 9 March 1924) addressing a group of social workers that founded the *Bahishkrit Hitakarini Sabha,* Dr Ambedkar had announced: "I would certainly not limit the use of the power of my intellect only to my family and my Caste. I will render them to the benefit of entire Depressed Classes, to help them build their social movement and struggle..."

Dr Ambedkar's speeches were not only inspiring but also purposeful, instilling self-respect among the Depressed Classes on some occasions and raising political awareness among others. He emphasized, "Lack of collective willpower is holding us back."

---

1 A number of highly distinguished office-bearers were involved: Sir Chimanlal Setalvad (President) and Dr R.P. Paranjpye as well as B.G. Kher as Vice Presidents. (Fourteen years later, Shri B.G. Kher became the Chief Minister of the Bombay Province.)

2 This is reminiscent of the work done by Booker T. Washington for the African American youth in the US in the late 19th and early 20th centuries.

On 1 January 1927, Dr Ambedkar addressed a meeting at the Koregaon War Memorial[3] near Pune and reminded his Untouchable *Mahar* followers how their forefathers had fought tenaciously and with magnificent courage.[4]

Importantly, Dr Ambedkar, for the first time, fully spelt out his vision for the Untouchables in the context of *Swaraj* (Home-rule) early on (24 May 1924) stating, "If *Swaraj* is coming, we must get equal political rights in it."

Explaining that Untouchability is worse than slavery, he said:[5]

> History is replete with examples wherein slaves were liberated and then became independent citizens of the State. But there is not a single example in India, where Untouchables became Touchable… Because of the strict rule that an Untouchable

---

3 The Marathi Speech delivered by Dr Ambedkar at the meeting held at the Koregaon War Memorial, Koregaon, near Pune on 1 January 1927 is documented in the English Report: BAWS, Vol. 17 (3), pp. 3-7.
The Koregaon War Memorial is a 65-foot high obelisk erected by the British to honour primarily *Mahar* soldiers who "fought tenaciously and with magnificent courage" in a great battle on 1 January 1818. This battle pitted the British forces (very small in number) against the army of Peshwa Bajirao II led by General Gokhale. Despite being significantly outnumbered, *Mahar* soldiers "fought without rest or respite, food or water, continuously for 12 hours." Their "heroic valour and enduring fortitude" earned them great admiration. The names of the Mahar soldiers who were killed or wounded in the battle are inscribed on the Monument.

4 There was a major incident at Bhima Koregaon (1 January 2018) where violence broke out during an annual celebratory gathering to mark the 200th year of the Battle of Bhima Koregaon victory.

5 The Marathi Speech delivered at the Conference of the Depressed Classes from Bombay Province, Barshi, District Solapur (24 May 1924). For English translation, see Jadhav (ed.), *Ambedkar Speaks,* Vol. III, pp. 49-53.

> is Untouchable by birth, centuries have passed and yet the situation has not changed at all. Untouchability is several times a greater hurdle in the path of progress of the Untouchables in India, than slavery was...

In the same speech, Dr Ambedkar underscored the need for an organization of Untouchables. He said: "What is more important is to create an institutional framework.... We must create a wide-ranging organization of Untouchables."

While concluding, Dr Ambedkar made an earnest appeal to his followers. He said: "My educated Brothers, if you want your future generations to remember you with respect and regards, if you want the condition of your children and grandchildren to be better than the situation that you have been in, please do come forward. It is your solemn duty to do...very best so as to rectify the situation."

Even in all these early speeches when Dr Ambedkar was laying the foundations of his mission, the underlying spirit of Republicanism is clearly discernible.

***

## In the Bombay Legislative Council

While the mass movement initiated by Dr Ambedkar was beginning to gain momentum, in December 1926, Dr Ambedkar was nominated as a Member of the Bombay Legislative Council (BLC). Under the Government of India Act, 1919, there was a provision for one Nominated Member to the Council representing the Depressed Classes. On behalf of the *Bahishkrit Hitakarini Sabha,* Dr Ambedkar was trying to persuade the British Government to increase the number of Nominated Members representing the Depressed Classes in the Province. In December 1926, the Government raised the number to two and appointed Dr Ambedkar and Dr P.G. Solanki to those positions. For Dr Ambedkar, this was going to be the beginning of a long and distinguished career as a Legislator.

As a nominated Member of the BLC, Dr Ambedkar quickly earned himself a reputation for his studious, analytical and comprehensive interventions. In his maiden speech at the BLC (24 February 1927), Dr Ambedkar critically dealt with the Provincial Budget 1927–28.

At the Council, Dr Ambedkar consistently emphasized the importance of both School and Higher Education. While speaking on School Education (on 12 March 1927), Dr Ambedkar argued that per capita expenditure on education must be raised. In a similar vein, Dr Ambedkar participated extensively in the debate on the Bombay University Act (Amendment) Bill. He analyzed the proposals before the Council and made suggestions so as to organize the University of Bombay into a better teaching University, promoting Higher Education and Research.

***

With his nomination to the Bombay Legislative Council as a Member, Dr Ambedkar's strategy for launching a mass movement for the upliftment of Untouchables started taking a concrete shape. Clearly, in that initial phase which was going to last for nearly a decade, Dr Ambedkar was going to fight for social justice, while remaining within the fold of the Hindu religion. He was going to orient his mass movement as a struggle for civic rights for the Untouchables.

It all began with the demand of getting to drink water from a public reservoir. The issue was one of asserting the elementary right to water for Untouchables and the setting was a small town of Mahad in Konkan.

For hundreds of years, Untouchables were prevented from collecting or drinking water from any of the points where the so-called Upper Castes did. In 1926, the Government of Bombay Province adopted a resolution abolishing such discrimination. As a follow-up action, the Mahad Municipality had passed a resolution to allow Untouchables full access to all waterfronts, including its largest reservoir, called Chavdar Lake. However, this resolution had remained only on paper, and the Hindu Untouchables were not allowed to draw any water from the lake, whereas Muslim and Christian Untouchables could do so. Others could even take their cattle to Chavdar Lake, but human beings such as the Hindu Untouchables could not. It was around this cause that Dr Ambedkar chose to launch a mass movement of the downtrodden.

## Chavdar Lake Struggle

Dr Ambedkar decided to hold a meeting at Mahad, where the Untouchables would exercise their right to water *en masse*. On 19 March 1927, the *Bahishkrit Hitakarini Sabha* sponsored a Conference of the Depressed Classes in Mahad. The response was simply unprecedented. Thousands of people of all ages, mostly wearing rags and carrying *bhakris* (round flat bread popular in Maharashtra and Gujarat) wrapped in cloth bags, assembled from different parts of the Province in response to Dr Ambedkar's call.

In that historic meeting, Dr Ambedkar first explained how the British had let the Untouchables down and urged the gathering to keep alive the (new) fire of awareness. Dr Ambedkar then added:[6] "Today, Untouchables ... have developed a habit of living on State food begged from house to house. They do it as if it is their great right; begging door to door for State food.... They have lost

6 For fuller version of the speech, see Jadhav (ed), *Ambedkar Speaks,* Vol. III, pp. 55-60.

their self-respect and dignity... It is most shameful to sell your humanity...."

Urging the assembled Untouchables to rebel against the humiliating and enslaving tradition of village duties, Dr Ambedkar made a passionate appeal. He said:

> Gentlemen, if not for you, at least for the sake of your children please listen to what I say. You may ask, 'why do all these difficult things when you are comfortable, maybe on half a bread?' You may ask me, 'why leave assured half bread for an imaginary full bread?' But I must warn you, if you do not do what I tell, you will not get even this half bread in times to come.

***

The first day of the Conference was a great success. The historic gathering of more than 10,000 Untouchables was visibly moved by the inspiring speech of Dr Ambedkar. Day One also witnessed the passage of several resolutions including, notably (a) that Touchables should bury their dead cattle themselves and not expect the Untouchables to do so any more, and (b) that the resolution allowing all Untouchables access to all water fronts should be made operational.

The next day (i.e., 20 March 1927), just as the Conference was about to conclude, a local Touchable Hindu leader Shri Anantrao Chitre suddenly announced: "Let's go to Chavdar Lake and implement the Mahad Municipality Resolution."

And there began the historic march!

The congregation of more than 10,000 people marched to Chavdar Lake with Dr Ambedkar leading the procession. The crowd marched in a disciplined manner, in rows of four, shouting slogans: "Educate, Unite, and Agitate!" The reservoir was surrounded by the houses of the so-called Upper Castes on all sides. Every door, window and terrace of every house was full of shocked people, who looked on at the huge, determined crowd gathered around their tank, "polluting" its sanctity.

After reaching the Chavdar Tank, Dr Ambedkar walked down the half-dozen steps with firm resolve and looking at the thousands of expectant followers, calmly bent down, cupped some water in his hands, and drank. The crowd roared and let loose cheers of *"Dr Ambedkar Ki Jay!"* (Victory to Dr Ambedkar) as everyone took a symbolic sip of water. A social rebellion had begun. While addressing the excited crowd, Dr Ambedkar proclaimed that the Untouchables were asserting their rights as human beings. They were making history.

A couple of hours later, a large crowd of so-called Upper-Castes armed with bamboo sticks gathered at the street corners, catching the delegates unawares. A rumour was afloat that the Untouchables were planning to forcibly enter the local Temple. The rowdies charged at the delegates who fled. They spared no one—men, women nor children—knocking their food into the dirt and pounding their utensils. The protesters were screaming with rage, itching for retaliation. A word from Dr Ambedkar, and Mahad would have turned into a battlefield. Dr Ambedkar, however, appealed for peace and discipline. He said that their struggle was to enforce the law, not to break it.

* * *

The "Mahad March" was a momentous event. For the first time, historically, the Depressed Classes had made a collective public attempt to assert the civic rights denied to them for generations.

Dr Ambedkar emerged as the saviour of the downtrodden, enkindling among them the flame of self-respect and self-elevation. Directly as result of the Mahad Conference, several of the Untouchables gave up eating carrion and skinning carcasses, and many stopped begging for crumbs.[7]

* * *

*Bahishkrit Hitakarini Sabha* convened a public meeting in Mumbai (on 3 July 1927) to protest against the oppression in Mahad. In the meeting, Dr Ambedkar announced his intention to do a *Satyagraha* in Mahad and said, "We need bold and self-respecting people for Mahad *Satyagraha.*"

As momentum was growing for the Mahad *Satyagraha*, some Untouchable activists initiated a Temple Entry *Satyagraha* at the Ambadevi Temple in Amravati, located in the Vidarbha region of Maharashtra. While the Temple Entry agitation was going on, a Conference of Untouchables from Berar (i.e., Vidarbha) was convened in Amravati. In his Presidential Address on 13 November 1927, Dr Ambedkar elaborated in detail on his philosophy behind the *Satyagraha* movement.[8]

Dr Ambedkar said:

> If Untouchables come out of that stigma and participate in nation-building, they will only contribute to the progress of the nation. Therefore, this movement for removal of Untouchability is in true sense a movement for nation-building and fraternity …
>
> …*Instead of abandoning the Hindu religion and causing its decline, they [Untouchables] want to remain within the Hindu religion and use all their energy to fight for the rights of humanity* [emphasis added]. They are *not* demanding any special rights and status; they are

7 At this point of time, Dr Ambedkar started a new fortnightly, titled *Bahishkrut Bharat* and began responding to critics of his mass movement and explaining his point of view to the general public.

8 For full English summary, see Jadhav (ed), *Ambedkar Speaks*, Vol. I, pp. 83-92.

demanding only equal treatment ... Their demand is only for equal rights with the Touchables. Now, if you apply the principles of the Gita, you will find that this movement of Untouchables is a movement for *Satyagraha.*

***

The symbolic march to the Chavdar Lake had kindled a flame of awakening in the Untouchables. On 4 August 1927, the Mahad Municipality revoked its earlier resolution granting Untouchables access to the water tank. Dr Ambedkar took this as a challenge and announced that he would intensify the struggle by holding another protest meeting in Mahad.

## The Mahad Satyagraha and Burning of Manusmriti

The Mahad *Satyagraha* Conference in December 1927 saw an even bigger gathering in Mahad where Dr Ambedkar explained, at length, that the Mahad *Satyagraha* was for laying the foundation of equality.[9] He said:

> The Touchables of Mahad are opposing Untouchables to draw water from Mahad Lake not because its water will get polluted or it will vanish in the thin air. They oppose it because they do not want to accept that the Untouchables are equal to them. ...
>
> Our objective is to prove that we are human beings just like others... this Conference is unique and historical. There is no parallel to this event in the entire history of India.
>
> We should remember ... principles of Versailles Conference for this Mahad Conference of ours. This Conference should follow the same path and same programmes to dismantle the frames of *Varnashram* in Hinduism; *we should adopt the programmes*

9 Presidential Address, Mahad *Satyagraha* Conference, 25-27 December 1927. For details, see Jadhav (ed), *Ambedkar Speaks*, Vol. I, pp. 93-101.

> *for unifying all the five Varnas and to form only one solid Class of all the Hindus* [emphasis added]. Unless it is done, the Untouchability will not vanish and there will be no equality and fraternity in our society.

In the same Presidential Address (25 December 1927), Dr Ambedkar specifically challenged the authority of all Hindu Scriptures. He said: "If you say your religion is our religion, your rights and ours must be equal. Is this the case? If not, on what grounds do you say that we must remain in the Hindu fold?"

Dr Ambedkar denounced the *Manusmṛiti*, which has traditionally governed the laws and lives of Hindus. Revered by the so-called Upper-Caste Hindus, it has been hated by the Untouchables, as it directed that molten lead be poured into the ears of Untouchables if they heard or read the sacred *Vedas*. Dr Ambedkar felt that the *Manusmṛiti* was not only a Declaration of Rights for the so-called Upper-Caste Hindus but also a Charter of slavery for the Untouchables. He condemned it as a symbol of tyranny among the Hindus. He therefore gave a call to publicly burn the copies of the Holy Book.

That evening (i.e., on 25 December 1927), the *Manusmṛiti* was placed on a special pyre and ceremoniously burned amid cheers from the Untouchables. This bold gesture was enacted essentially to demonstrate that Untouchables were no longer willing to abide by the religious and ritualistic servitude imposed on them.

* * *

The next day (i.e., on 26 December 1927) all the assembled people took out a massive rally on the roads of Mahad, went to the Lake and encircled it. The rally was of such magnitude that it took over two hours to navigate through the relatively small area. It was very disciplined. Touchable Hindus largely remained indoors and all the shops were closed. Although the *Satyagrahis* did not physically enter the Mahad Lake, they had virtually captured it by surrounding it from all sides.

Ironically, following the Chavdar Lake struggle earlier, the orthodox Upper-Caste Hindus of Mahad had the Brahmin priests "purify" the "desecrated" reservoir by pouring into it 108 pots of curd, milk, cow dung and cow urine amid loud religious chants!

By burning the Hindu scriptures at the same place only a few months later, Dr Ambedkar had succeeded in converting the fight for the right to drinking water into a socio-cultural struggle of the downtrodden masses for equality.

It was around this time (December 1927) that Dr Ambedkar formed the *Samata Sainik Dal* (Social Equality Corps) with a view to aggressively pursue the agenda of social equality.

***

During the years 1928 and 1929, Dr Ambedkar, in the aftermath of the Mahad *Satyagraha,* delivered some very important speeches.

In one of them, he said:[10] "Those who accuse us of being aggressive should be ashamed of themselves. There is no other community in the world as modest as Untouchables… Haven't we remained meek under the most humiliating and inhuman circumstances, for ages?…"

In yet another speech,[11] Dr Ambedkar told his followers: "… Another method to remove the injustice caused to us is to capture

---

10 For full English summary, see Jadhav (ed), *Ambedkar Speaks*, Vol. I, p. 11. The original Marathi speech was delivered at a Ganesh Festival in Mumbai on 25 September 1928.

11 For English summary, see Jadhav (ed), *Ambedkar Speaks*, Vol. III, pp. 64-5. The original Marathi speech was delivered at the Social Conference of the Depressed Classes, in Belgaum.

the power. We need to have the political power to dismantle this frame of *Chaturvarna....*"[12]

In yet another hard-hitting speech, Dr Ambedkar maintained that the Depressed Classes will not get human rights unless they declare war against the oppression.[13]

***

## *Kala Ram Temple Satyagraha*

The next stage of Dr Ambedkar's mass movement for social cause came in the form of a temple entry agitation at the Kala Ram Temple at Nashik.[14] A call was issued to Untouchables all over Maharashtra to come to Nashik on 1 March 1930 and assert their right to worship Lord Ram at the Kala Ram Temple. Thousands of Untouchables had flocked to Nashik in response to Dr Ambedkar's call. The mass movement initiated by Dr Ambedkar had gathered further momentum.

In the public meeting, Dr Ambedkar explained the purpose of the struggle and recounted his efforts towards peaceful negotiations. "We will not die if we are not allowed in the Temple, nor are we going to be immortalized by gaining entry. We are fighting for equal rights as human beings, and we are not going to accept anything less," he said to a thunderous applause.

Soon after the public meeting, Dr Ambedkar led a procession to Kala Ram Temple. He was followed by a band playing martial tunes and hundreds volunteers. Following them were around 500 women. This was a revolution in itself, as it was for *the first time that*

---

12 Dr Ambedkar formally joined politics much later, in 1936.

13 Presidential Address (Marathi) in Chittegaon, Nashik (21 June 1929).

14 The Kala Ram Temple in Nashik, Maharashtra, was constructed in 1782 at the site believed to have been inhabited by Ram, Sita and Laxman during their exile.

*Untouchable women were participating in a mass movement* [emphasis added]. Behind them were thousands of orderly protesters, walking with discipline and determination. When the procession reached the Temple, the gates were closed and barricaded. A contingent of armed police was guarding the main entrance. Dr Ambedkar spoke to the Police Superintendent and then directed the procession to the Godavari River where another rally was held.

A peaceful agitation in front of the Temple gates began the next day. There were four gates with hundreds of armed policemen at each gate. The Police Superintendent had set up an office in a tent pitched right in front of the Temple, and had camped there expecting the agitators to strike in the dead of night. With thousands of protesters taking turns and forming a human barricade, the Temple was sealed and nobody was allowed to enter. The agitation continued for several days.

Towards the end of March in 1930, as Ram Navami, Lord Ram's birth anniversary, approached, the trustees decided to reopen the Temple nearly a month after it had been sealed. Upon hearing this news, the protesters sprang into action. They formed a human barricade at the entrance, insisting that worship should be allowed on a first-come, first-served basis. In response, the gates were hurriedly closed once again. Thousands willingly courted arrest. With baton blows by police raining, the protesters were packed into police vans and taken to local jails, which quickly became overcrowded. They were then driven outside the city and dumped there, without food, water or shelter. Despite these hardships, they remained unfazed. They defiantly marched right back, singing and chanting along the way.

Two days after Ram Navami, tradition called for a procession of Lord Ram's chariot through Nashik city. While Untouchables were not allowed inside the Temple, tradition permitted them to participate in pulling the chariot. However, due to the disturbance, a hasty compromise was reached: the Upper Castes would pull the chariot up to the Temple's main gate, and from there, it would be carried by the Untouchables.

The priests had announced a specific time for the procession to start, but then quietly the so-called Upper-Caste Hindus gathered much earlier. They hastily led the chariot, cheered on by the priests, and went well past the main gate. The protesters were caught unawares, but they quickly got into action and collectively forced the chariot to a halt midway. The chariot was sidetracked as fights ensued. The police beat the protesters, pushing them into alleys. Their batons flew freely and they spared no one, not even women and children. There was rioting and a few agitators set some shops on fire. The fire spread rapidly, damaging a lot of property, bicycles and cars. Many protesters, including Dr Ambedkar, were injured.

A majority of those injured were Untouchables. They were furious and wanted revenge, but Dr Ambedkar, injured though he was, addressed and pacified them. All gatherings near the Temple were then forbidden and would warrant arrest. The matter went to the court and, pending the court decision, the agitation was temporarily suspended.

***

Almost precisely at that point of time, it was announced that Mahatma Gandhi had defied the salt laws imposed by the British in a town called Dandi in today's Gujarat. Gandhiji had also announced a nationwide Civil Disobedience Movement against the British Rule on behalf of the Congress Party.

The parallel between the movements led by Mahatma Gandhi and Dr Ambedkar, respectively, becomes apparent here. Indeed, Dr Ambedkar's declaration of social independence for Untouchables coincided with Mahatma Gandhi's declaration of political independence for the people of India.

# PART II

# Making of Mahatma Gandhi

# CHAPTER FOUR

# Mohandas Gandhi: The Early Days

Rabindranath Tagore bestowed the honorific of *Mahatma* (A Great Soul) on Mohandas Karamchand Gandhi in 1915 and, in turn, Gandhiji called Rabindranath, who was eight years older than him, as *Gurudev*.

In India, Mahatma Gandhi is regarded as the Father of the Nation. His birthday, i.e., 2 October, is celebrated in India as Gandhi Jayanti and around the world as the International Day of Non-Violence

Mohandas Karamchand Gandhi[1] was born on 2 October 1869 in the capital city of a small Princely State of Porbandar. His father, Karamchand Uttamchand Gandhi, worked as the *Diwan* (Chief Minister) of the Porbandar Princely State. Karamchand's father (i.e., Mohandas's grandfather) was also the *Diwan* of Porbandar. With education limited only to the Elementary level, Karamchand had a modest start in Porbandar State. In 1874, when Mohandas was around five years old, Karamchand joined another small

1 Three chapters, i.e., Chapters 4, 5 and 6, are essentially background materials put together on the basis of standard sources.

Princely State of Rajkot as a Counsellor to the local ruler. Within two years, he became the *Diwan* of Rajkot. At that time, Mohandas was seven years old. Later on, Karamchand succeeded his father Uttamchand as the *Diwan* of Porbandar.

Mohandas, the youngest child, was born to Karamchand and his fourth wife, Putlibai. They had three other children: a son named Laxmidas (born in 1860), a daughter named Raliatbehn (born in 1862), and another son named Karsandas (born in 1866). Thus, Mohandas's brother and sister were nine and seven years older than him, respectively, while his immediate elder brother was around three years older.

The Gandhi family had somewhat unusual religious background. While it was a Hindu family, the father belonged to Modh Baniya Caste (in the *Varna* of *Vaishya,* the trader class among the four *Varnas*) and his mother came from a *Pranami Vaishnava* sect of Hinduism. The *Pranami* sect follows the Krishna *Bhakti* (worship) cult and their religious texts include the *Bhagavad Gita* and *Bhagavata Purana*.

While growing up, the dominant influence on Mohandas was that of his mother Putlibai. She was known to be a very pious lady who "would take the hardest vows and keep them without flinching. To keep two or three consecutive fasts was nothing to her."[2]

No wonder the Indian classics generally and the stories of King Harishchandra and Shravana in particular had a great impact on Mohandas in his childhood. In his autobiography, Gandhiji has indicated how these classics left an indelible impression on his mind. He wrote: "It haunted me and I must have acted

---

2 Ramachandra Guha, *Gandhi Before India* (Gurugram: Penguin Random House, 2016), p. 23.

Harishchandra to myself many times."[3] Some scholars believe that Gandhiji's self-identification with truth and love as supreme values is traceable to these epic characters.[4] Apparently, Mohandas asked himself why everyone could not be as truthful as Harishchandra and was fascinated by Shravana's devotion towards his parents.

## Mediocre Child

Mohandas was shy from a young age, a trait which is said to have impacted him in the long run when he was trying to establish a successful legal practice in India.[5] He kept to himself and largely avoided classmates, whom he described as being taller, heavier and more social than him. He was known to be scared of the dark, ghosts and spirits. He ensured that the light in his room was always on, and often asked his maid for help. She would tell him to repeat the words *Ramanama*.

Mohandas was playful at home. He used to tease his dog as well as his sister Raliatbehn who was supposed to take care of him at home. Mohan was given the nickname *Moniya* by his family, and they deeply loved and adored him.

In school, Mohan struggled. He attended *dhooli shala* (Pre-Primary School) at Porbandar, where he took very little interest in trying to excel. He used to memorize multiplication tables and other required material so as to pass and perform decently in tests.

---

3 M.K. Gandhi, *An Autobiography or The Story of My Experiments with Truth.* The first edition of the autobiography (which was in Gujarati) was published in two volumes—Vol. 1 in 1927 and Vol. II in 1929. The quotes used here are from its English translation by Mahadev Desai in 1940 (revised and reprinted by General Press, New Delhi in 2018).

4 See, for example, see Pitirim Sorokin, *The Ways and Power of Love* (West Conshohocken, PA: Templeton Press, 2002), p. 169.

5 A.M. Todd, *Mohandas Gandhi* (New York: Infobase Publishing, 2004).

A major reason for this was his difficulty in fitting in with his schoolmates. From a young age, he was much disciplined and did not engage in mischief. Moreover, he adhered strictly to his principles, regardless of the circumstances. This was not very well received by his friends, with whom he struggled to converse and fit in.[6]

This distinction from his peers and mates did not deter his strong sense of self, and he took pride in the fact that he was different from the rest. He took it to be an inherent part of his identity.

When Mohan was seven, his family moved to Rajkot. His father had become the *Diwan* of Rajkot. There Mohan missed the blue ocean and ships in harbour.[7] At Rajkot, he was sent to a primary school where English was emphasized upon. Mohan faced issues in learning and largely remained a mediocre student. He was shy and did not blend well with the school crowd.[8] His books were his sole companions, and he used to rush back home to them after school.

Soon after completing his primary education, Mohan joined Alfred Boys High School when he was 12, following in the footsteps of his elder brothers. Here, English was the primary medium of instruction, and Mohan struggled to grasp the concepts. It was during this period that the Hindu epics began to profoundly influence him. He was not particularly fond of learning by heart, and struggled with both English and *Sanskrit*. On the other hand, he enjoyed Geometry as it involved logic and reasoning.[9]

---

6 Ibid.

7 Rajkumari Shanker, *The Story of Gandhi* (New Delhi: Children's Book Trust, 1969), https://www.mkgandhi.org/ebks/The%20Story%20of%20Gandhi.pdf.

8 Ibid.

9 Ibid.

Quite unusual for Mohan's family status, he had an early exposure to the Caste system and Untouchability. He had a friend named Uka, an Untouchable sweeper-boy, at his school. One day, Mohan approached Uka to offer him some sweets. Uka, aware of their Caste differences, told him not to come too close. Yet, Mohan extended his hand and gave him some of his sweets. This scene was observed by Mohan's mother from a window above, and she immediately called him back inside. She explained that according to Hindu traditions, an Upper-Caste Hindu should not touch someone from a lower caste. Mohan, however, failed to see the rationale behind this custom and asked her what made Uka different and why he was forbidden to touch him.[10]

## Mohandas Gets Married

A year after enrolling into the High School, there was a sudden change in Mohan's life. He was told that he was to be married to Kasturbai Makanji. She was one year older than him and lived in Porbandar. Her father was a rich merchant friend of Mohan's father Karamchand.

The wedding was an elaborate affair. It took months of preparations. Mohan had no clue that the wedding was to take place till the time the preparations were already underway. Later, in his autobiography, he wrote that the wedding, at that time, did not mean "anything more to me than the prospects of good clothes to wear, drum beating, marriage processions, rich dinners and a strange girl to play with".[11]

During the wedding ceremony, the bride and groom took the traditional vows of devotion and fidelity. As described later in his

---

10 Ibid.

11 Gandhi, *The Story of My Experiments with Truth.*

autobiography, the vows of faithfulness had an untoward effect. He wished that his wife reciprocated his faithfulness and trust, and a tinge of jealousy grew inside him. He was always watchful of her movements, and demanded that she could not leave without his permission. Here, a rift became evident between the married couple.

Kasturba disregarded these demands and made it a point that she could do as she pleased, and move around as she liked and when she desired. According to his autobiography, the restraints Mohan imposed on her were met with rebellion and she would try harder to stay free. A large part of their daily routine thus became refusal to speak to each other, and some bitter exchanges. Years later, Gandhiji acknowledged that it was improper of him to have made such large demands; however, at that point of time all he wished for was to be a strict husband.

The rift had long-standing effects on him. Mohan also became increasingly lustful of his wife and wished to be with her at all times. At school, he constantly looked at the clock and wished for school to be over, so that he could go and be with his wife. As a result, his grades started falling.

Mohan was also disturbed by the fact that Kasturba was an illiterate. He made many attempts to teach her, but to no avail. Although he wanted her to learn how to read and write, she showed no interest at all. This left him frustrated.[12]

After some time, Kasturba left him to live with her parents for a while. During this time, they were able to re-examine their values and priorities. The positive feelings that the two felt for each other surfaced over the years, especially after Mohan's possessive attitude and jealous feelings changed into those of trust. Later on, Kasturba became one of the main supporters of Gandhiji and his movement.

---

12 Ibid.

She actively took part in his social activities, and supported her husband throughout their long marriage.

## Mohandas Goes Astray

While he was still in High School, Mohan met a friend of his brother called Sheik Mehtab.[13] Although Sheik had a bad reputation amongst his friends and within his school, Mohan was fascinated by him because he had a strong physique. When he asked Sheik what made him so strong, he said that if Mohan ate meat (just as Sheik did), he too would grow tall and strong. In his orthodox Hindu family, meat-eating was forbidden but Mohan tried meat. This was much against the traditions that prevailed amongst his family and household. At first, the taste did not appeal to him; however, gradually meat curries tended to grow on him.

At that point, Mohan started lying to his family. He made excuses for not eating his dinner whenever he ate outside. He knew that his family would not allow him to eat meat, and would not forgive him. Soon, the guilt of lying to his family started affecting him and he decided to never touch meat again. Even though he felt no guilt for eating meat or breaking traditions, he felt bad for lying to his mother.[14]

At other instances, Mohan had used small amounts of money that he possessed to buy cigarettes to smoke along with Sheik and his brother. One day, he ended up stealing a piece of gold. He knew that he had committed a crime and felt very guilty for his sins. He resolved that he would never steal again and wrote a letter of confession to his father. Karamchand read the confession and,

---

13 Todd, *Mohandas Gandhi.*

14 Shanker, *The Story of Gandhi.*

with sorrow, immediately tore it up. Mohan left the room at once, crying intensely.

In 1885, his father suffered an attack of fistula, and his condition started to deteriorate day by day. The doctors administered some treatment, but it proved ineffective. On 16 November 1885, Karamchand Gandhi died at the age of 63.

During this time, Mohan was around 16 years old, while his wife was 17. They had recently welcomed their first child, who tragically passed away shortly thereafter. These two losses deeply saddened and troubled Mohan. The family found it hard to meet even the day-to-day household expenses during this period. Mohan still had about two years of High School ahead of him, and his eldest brother was unemployed. They relied on financial assistance from their uncles to make ends meet.[15]

***

In January 1888, shortly after completing High School, Mohan joined Samaldas College in Bhavnagar. However, he soon lost interest in his studies and became so stressed that he decided to drop out after finishing his first term. Upon returning home, he was surprised to find that his elder brother Laxmidas and his cousin Mavji Dave Joshi urging him to go to the UK to continue his education.[16] Mohan saw this as a chance to travel and explore the world. Meanwhile, Kasturba had given birth to their first healthy child, Harilal.

Mohan was advised that getting his education from Britain to become a lawyer or a barrister would take him only three years, as opposed to the longer four-year course that prevailed in India.

15 Anne Shraff, *Mahatma Gandhi [20th Century Biographies]* (California: Saddleback Educational Publishing, 2008).

16 Guha, *Gandhi Before India*, p. 32.

However, the cost of his Higher Education would be Rs 13,000, which was a very large sum for the family then. There were no scholarships either, so they would have to incur the entire cost.

Moreover, his mother Putlibai was opposed to the idea of her son travelling to the UK. She did not want her son to leave her and stay so far away from her. Her main fear was that he would end up losing his Caste and morality. According to her, he would be making friends with the wrong kind of people and lose his morality.[17] She was afraid of him abandoning all his Hindu traditions by eating meat, seeing other women and consuming alcohol. Kasturba was not to accompany Mohan to England, and this further aggravated Pultibai's fears.

Mohan pleaded with his mother to let him go to England, and took a vow to "not eat meat, not drink, and not touch a woman".[18] Finally, he was allowed to travel. Laxmidas had to sell off the family jewels to get enough money to pay for Mohan's education.

On his way to England, Mohan stayed at a local Modh Baniya community lodging in Mumbai before departing. There, the community elders expressed apprehension about his plans and told him that it was unnatural and improper for him to travel across the sea. Mohan told them about his vows to his mother; however, they did not take this into account. He was excommunicated from their Caste.

## Mohandas in London

In England, Mohandas first arrived at Southampton. He saw many people in overcoats, black clothes and bowler hats, and was embarrassed that he was the only one who was wearing white

---

17 Shraff, *Mahatma Gandhi.*

18 Ibid.

flannel. Luckily, he had some family friends in England. On his arrival, he met Dr P.J. Mehta, a family friend. Given Mohan's unorthodox behaviour and clothing, Dr Mehta advised him on European manners. Dr Mehta advised him not to speak loudly, not to abruptly touch other people's things and not to keep addressing people as "sir", since only servants spoke that way to their masters.

Mohan found this very peculiar, yet he tried his level best to assimilate. He struggled to adopt the European customs, even going as far as buying tailored clothes and a top hat while renting a suite of rooms. He also took dancing lessons, but soon discovered he lacked rhythm. Moreover, he found it hard to like the European food and became homesick. Luckily, he discovered a local vegetarian restaurant where he could enjoy simple, vegetarian meals. To manage his expenses, he opted to travel on foot whenever possible.

He enrolled at the University College London (UCL) which was a part of London University.[19] He could not attend premier institutions such as Oxford or Cambridge as they were too expensive and elite. He studied law, with the intention of becoming a barrister. During this time, he appeared for the London Matriculation Exam, where he passed in Chemistry, French and English, but failed in Latin. Later on, he was able to pass in Latin too. He was admitted to the Inner Temple in November 1888.

At that time, Mohan joined the London Vegetarian Society (LVS), and was also elected as a member of its Executive Committee. He worked under Arnold Hills, a British businessman and vegetarianism promoter. Some of the members were also part of the Theosophical Society, which aimed at promoting universal brotherhood. Among other things, they also promoted the study of Hinduism and Buddhism. Thus, they were able to encourage Mohan to join them in reading the *Bhagavad Gita*.

---

19 Thomas Weber, *Gandhi as Disciple and Mentor* (New York: Cambridge University Press, 2004).

## Tongue-tied Barrister

A major problem that Mohandas faced was his tongue-tied and shy nature. It largely prevented him from speaking up for his beliefs and voicing his opinions in the LVS meetings. Once, a senior colleague in the LVS, Dr Oldfield, said to him: "You talk to me quite all right, but why is it that you never open your lips at a committee meeting? You are a drone."

It was not that Mohandas had nothing to speak about, yet he had no way to muster up the courage or words to speak up at these meetings. Everyone else appeared to be more informed, and whenever he was ready to articulate something, another topic of discussion would come up and his statements would be sidelined.

Hill was a puritan. Moreover, he was a major financier of the LVS. Many members in the Council were also his students and worked under him. At that time, new means of birth control had come up. Certain members of the Society considered this to be immoral; however, one member, Thomas Alison, was an ardent promoter of it. Due to this, Hill wished that Thomas be removed from the Society. He viewed vegetarianism as an inherently moral movement, and wished for it to stay in that way. Mohandas felt differently. As he described later in his autobiography, Mohandas believed that "any vegetarian could be a member of the Society irrespective of his views on other morals".[20]

A motion was raised to remove Thomas from the LVS. Although there were others in the Society who shared Mohan's views, he felt as if he had an obligation to present them himself. He prepared his arguments and appeared at the meeting that day. However, his fear and shyness prevented him from uttering a single word. Finally, the Chairman told another member of the Committee to read out

20 https://www.mkgandhi.org/autobio/chap18.htm

Mohan's document. This incident brought ridicule to Mohandas and he became the face of mockery.

Looking back, Gandhiji later admitted that at that time he felt ashamed due to his mannerisms. They prevented him from speaking up and actually voicing his opinions. They also caused him financial loss and ridicule and made him come off as unintelligent in the eyes of his peers. However, in his Autobiography, he stated that it was not to his disadvantage, for he learnt about the "economy of words". His hesitancy became a pleasure, as a thoughtless word was never penned down or uttered by him. This nature ensured that he never regretted anything he said or wrote. His shyness allowed him to be shielded and grow as an individual, and ensured that everything he said was thoughtful.

In the meantime, Mohandas had devoted most of his attention to studies. He keenly prepared for the Bar exam. He passed with fairly high marks, and on 10 June 1891, he was called to the Bar. After being admitted as a barrister and enrolled with the High Court, Barrister Mohandas Karamchand Gandhi sailed for India on 12 June 1891. He was 22 years old.

***

## Barrister Gandhi Returns to India

As his ship docked in the Mumbai harbour, Mohan spotted his brother Laxmidas waiting for him with a sombre expression. Concerned, Mohan asked if there was any distressing news to share. To his dismay, Laxmidas revealed that their mother, Pultibai, had died a few weeks before. His family did not wish to disturb him during his examinations and knew that he would return if he heard the news. Hence, they did not inform him. Shocked, Mohan began to cry. His mother meant the world to him and had a great influence on him. Upon returning from London, he was eager to tell his mother that he had upheld his vows of not eating meat or drinking wine. This was definitely not the kind of homecoming that he had wished for.

Barrister M.K. Gandhi set up a small practice in Rajkot. The occupation was not what he was looking out for. He was shocked at the sporadic problems that prevailed in Indian courts. Poor subjects were unable to access justice, and problems such as corruption and bribery were rampant.[21] His attempts to set up a practice in Mumbai also failed, when he was unable to cross-examine a key witness in a trial.[22]

Mohandas was not too happy with his life in Rajkot and longed to move away. Here, he was even refused odd jobs and smaller roles. He learned of an opening for a teacher's job in a nearby school and wished to apply for it. It paid Rs 75. Mohandas went there in high spirits and was sure of getting the job, given his British degree and foreign education. However, the principal of the school denied him the job on the grounds that he was not a graduate. He could not find any work in Mumbai either.

Finally, there was a ray of hope. Mohandas found an opportunity to move to South Africa on behalf of Dada Abdullah, a Muslim merchant in Kathiawar, who owned a shipping business in South Africa. His cousin in Johannesburg needed a lawyer of Kathiawar heritage, and wished to employ Mohandas. He was offered a total salary of £105.[23] It was to be a one-year commitment in the Colony of Natal, which was then a part of the British Empire.

In April 1893, Mohandas set sail for South Africa. Instead of a short stay of one year, however, he ended up spending nearly 21 years in South Africa.

---

21 Shanker, *The Story of Gandhi.*

22 D.G. Tendulkar, *Mahatma: Life of Mohandas Karamchand Gandhi* (Bombay: Vithalbhai K. Jhaveri, 1951).

23 Ibid.

## CHAPTER FIVE

# Barrister Gandhi: Struggle in South Africa

In late May 1893, Barrister Mohandas Gandhi arrived at the Port of Natal, where he noticed that, along with other Indians, he was clearly being treated differently with little or no respect.

Soon after arriving there, Gandhi began to represent Abdullah & Co. at the court. In the first week of his landing at Durban, he went to a court with Dada Abudullah. There he faced the first of many instances of racial prejudices and injustices against him, as well as South Africans at large.

When Gandhi sat down in the court, the Magistrate stared down at him and pointing his finger he asked Gandhi to remove his turban. Even though several Parsis and Mohammedans wore their turbans without any objection, he was being singled out. When Gandhi refused to remove his turban as he saw no reason to do so, the Magistrate yelled at him. At this, Gandhi left the court. Abdullah rushed after him, trying to explain why the Magistrate acted in such a way. According to Abdullah, the Whites considered Indians to be inferior and called them "coolie" or *sami*. Parsis and

Mohammedans were allowed to wear their turbans because the Whites considered it to be a part of their religion.

Gandhi was enraged and wished to protest. He proclaimed that he was a free man and had to be treated as such. He said he would reach out to the Durban Free Press to protest against such rules. The letters he wrote to the Press were published, but he was openly ridiculed and papers described him as an "unwelcome visitor".[1] He came to be known as the "Coolie Barrister".

## Pangs of Racial Discrimination

A week later, Gandhi had to travel from Durban to Pretoria, where he faced another form of discrimination—one which he took to heart. This experience became a turning point, prompting him to make it his mission to fight against such discrimination.[2]

Abdullah had advised Gandhi to spend five shillings to reserve a bed on the train. However, Gandhi chose to save the money and did not make the reservation. He boarded the train with a valid first-class ticket. Shortly after, an Englishman entered the compartment. Around 9 p.m., when the train reached the next station, the man took a closer look at Gandhi. Realizing that he was a "coloured" Indian, the man grew agitated and left the compartment. He soon returned with two White railway officials. Though they said nothing, a third official appeared and ordered Gandhi to move to the van compartment.

Gandhi calmly showed his first-class ticket, explaining that he had boarded the train in Durban with full permission and had every right to remain seated in peace. Nevertheless, the official insisted that Indians were not allowed in first class and told him to leave.

---

1 Tendulkar, *Mahatma.*

2 Shanker, *The Story of Gandhi.*

When Gandhi refused, they threatened to call the police. Gandhi stood firm, stating that he would not leave voluntarily and they would need to call a constable to remove him.

A police constable was summoned and promptly forced Gandhi off the train. His luggage was taken by the railway authorities, and he was left to spend the night in the station's waiting room with only his handbag.[3] The place, Pietermaritzburg, was at a high altitude and bitterly cold. Gandhi did not even dare to ask for his overcoat, which was in his luggage. He feared being further insulted if he made such a request.

That night, Gandhi was faced with a dilemma: Should he stay and fight for his rights, or return to India and wait until the case was over? Should he protest the injustice or simply proceed to Pretoria despite his current circumstances? As Gandhi later reflected in his Autobiography, he believed it would be cowardly to retreat to India without fulfilling his obligations. He reminded himself: "The hardship to which I was subjected was superficial, only a symptom of the deep disease of colour prejudice. I should try, if possible, to root out the disease and suffer hardships in the process."[4]

Gandhi then took the next train to Pretoria and decided to take action against the injustice he had experienced. He informed Abdullah and sent a telegram to the General Manager (GM) of the Railways, and asked Abdullah to meet with the GM. However, the GM justified the actions of those on board, stating that it was common practice and a well-established rule that Indians or coolies could not sit in the first class, regardless of whether they held a valid ticket. This response deeply affected Gandhi, and he vowed to pursue further action. When the evening train arrived, there was

---

3 Gandhi, *My Experiments with Truth*.

4 Ibid.

a specific berth reserved for him. This time, he used five shillings to purchase the bedding compartment he had previously declined.

The subsequent leg of the journey proved even more harrowing. White passengers objected to Gandhi sitting among them in the stagecoach. The leader of the stagecoach (White, of course) was called to remove Gandhi. When he arrived, he instructed Gandhi to sit in a distant spot where the leader himself usually sat. It was a spot in the coachbox. The leader then took Gandhi's place in the main coach, an act that Gandhi perceived as a major insult.

After some time, the coach leader wished to smoke and needed the seat Gandhi was occupying. He took a dirty "sackcloth", laid it on the floor and asked Gandhi to sit on it, addressing him dismissively as a *sami*. Gandhi protested, explaining that it was the coach leader who had directed him to sit there, and now, simply because he wanted to smoke, he was asking Gandhi to sit at his feet. Gandhi firmly refused, saying he would be happy to return to his rightful seat in the coach.

At this, the coach leader became violent. He struck Gandhi, boxing his ears, and attempted to drag him down by his arms. Gandhi trembled and struggled to speak but managed to steady himself by grabbing onto the brass railings.[5] The man began swearing at him and belittling his Indian origin, all while the White passengers watched the scene in silence.

Fortunately, a few passengers intervened. They told the coach leader to stop beating Gandhi, saying that Gandhi was in the right and should not have been assaulted.

Once the coach resumed its journey, the leader again threatened Gandhi, saying he would beat him up upon arrival at Standerton. Luckily, a group of Indians sent by Abdullah met Gandhi at the station and quickly whisked Gandhi away.

---

5 Ibid.

On the next train through the Transvaal, the situation was even worse. Indians were not issued first- or second-class tickets at all. Nevertheless, Gandhi did his best to understand the regulations and, after some effort, managed to purchase a first-class ticket at a train station.

At Germiston, a guard approached Gandhi and became angry upon seeing him in the first-class compartment. He signalled for Gandhi to move to third class. When Gandhi showed his valid ticket, the guard dismissed it, insisting that he still had to leave.

Fortunately, an Englishman seated next to Gandhi intervened. He stood up, threw the guard's papers to the ground and told him not to harass Gandhi. He then helped Gandhi feel comfortable in the compartment.

## Crusade Against Racial Discrimination

After the court case in Pretoria had been concluded, Gandhi went back to Durban. Here, he came to know about a forthcoming Bill in the Natal Legislative Assembly.

At a farewell party hosted for Gandhi, he read in the newspaper that this proposed legislation aimed at depriving Indians of their right to elect members to the Legislative Assembly, thereby disenfranchising them. Gandhi brought this to the notice of all Indians who had gathered there. When Abdullah asked him why this affected him, or why they should take any action, Gandhi explained that it was one of the first nails in the coffin and that it was aimed at striking them at the root of their self-respect. When Gandhi explained what it meant, and how this policy would have long-standing impact on the Indian community at large, they asked him to stay back in Durban for longer in order to protest against the Bill.

The Natal Indians did their best to ensure that the Franchise Bill would not pass in the Legislative Assembly. They sent telegrams to the Speaker of the Assembly who ensured that discussions would proceed for two days on the matter. They also used petitions to get public support for their stand. They drew up a petition to the Legislative Assembly pleading against the Bill, and one even to Lord Ripon, the then British Secretary of State for Colonies. Their movement gained a lot of traction as tens of thousands of Indians signed the petitions. Moreover, their movement was also recognized in Britain and India, besides South Africa. Although a lot of sympathy was gained for the Indians, the movement fell short in preventing a law from being enacted. Sadly, the movement came too late.[6]

Due to this, Gandhi became well known in South Africa, especially amongst the Indian community. He also helped in the formation of the Natal Indian Congress. As a result, the Natal Indians pleaded that Gandhi should not leave and take up their legal matters as well. This way, he would be able to guide them properly. Gandhi agreed.

Gandhi soon applied to become an advocate, but the entire Bar was composed of Whites and they refused to grant him permission to practice before a court. However, the Supreme Court overruled and overturned their decision and Gandhi was allowed to argue before a court. Gandhi, at once, became one of the busiest lawyers in Durban as he took up many cases for Indian merchants.

After the formation of the Natal Indian Congress, Gandhi's crusade against racism and to get equal treatment for Indians in South Africa started. At that time, the Government aimed at imposing an "annual poll tax" on indentured Indians. They were Indian labourers, who, on a five-year contract, worked on minimal

---

6 Shanker, *The Story of Gandhi.*

wages. In effect, they were virtually slaves. Like other slaves in those times, the White colonizers had taken them to cultivate fields and used them for agricultural purposes. However, due to their hardworking and innovative nature, they rose to the level of common labourers. They had gained enough wealth to buy their own lands and had started to cultivate them. As a result, the White government aimed at instituting a poll tax of around 25 pounds. Gandhi considered this an "atrocious tax".[7]

The Natal Indian Congress led a strong agitation against this. Upon Lord Eglin's intervention, this tax was reduced to three pounds. It took 20 years for this tax to be withdrawn.

Gandhi was the Secretary of the Natal Indian Congress. He streamlined it and organized its working very well. Gandhi's mission against the Law Society and their racist nature, his appeal to the Supreme Court and his other initiatives against discrimination were very well received and documented. Many people came forward in his support, and he became a big name in Durban, especially amongst the Indian community.

In 1896, Gandhi set sail for India, and after a 26-day sail he landed in Calcutta (now known as Kolkata). He then went to Rajkot where his whole family awaited him. He was joyous to meet Kasturba and his two sons.

In India, he took up the duty of informing the country about the plight of the Indians who lived in South Africa. To this end, he met writers and editors of top Indian newspapers. He also met Indian leaders such as Bal Gangadhar Tilak as well as Gopal Krishna Gokhale.[8] Around this time, the Bubonic plague had broken out in Bombay Province and it was spreading to the neighbouring

---

7 Gandhi, *My Experiments with Truth.*

8 In his Autobiography, Gandhiji has referred to Gokhale as his mentor and guide.

Provinces. Gandhi volunteered to join a group in Rajkot that worked for creating awareness among people about the sanitary conditions and measures to prevent the spread of such dreadful diseases.

By November, there were certain developments in Durban and Natal and Gandhi was requested to return soon, which he did.

***

By the methods and outcomes of Gandhi's work in Natal, he had enraged a large community of Whites living there. As a result, they held meetings and demonstrations to deal with Gandhi when he arrived. Moreover, a rumour spread that Gandhi was bringing two ships with Indians to Natal. This further angered the Whites, who decided to take some action.

On 18 December 1897, Gandhi's ship arrived at the port of Durban. However, the passengers were not allowed to leave before a thorough medical examination, which was warranted due to the fact that Bombay was infested with the dreadful plague.

At that time, the Whites in Durban protested against the repatriation of Gandhi. They were angry with him because they thought that he was spreading anti-European sentiments and propaganda. This had caused a long delay, and after 23 days, the ship was allowed to dock. Gandhi was advised not to leave the ship, as there was a large, angry mob of White men at the docks. His family was sent to a Parsi businessman Rustomji's house while he stayed on the ship.

Soon, Laughton, the legal advisor of Dada Abdulla, came to the docks to escort Gandhi out from the ship. Initially, the atmosphere was calm, with no disturbances. Soon, some young men began making some nasty remarks as Gandhi walked by. This escalated into loud shouting, drawing a large crowd. They blocked Gandhi and his companion from going any further. They separated Laughton and Gandhi, and started to pelt him with stones, bricks and rotten eggs. While he tried to stand up for his breath, he was boxed and battered and was unable to stand by himself.[9] They also removed and took away his turban. At that time, luckily, the Police Superintendent's wife came on the scene and saved Gandhi from getting hurt. She told the mob to stop, and called them cowards for what they were doing.

In the meantime, an Indian youth who had witnessed these wrongdoings went to the nearest police station and informed the Police Superintendent about the incident. The Police Superintendent soon sent a posse of men to surround Gandhi and transport him safely. When the police arrived at the scene, the crowd dispersed. Then, the police escorted Gandhi safely to Rustomji's house. The police station was on the way, hence they offered him sanctuary at the station, but Gandhi declined and proceeded straight to Rustomji's house. He did not face any further abuse or harm. At his house, Dr Dadibarjor, the ship's doctor, administered the medical treatment to tend to the wounds.

Soon thereafter, the Whites began to surround the house. They wished to take Gandhi away. Although the Police Superintendent tried to maintain calm by humouring the crowds, it was of little avail. Finally, he advised Gandhi and his family to escape in disguise. On the other hand, a friend suggested that he bravely face the crowd and deal with the threat. Another dilemma appeared before Gandhi. If he stayed and did nothing, his family and friends would be in danger. Finally, Gandhi decided to leave the scene in disguise.

Subsequently, a letter from Joseph Chamberlain, the Secretary of State for Colonies, directed the Natal Government to prosecute

---

9 Gandhi, *My Experiments with Truth.*

all those responsible for the attacks on Gandhi. The Natal Government also assured Gandhi that nothing like this would happen again, and asked him to come to identify the perpetrators. Gandhi did not do so, as he did not want the assailants to be blamed and felt that the real blame rested with the media and their characterization of him. False reports and hearsay were responsible for what had happened. After this, the whole narrative changed. More and more media reports started proclaiming Gandhi as innocent and the overall level of sympathy for Indians rose significantly.

In the course of time, Gandhi took up various initiatives to ensure that the improper narrative about Indians was corrected. There prevailed a stereotype amongst the British that the Indians were not manly or strong enough to be part of the army, unlike Muslims, who were naturally the "Martial Race". Gandhi took up the challenge of correcting this stereotype. In 1900, during the onset of the Boer War, Gandhi formed the Natal Indian Ambulance Corps.[10] He was able to raise around 1100 Indian volunteers to support the British fight against the Boers. During the Battle of Colenso, they acted as auxiliaries to another British ambulance, whereas during the Battle of Spion Kop, they were at the frontlines. This task was so demanding that they had to carry the wounded soldiers for miles due to the rough terrain. On account of their valour, 74 of the volunteers were granted the Queen's South Africa Medal. Newspapers also praised the efforts of the Indians.

Besides this mainstream work, Gandhi kept on working on issues of the Indians in South Africa. At this point, Kasturba worked alongside him while he carried out his mission in the region.

---

10 P.F. Power, "Gandhi in South Africa", *The Journal of Modern African Studies*, Vol. 7, No. 3 (1969), p. 7.

## Satyagraha as a Strategy

In 1906, another arbitrary law was introduced by the Transvaal Government. It required that all Indian men, women and children register for a special form of certification which bore their name and thumb impression. It had to be carried by Indians at all times, and if someone was unable to produce it on demand, he or she could even be imprisoned or heavily fined. The police could enter houses to conduct inspections to check whether these laws were being abided by.

Gandhi considered this law to be an "absolute ruin" for Indians in South Africa. This incident turned out to be the early origins of *Satyagraha*.[11] Gandhi knew that the police and other authorities would do whatever it takes—resorting to violence, arresting people and even jailing protestors—to enforce this law. He realized that all of this must be handled with peace and without violence. Gandhi's movement now had to rest on non-violence. Indians would have to purposely disobey the law and not abide by it.

When hundreds of Indians disobeyed the "Black Act", they were imprisoned and put on trial. Here, none of them put up a defence and all pleaded guilty. Amongst them was Gandhi, who was sent to prison, and also to see General Smuts in Pretoria.

When the General told him that the movement that he had started must obey the law, Gandhi proclaimed that he would rather die than obey a law which purposely meant to belittle and disregard Indians. However, during their meeting, they reached a compromise. If Smuts repealed the "Black Act" and released all the prisoners, Gandhi would end his *Satyagraha* movement. Gandhi also agreed that Indians would register themselves on their own accord.

---

11 Shanker, *The Story of Gandhi.*

Gandhi then explained to his followers that if the Indians showed signs of goodwill and cooperation, General Smuts would repeal the arbitrary law and there would be peace. To this, he received backlash from some Indians such as Mir Alam. Alam was shocked and considered Gandhi's sudden change in attitude to be contradictory and hypocritical.

The next morning, Gandhi and his *Satyagrahis* set out to the local registration office. They were attacked by Mir Alam and his group of associates. Gandhi did not blame Mir Alam and asked the Indians to get registered. Hundreds of his followers did so. However, General Smuts did *not* repeal the law. In turn, the Indians demanded that their applications be rescinded and withdrawn. Under Gandhi's leadership, the Indians gave an ultimatum: "If the 'Black Act' is not repealed before a fixed date, the certificates collected by the Indians will be burnt."[12]

Smuts and his Government ignored this threat. The Indians went ahead; a large bonfire was held and nearly 2000 certificates were burned. Indians also crossed the border into Transvaal where their presence was banned. They were imprisoned, and a new *Satyagraha* movement began. In the meantime, Gandhi and Seth Haji Habib were advised to travel to London to ventilate their grievances. Although they did so, their mission on the whole was a failure.[13]

Gandhi took several other initiatives. He established the Tolstoy Farm, which was one of the first of the *Ashrams* he established. It was a place where "people who were different in nationality, religion and colour lived together like one family. They worked hard and shared the fruits of their labour." He taught children at the farm, and did other activities.

---

12 Ibid.

13 Ibid.

In 1913, Gandhi held a march of over 6000 Indian workers from Natal to Transvaal, where they were traditionally not allowed by law. Throughout this movement, his strategy and modus operandi were as expressed here:

> We are going to march peacefully together across the border into the Transvaal. The Government will arrest us and put us in prison. We are to remain peaceful. This is the non-violent way of protesting against the poll tax, against the government's decision not to recognize our marriages and against all the laws that are made against us. We are fighting for just causes, we will not harm anyone.[14]

In response, General Smuts appointed an Inquiry Commission to look into the matter. The Commission reported in favour of Indians and their demands. It allowed the marriages to take place and removed the duties and laws against inter-state travel. Moreover, the Relief Bill by the Indians was also passed by the Governor and signed into law.

In sum, Gandhi's crusade in South Africa was a major success. He had become a famous name and a messiah not only for Indians in South Africa, but also for Indians throughout the world. People in India, UK, Africa and all across the world came to know of Gandhi and his missionary work. Many years later, Gandhi was also honoured in South Africa through the construction of national monuments.[15]

Now time had come to move on, to spread his movement in India and to fight for independence for the Indian people.

---

14 Shanker, *The Story of Gandhi*, from www.gandhiashramsevagram.org, Chapter 11.

15 C. Smith, Mbeki: Mahatma Gandhi Satyagraha 100th Anniversary (2006).

# CHAPTER SIX

# The Advent of Gandhi in India

Gandhiji returned to India in 1915, apparently on the request of Gopal Krishna Gokhale (who was the Congress President in 1905). Gokhale was known for his restraint and moderation, and Gandhiji regarded Gokhale as his *Guru*.

Before leaving for India, Gandhiji intended to fulfill a promise by visiting Gokhale in London. Accompanied by Kasturba and a friend Kallenbach, he sailed for England on 18 July in 1914. Two days before his arrival, however, World War I was declared.[1] Upon his arrival, Gandhiji learnt that Gokhale was in Paris for medical treatment. He could not reach out or communicate with Gokhale due to the War, and was utterly disappointed.

In the meantime, a meeting of Indians was held in England. During this meeting, Gandhiji argued that Indians should support the War effort as a gesture of goodwill and friendship. He proposed that Indian students should also join the army. However, some attendees believed that this was an opportunity to exact freedom for India from the British and get their due rights. Gandhiji did not find it fair to exploit England's weakened state for India's gain.

---

1 Gandhi, *My Experiments with Truth.*

In fact, he even organized ambulance corps to support the British War effort.

By this time, Gokhale had returned to England. However, before Gandhiji could meet him, he had an attack of pleurisy and was advised to go to India to get the necessary medical treatment.

Once in India, Gandhiji set out the process of the formation of various *Ashrams* in order to spread his message. He told Gokhale that he wished to form an *Ashram* to settle down with his Phoenix Family. The best model suggested was Rabindranath Tagore's *Santiniketan*. When Gandhiji was visiting *Santiniketan*, he learnt that Gokhale had passed away. Distraught, he set out for Pune along with C.F. Andrews.[2]

During this trip, Andrews spoke to Gandhiji about his freedom movements in South Africa, and asked whether it would be possible for a *Satyagraha* movement in India. Gandhiji told him it would be difficult to do anything for a whole year because of his promise to Gokhale that he would observe and learn about the nuanced situation in India. He was unable to express any of his opinions during this period of probation.

After Gokhale's death, Gandhiji travelled all over India to meet leaders and interact with the masses. He even visited Gokhale's Servants of India Society. He had an intention to join it, out of sheer respect for Gokhale. However, he could not do so due to opposition by some members of the Society.

Around May 1915, Gandhiji established an *Ashram* in a village near Ahmedabad, the centre of handloom weaving. The *Ashram* had an environment of spirituality and devotion. Everyone wore the same kind of clothing, cooked in one kitchen and lived together

---

2 C.F. Andrews (also called *Deen Bandhu*) was a Christian missionary who had aligned himself with the cause of India's Independence. He was a personal friend of both Gandhiji and Rabindranath Tagore.

as one family. Gandhiji would tell his followers: "If you want to serve the people, it is essential to observe the vows of truth, *Ahimsa*, celibacy, non-stealing, non-possession and control of the palate."[3] Once, some Untouchables wished to join the *Ashram*. They wrote a letter to Gandhiji who responded saying that they were most welcome. However, this caused controversy amongst those in the *Ashram*. They did not wish to live with the Untouchables. Nevertheless, Gandhiji's mind was made up. The patrons did not appreciate this move and pulled out their financial support. A little later, a rich man gave a large sum of Rs 13,000 to the *Ashram* as a donation.

In February 1916, Gandhiji was invited as a keynote speaker at the commencement of the Banaras Hindu University. Here he wore a Kathiawad long coat and turban. In his speech, he extolled the importance of the Hindi language and how Indians had forsaken their mother tongue to a large extent. He said, "It is a matter of deep humiliation and shame for us that I am compelled this evening under the shadow of this great college, in the sacred city, to address my countrymen in a language that is foreign to me."[4]

Most British officers and dignitaries present were angered by these remarks. Gandhiji also criticized the Indian rulers for having plundered the wealth of the common man. His speech was filled with outspoken criticism. To this, Ms Annie Besant pleaded with him to stop speaking; however, the audience was excited and Gandhiji went on. This speech was proclaimed by many as Gandhiji's first political speech for the freedom struggle. It also laid the foundation of his struggle and *Satyagraha* movement in India.

---

3 Shanker, *The Story of Gandhi.* pp. 42-43.

4 Ibid.

## Launching Satyagraha Movement in India

Gandhiji initially organized several *Satyagraha* movements on various issues that plagued the Indian society, such as the Champaran *Satyagraha* and the Ahmedabad Mill Workers *Satyagraha*. These set the foundation for a larger, more pervasive movement and consolidated Gandhiji's influence upon the Indian masses.

In Champaran, a district of Bihar, a peculiar system of agriculture prevailed. Cultivators were being exploited by the European settlers and were forced to grow indigo, a blue dye. These cultivators relied on their own produce, and the Europeans had disallowed them from growing food which was vital for their own survival. They did not receive proper payments either. This exposed the Colonial and exploitative nature of the British settlers, something that Gandhiji took up to fight against.

In 1917, Gandhiji visited Champaran and saw that he was not welcome. The District Magistrate (DM) told him to leave by train at once.[5] Gandhiji openly defied the order and was summoned to court, where the DM told him that if he left the district at once and did not return, he would be left alone. Outside the court, many Indians had gathered, chanting slogans in his support. Gandhiji told the Judge that he could pacify the crowd, and told the mob that the DM had the right to arrest him for disobeying the order. He urged them to accept it if he was jailed. Witnessing this, the authorities withdrew the case against Gandhiji and allowed him to stay in the district.

Gandhiji surveyed the farmlands and interviewed several cultivators to understand how such a large number of people could be exploited by the British. The cultivators' lack of awareness and their dire economic conditions had essentially made them

---

5 R. Prasad, *Satyagraha in Champaran* (Ahmedabad: Navajivan Publishing House, 1949).

slaves to the settlers. To address these issues, he set up multiple organizations aimed at improving the economic and educational status of those people. He opened schools and provided sanitary education.[6] Recognizing Gandhiji's dedication and commitment to the cause, the Government formed a Committee to investigate the cultivators' plight. Gandhiji was invited to participate in the Committee meetings. After a few months, the Committee proposed and passed the reformed Champaran Agrarian Bill. It brought great relief to both landowners and cultivators alike.

In the surrounding areas of Ahmedabad, a severe outbreak of Bubonic plague had broken out. Gandhiji rushed back from Bihar to clear evacuate his *Ashram*. Fortunately, another generous donor was able to secure a good piece of land for the *Ashram*. Even before Gandhiji had established his *Ashram*, he had friendly relations with various mill workers and mill owners.

The economic conditions in Ahmedabad were marked by rising prices for the daily wage workers, who were demanding higher wages. Most of these labourers were unable to even afford the basic necessities and get food on the table. This was especially true for those who worked in the textile mill industry. Witnessing their plight, Gandhiji committed himself to their cause.[7]

Gandhiji launched a non-violent strike and urged the workers to join him in peaceful demonstrations. He asked them to vow not to work until their demands were met, something he was unsure if they would comply. Gandhiji declared his intention to fast until an agreement was reached. Inspired by his commitment, the workers joined hands in this strike. This pressure compelled the mill owners to concede, and within three days, the strike came to an end.

---

6 Ibid.

7 M. Mehta, "Gandhi and Ahmedabad, 1915-20", *Economic and Political Weekly*, Vol. 40, No. 4 (22 January 2005).

After this came the Kheda Satyagraha of 1918. Under Gandhiji's leadership, several prominent figures such as Vallabhbhai Patel, Shankarlal Banker, Mahadev Desai and others took an active part in this struggle to support the peasants. A famine had gripped parts of Gujarat. The situation was appalling in Kheda district, where impoverished communities, who could barely manage their daily meal, faced the burden of taxes they couldn't pay.

Gandhiji's lieutenants like Vallabhbhai Patel mobilized a tax revolt. They toured across the district and gave the peasants political guidance. The peasants of Kheda united, signing a petition demanding the abolition of taxes for the year. The Government of Bombay Presidency initially rejected their plea. The police confiscated their lands but the farmers did not retaliate or resist arrest.

However, the Government eventually yielded to pressure. A compromise was reached, suspending the taxes for two years and returning all confiscated lands and property. Within four months, this movement was also successfully concluded.

## Supporting the British War Effort

From 1914 till 1918, the world powers at large were grappling with World War I. During 1917-18, both Britain and France were in an exceedingly difficult situation. In the spring of 1917, the British and French troops were defeated by German forces. The Russian War effort was heavily affected due to the Communist October Revolution. Although America had entered the War, their troops were not present at the battle fields as yet.

At this point, Lord Chelmsford, the Viceroy of India, invited Gandhiji and various Indian leaders to a War Conference. Here, a resolution was tabled to recruit Indians into the War effort.

Gandhiji wholeheartedly supported this move. Most Indian rulers and dignitaries opposed Gandhiji on the ground that it was a policy contrary to his *Ahimsa* and non-violent struggle. They also doubted the efficacy of this policy in actually bringing about freedom; yet, Gandhiji held that cooperating with and helping the British at their vulnerable moment would go a long way in bringing about British sympathies for the Indian cause.

Gandhiji not only supported the British War effort in principle, but he also spearheaded a major recruitment programme and spread information through speeches and leaflets.[8] These drives ended up adversely affecting Gandhiji's health.

## Rowlatt Act of 1919

While recuperating from poor health in Ahmedabad, Gandhiji stumbled upon the published report of the Rowlatt Committee, which proposed highly controversial amendments to India's criminal law.[9] These recommendations included provisions for arbitrary arrests and indefinite detentions of Indians. As Gandhiji wrote in his autobiography (1927), "They were unjust, subversive of principles of liberty and justice, and destructive of the elements of the individual."[10]

Despite his declining health, Gandhiji summoned several leaders to his *Ashram* and announced a new *Satyagraha*. A pledge

---

8 www.mkgandhi.org, accessed on 22 July 2020.

9 The report essentially entailed indefinitely extending the emergency measures of preventive indefinite detention, incarceration without trial and judicial review incorporated in the Defence of India Act of 1915 during World War I.

10 Gandhi, *My Experiments with Truth.*

for the *Satyagraha* was drafted and signed by all, and a separate *Satyagraha Sabha* was established with its headquarters in Mumbai. Nevertheless, in 1919, the Government of India introduced the Bill in the India's Central Legislative Assembly, which was passed as The Anarchical and Revolutionary Crimes Act of 1919 (commonly known as Rowlatt Act of 1919) on 16 March 1919.

After the Bill was passed, Gandhiji considered hosting an all-India *Hartal* as a commencement of the *Satyagraha* movement nationwide. The date was set for 6 April 1919. Newspapers, publications and the leaders gave a lot of publicity to this *Hartal.* Gandhiji first went to Mumbai to demonstrate, while in Delhi, Lahore and Amritsar, a large-scale *Hartal* had commenced. In Mumbai, the *Hartal* was a big success. However, in Delhi, things took a violent turn. Delhi Police did not allow free movement of people, which led to shootings and firings, causing human casualties. Although Gandhiji had requested all to be peaceful and not engage in violence, there were several violent instances in Delhi, Punjab and Ahmedabad. In Ahmedabad, Gandhiji requested the Commissioner to allow holding a procession in the Sabarmati *Ashram*. Here, he announced the suspension of the Civil Disobedience Movement, as it had taken a drastically violent turn.

Gandhiji again felt that he had started this movement a bit too soon, without any proper training for people. He expressed his regret, and went around giving speeches and training people about the true motives and means of *Satyagraha*. He believed that it was essential that people understood his motives and abide by them. His decision of the suspension of the Civil Disobedience Movement turned out to be a highly controversial move, and was opposed by many leaders and even friends who had all along stood with Gandhiji.

## The Jallianwala Bagh Massacre

The Jallianwala Bagh Massacre (13 April 1919) is often cited as the turning point that transformed Gandhiji's mindset and ideology in the struggle for freedom. This event appears to have marked Gandhiji's transition from a supporter of British rule to a staunch opponent.[11] The tragic event unfolded as follows:

The situation in Punjab was very volatile, and the measures taken by the Government were drastic. In Amritsar, no one was allowed to move about freely and there was an order that forbade all kinds of meetings and gatherings. Since these orders were issued in English, most people were unaware of these.[12]

A meeting was called in the Jallianwallah Bagh (park) in Amritsar to protest the Government's decision. General Dyer, a British army man, allowed the congregation to take place and did not prevent people from entering the park. However, once the demonstration started, he surrounded the park and shut all doors. He told his soldiers to fire at will and to keep firing till the ammunition had been exhausted. In all, over 1600 rounds were fired at the gathering of unarmed people. Officially, 379 were killed and 200 wounded.

Shockingly, General Dyer had ordered that Indians were to alight from vehicles and crawl on their hands when an Englishman walked past and salute/ do *salaam*. Marriages were prevented, and water and electrical supplies were stopped. Children were forced to participate in parades, walk miles for roll call and salute the British flag.

---

11 Pravat Ranjan Sethi, "Gandhi and the Jallianwala Bagh Massacre and Beyond", *Mainstream Weekly*, New Delhi, Vol. LVII, No. 18, 2019. https://www.mainstreamweekly.net/article8659.html (accessed on 22 July 2020).

12 Shanker, *The Story of Gandhi*.

C.F. Andrews had reached Punjab. He wrote to Gandhiji, and pleaded that he should visit Punjab. Although he tried, Gandhiji's requests were denied by the Viceroy. Only some time later he was allowed to visit. Gandhiji noticed that the Government had taken action to hide individuals responsible for violence and killings. When Gandhiji arrived, the Indian National Congress (INC) had formed a Committee to look into the atrocities and investigate what exactly had happened. This was called the Punjab Subcommittee of the INC.

During that time, there was a considerable polarization regarding the accountability for the atrocity that had occurred. On one side, the responsibility of the massacre resided with a single individual: General Dyer. The Government contended that the General misunderstood his duties and may have been psychologically unbalanced. On the other hand, the Congress asserted that the massacre epitomized the oppressive nature of British rule in India.[13] The Committee's Report confirmed that the Government had taken measures to protect certain individuals from punishment.

## Non-Cooperation Movement

Given the apparent disillusionment with the policies and actions of the British in India, Gandhiji launched another *Satyagraha* Movement. For this, he appealed to everyone not to cooperate with the British. He told them not to accept honours, and return any they had received from the British. He told families to boycott British goods and to pull students out of British schools. The massive Non-Cooperation Movement had begun.

---

13 Richard McCutcheon, "The Impact of the Jallianwala Bagh Massacre on Gandhi" (1989), McMaster University Thesis, Available from http://hdl.handle.net/11375/11927.

On 1 August 1920, Gandhiji wrote to the Viceroy of India, signalling the start of the Non-Cooperation Movement. Gandhiji returned his Kaiser-i-Hind Medal, and extensively wrote about non-cooperation in the columns of *Young India*. He actively travelled with leaders and preached the meaning of *Satyagraha* at large meetings. In a Special Session of the Congress, a resolution was passed for non-cooperation as a means of attaining *Swaraj*.

During the year, Gandhiji advocated a three-pronged form of boycott in which he wished to boycott all schools, Government institutions and colleges run or aided by the British. On 26 December 1920, in the Nagpur Session of the Congress, Gandhiji's proposals were passed with overwhelming majority.

While the nationwide Non-Cooperation Movement was on, the infamous Chauri Chaura incident took place on 12 February 1922. In the Gorakhpur district of UP, in the village of Chauri Chaura, demonstrations had turned violent. The police had fired at demonstrators, who ended up attacking the police station and confining the police in city hall. They set fire to the hall, which caused many deaths. British authorities declared Martial Law in and around Chauri Chaura and arrested hundreds of people.

This incident hurt Gandhiji very much. He went on a five-day fast as penance as he perceived his accountability in the bloodshed. He had expected people to have been responsible and ready for a new *Satyagraha* movement.

Gandhiji felt that he had acted rather hastily in encouraging people to revolt against the British *Raj* without adequate emphasis on the importance of non-violence and without sufficient training to exercise restraint in the face of an attack. Gandhiji was convinced that the Indian people were ill-prepared and not yet ready to do what was needed to achieve Independence.

On 12 February 1922, the Indian National Congress indefinitely suspended the Non-Cooperation Movement at the national level.

Gandhiji was arrested on 10 March 1922. He was tried for sedition and sentenced to imprisonment for six years commencing 18 March 1922 in the Yerawada prison in Pune.

***

In 1924, Gandhiji fell very ill due to appendicitis. He was in great pain and even the prison staff and guards were worried about him dying in the jail. This would cause further political upheaval and outrage in India. The British then called in a doctor to operate on him, which was done successfully. Yet, his recovery was slow and his health steadily deteriorated. As a result, he was released from the jail.

The Congress, in the meantime, was divided into two camps: *Swarajists* and No-changers. While *Swarajists* advocated the Central Legislative Council entry (through election) with an aim to end or mend the working of the Council, the No-changers advocated constructive work.[14] The *Swarajists* camp, led by Chittaranjan Das, Motilal Nehru and Ajmal Khan, in fact, established a new political party, called the *Swaraj* Party in January 1923. The No-changers were led, among others, by C. Rajagopalachari, Vallabhbhai Patel, Rajendra Prasad and M.A. Ansari.

The timing of the formation of *Swaraj* Party was strategically important. The term of the first Central Legislative Council was coming to an end, and the Second General Elections in British India were just round the corner. The Second General Elections were actually held in November 1923. The Central Legislative Assembly had 145 seats, of which candidates on 105 were elected by the public.[15] The *Swaraj* Party fought the elections and achieved

14 Bipan Chandra, Mridula Mukherjee, et al., *India's Struggle for Independence, 1857-1947* (New Delhi: Penguin Books, 1989), pp. 223-24.

15 "Indian Election Results. Strength of Extremists", *The Times*, 15 December 1923, Issue 43525, p. 11.

considerable success. The Party won 48 seats in the Central Legislative Assembly, the largest number of seats by any Party.[16] The Central Legislative Assembly was inaugurated in January 1924 by the then Viceroy Lord Reading.

When Gandhiji was released from jail in 1924, he was elected as the President of the Congress Party. As the President, he tried to reunite the camps but achieved only moderate success, initially. However, the *Swaraj* Party and its mission suffered a major setback with the death of Chittaranjan Das in 1925. This was reflected in the performance of the Party in the Third General Elections held in 1926. At the national level, the number of elected representatives of the *Swaraj* Party dwindled. Over the next year, the *Swaraj* Party witnessed a further decline due to lack of leadership, and retreating of leaders back to the Congress fold.

## Simon Commission

In 1928, a Commission to study the Indian conditions and Constitutional reformation was appointed; it was led by Sir John Simon. The Viceroy informed Gandhiji that no Indians would be part of this body; this was opposed throughout India. Gandhiji appealed to all political leaders and his followers to boycott this Commission as it was arbitrary and did not adequately represent the true needs of Indians at the grassroots level.

When the Simon Commission landed in India, a *Hartal* was observed in Mumbai and the whole country witnessed black-flag demonstrations. The call of the slogan "Simon Go Back" reverberated throughout the country.

During this time, the peasants in Gujarat were affected by the enhancement of land taxes. Gandhiji suggested that a non-violent

16 "Indian Election Results: Strength of the Swaraj Party", *The Times*, 1 January 1924, Issue 43537, p. 11.

protest be held to challenge the taxes. He made Vallabhbhai Patel in charge of that protest, and ensured that it remained non-violent in nature. After a point of time, Patel did make some progress, and negotiations were held in Bardoli. Once Gandhiji arrived on the scene the issue was resolved in a month's time.

Having seen the great influence that Gandhiji now wielded, and the level of resentment and unrest in India, the Viceroy called a meeting of Indian leaders and announced that India would be given a Dominion Status, as was done in Canada. Although some were convinced of this step, Gandhiji wished for an immediate plan to frame the Constitution for India. The Viceroy did not promise anything of such a nature, and it soon became clear that they were merely trying to stall the protests and pacify the leaders.

After these events, Jawaharlal Nehru was elected as the President of the Indian National Congress, seemingly on the approval and suggestion of Gandhiji. The Lahore Session of the INC was held on 31 December 1929. Here, the famous resolution proclaiming *Poorna Swaraj* (total self-rule) was tabled and supported by all present. The Congress now worked to get *Poorna Swaraj* – "Full Independence".

This marked the start of the Civil Disobedience Movement. Through this, Gandhiji announced and called for the deliberate breaking and disobeying of the British laws. He then turned to the Salt laws which prevailed then.

## Salt Laws and the Dandi March

At that time, the British Government held a monopoly on salt production and imposed excessively high excise tax that made salt unaffordable for the common Indian. In response, on 2 March 1930, Gandhiji wrote a letter to Viceroy Lord Irwin, condemning the living conditions imposed on Indians and indicated that the "British rule has impoverished the dumb millions by a system of progressive exploitation, and by ruinously expensive military and civil administration which the country can never afford. It had reduced us politically to serfdom. It has sapped the foundation of our culture." Gandhiji announced that starting from 11 March, he would "proceed with…co-workers of the *Ashram*…, to disregard the provisions of the salt laws."[17]

Therefore, on 12 March, Gandhiji and 78 of his followers began marching from his *Ashram* to Dandi, covering about 400 km. They marched through villages and informed the peasants of the new *Satyagraha* movement. This act of defiance was viewed all over the world as a major sign of opposition to the British rule.

Due to the immense popularity of the march, the British authorities refrained from arresting Gandhiji and allowed the procession to proceed uninterrupted until they reached Dandi. Finally, on 5 April, accompanied by thousands of leaders, followers and family members, Gandhiji openly defied the salt laws. This marked the official commencement of the Civil Disobedience Movement.

* * *

As previously mentioned (Chapter 3), the parallelism between Mahatma Gandhi's advocacy for India's political independence and Dr Ambedkar's call for social independence for the people of India becomes strikingly apparent at this juncture.

For a long time, the Congress Party had held a view that the issue of the Depressed Classes is a "social problem" and that its solution lies elsewhere, not in politics. In contrast, Dr Ambedkar

---

17 Shanker, *The Story of Gandhi.*

firmly believed that the plight of the Depressed Classes was "eminently a political problem and must be treated as such".[18]

With such starkly contrasting views on the issue of the Depressed Classes, a major conflict between Mahatma Gandhi and Dr Ambedkar appeared inevitable. Indeed, that is precisely what happened thereafter.

18 Dr Ambedkar's speech in the opening Plenary Session of the First Round Table Conference. See Jadhav (ed), *Ambedkar Speaks*, Vol. III, pp. 101-07.

# PART III

# Gandhi–Ambedkar: Conflicts and Compromises

## CHAPTER SEVEN

# Gandhi–Ambedkar Conflict: The Setting

The setting for the historic confrontation between Gandhiji and Dr Ambedkar was provided by the Simon Commission Report which came out in May 1930. The Report recommended the establishment of a representative government in the Provinces. It also advised that separate communal electorates be retained until tensions between the Hindus and Muslims die down. Since the educated Indians were opposed to the Simon Commission and there were no signs of communal tensions between Hindus and Muslims coming down, the British Government opted for another method of dealing with the Constitutional Reforms in India and that involved taking into account the Indian public opinion.

This laid the foundation of the three Round Table Conferences (RTCs) organized by the British Government at London during the period 1930–32. The Indian National Congress boycotted the First (and the Third) RTC. Dr Ambedkar, along with Rao Bahadur Srinivasan, represented the Depressed Classes of India and participated in all three RTCs.

The RTCs primarily focused on two main questions regarding the proposed Constitutional Reform:

i.) Should India have a responsible government and, if so, when and to whom that government should be responsible?

ii.) What should be the form of the proposed representative government?

## The First Round Table Conference

The First RTC, held in November 1930, was chaired by the then British Prime Minister Ramsay MacDonald. The three British political parties were represented by 16 delegates while the Indian delegation consisted of 89 delegates (including 57 political leaders from the British India, and 16 delegates from the Princely States).

Dr Ambedkar participated extensively in the Plenary Sessions as well as in various Sub-Committees.

## Opening Plenary Session

In the opening Plenary Session of the First RTC, Dr Ambedkar forcefully made out a case for political power for the Depressed Classes. At the outset, Dr Ambedkar presented a perspective on the position of the Depressed Classes in India.[1] He said that the "Depressed Classes form a group by themselves". Although they are included among the Hindus, "they in no sense form an integral part of that community..." Their Untouchability involves both—"discrimination in public life", as well as "denial of all equality of opportunity and...most elementary of the civic rights on which

---

1 For full text of the Speech, see Jadhav (ed), *Ambedkar Speaks,* Vol. III, pp. 101-07. All quotes in this section are from the same speech.

all human existence depends…" He emphasized that such a community, as large as the population of England or France, and "so heavily handicapped in the struggle for existence," must have some influence on the possible solution to the political problem.

Then Dr Ambedkar opened a fearless direct attack on the British Rule. He said that the British Government of India "instead of marching on" is only "marking time". The British Government has done absolutely nothing, he said, to remove "the social evils which are eating into the vitals of Indian society and have blighted the lives of the Downtrodden Classes for so many years… Yet it is the most painful thing that it has not dared to touch any of these evils." He alleged that the British Government was "afraid that its intervention to amend the existing code of social and economic life will give rise to resistance." "Of what good is such Government to anybody?" he asked.

Dr Ambedkar, at this point of his intervention, made a passionate appeal for a democratic Republic for India. He said:

> …We must have a government…which…will not be afraid to amend the social and economic code of life which the dictates of justice and expediency so urgently call for. This role the British Government will never be able to play. It is only a government which is of the people, for the people and by the people that will make this possible….

Dr Ambedkar proceeded then to emphasize the need for a *Swaraj* Constitution. He said: "…We feel that nobody can remove our grievances as well as we can, and we cannot remove them unless we get political power in our own hands. … It is only in a *Swaraj* Constitution that we stand any chance of getting the political power into our own hands, without which we cannot bring salvation to our people."

Dr Ambedkar, then, raised a series of issues regarding uncertain future of the Depressed Classes. While supporting the Dominion Status for India, he asked, "How will Dominion India function? Where will the centre of political power be? Who will have it? Will the Depressed Classes be heirs to it?"

Emphasizing that these questions are "chief concerns", he argued that the Indian society is a "gradation of Castes forming an ascending scale of reverence and a descending scale of contempt, a system which gives no scope for the growth of that sentiment of equality and fraternity so essential for a democratic form of government." He maintained that the Indian intelligentsia comes from the so-called Upper Castes which "speaks in the name of the country and leads the political movement," (but) "has not shed the narrow particularism of the Class from which it is drawn..."

Dr Ambedkar even drew contours for the future Constitution. He said: "What the Depressed Classes wish to urge is that the political mechanism...must have a definite relation to the psychology of the society for which it is devised. Otherwise, you are likely to produce a Constitution which, however symmetrical, will be a truncated one and a total misfit to the society for which it is designed..."

While referring to a criticism by the Congress Party that the problem of the Depressed Classes is essentially a social one and that "its solution lies elsewhere" and not in politics, Dr Ambedkar forcefully contended that "the problem of Depressed Classes is... eminently a political problem and must be treated as such...."

Looking into the future, Dr Ambedkar explicitly recognized that "political power is passing from the British into the hands of those who wield such tremendous economic, social and religious sway over our existence." While admitting that "the idea of *Swaraj* recalls to the mind...the tyrannies, oppressions and injustices practiced upon us in the past, and fear of their recurrence under

*Swaraj,"* he said, "we are prepared to take the inevitable risk of the situation in the hope that we shall be installed, in adequate proportion, as the political sovereigns of the country along with our fellow countrymen…."

Resuming his scathing attack on the British Rule, Dr Ambedkar said that at "every successive step taken by the British Government…towards Constitutional Reforms, the Depressed Classes have been systematically left out." He gave a warning without mincing his words, "I protest with all the emphasis I can that we will not stand this any longer…."

Dr Ambedkar supported *Swaraj* but with an important caveat. He said: "Although we want responsible government, we do not want a government that will only mean a change of masters. Let the Legislature be fully and really representative if your Executive is going to be fully responsible."

Dr Ambedkar concluded his intervention with a passionate outburst: "…Depressed by the Government, suppressed by the Hindu and disregarded by the Muslim, we are left in a most intolerable position of utter helplessness to which I am sure there is no parallel…"

Dr Ambedkar's speech was very well received. The clarity and lucidity of his exposition, and the fearless manner of his delivery won Dr Ambedkar many admirers. The *Indian Daily Mail* described the speech as one of the finest bits of oratory during the whole Conference.[2]

***

## On Franchise and Suffrage

While participating in the Sub-Committee on Franchise (22 December 1930), Dr Ambedkar made out a strong case for

2 Keer, *Dr Ambedkar: Life and Mission*.

adult franchise and also discussed the "thorny" question of joint electorates *versus* separate electorates. Dr Ambedkar first firmly expressed his view that the then proposed Dominion Status must be responsible to the people of India. He said:[3] "Speaking on behalf of the Depressed Classes, I cannot honestly consent to responsible government or to Dominion Status unless I can be sure that the people for whom I speak are to have a place in that Constitution...."

Then, focusing on the issue of adult suffrage, Dr Ambedkar referred to it as the inherent right of every individual. He argued that "the suffrage and franchise are nothing but the right of self-defence..." Giving the franchise to an individual means giving "the power to regulate the terms on which he will live in a relationship with other individuals in society."

Dr Ambedkar emphasized: "...surely you cannot give...(the adult franchise) to only the higher Classes, or the propertied Classes...and leave the lower Classes at their mercy. ...The (adult) franchise is something which must be regarded as the inherent right of every individual in the State...."

Dr Ambedkar's spirit of Classical Republicanism becomes clearly evident here. He pointed out that if there are administrative difficulties in the "effectuation" of the universal adult franchise, "then the remedy is not to curtail the franchise, but to provide the necessary machinery...."

Dr Ambedkar emphatically maintained that "You cannot have in India any system of suffrage short of adult suffrage which will give equality of representation to all the Castes and communities..." Dr Ambedkar warned against creating a "system of political government in which only some Castes and some communities will predominate," which, he said, would amount to "creating in

3 Proceedings of Sub-Committee No. VI (Franchise), Govt of India, Central Publication Branch, Calcutta, 1931, pp. 28-35. All quotes here are from the same intervention.

India, a South Africa where only some people will have the vote and the rest will not."

## On Joint *versus* Separate Electorates

Moving on to the "thorniest" question of Joint *vs* Separate Electorates,[4] Dr Ambedkar observed that the issue is "inextricably bound up with the question of franchise". No minority is going to agree to joint electorates "unless that minority has adult suffrage".

Dr Ambedkar made it abundantly clear, "I am not going to place myself under the thumb and authority of any majority government, unless I am certain that I can exercise electoral power in elections which is commensurate with my social power...."

## On the Issue of Minority Representation

Dr Ambedkar and his colleague Rao Bahadur Srinivasan thought it advisable to submit a written Memorandum clearly and explicitly delineating what the Depressed Classes desire by way of political safeguards in the future Constitution of India.

The Memorandum titled "A Scheme of Political Safeguards for the Protection of the Depressed Classes in the Future Constitution of a Self-governing India" was circulated among the Members of the Sub-Committee on Minorities.[5]

---

4 Under Separate Electorates, the voters of a country are divided into different electorates, based on well-defined criteria such as religion, caste, gender, etc. Voters in each electorate vote only to elect representatives for their electorate. In contrast, under Joint Electorates there is no such sub-division of voters.

5 For full text of the Memorandum, see Jadhav (ed), *Ambedkar Writes*, Vol. I, pp. 84-92; For full text of the relevant speech, see Jadhav (ed), *Ambedkar Speaks,* Vol. III, pp. 122-28.

The Memorandum sought for the Depressed Classes the rights of citizenship common with other citizens and an appropriate "Fundamental Right" to be introduced in the Constitution aimed at securing the abolition of Untouchability and creating the equality of citizenship including a redressal mechanism. Further, it spelt out the conditions regarding electoral law—Right to adequate representation in the Legislatures, both Provincial and Central; Right to elect their own people as their representatives, by (1) adult suffrage and (2) by separate electorates for the first ten years and then joint electorates with reservation.

## Closing Plenary Session

Dr Ambedkar's remarks in the closing Plenary Session were remarkably sharp, analytically cogent and yet passionate in their appeal.[6] Expressing his views on the Committee's report that did not grant franchise to all adults, Dr Ambedkar reiterated his demand that responsible government must be truly representative and expressed his "disillusion" after finding that "it was difficult to persuade even the Indian Liberals to consent to enfranchise 25 per cent of the population for Provincial Legislatures."

Voicing his apprehension about the same in respect of the Central Legislature, Dr Ambedkar warned: "A franchise so

---

Also, in Proceedings of the Sub-Committee No. III (Minorities), Govt of India, Central Publication Branch, Calcutta, 1931, pp. 73-80; BAWS, Vol. 2, pp. 528-56.

6 For full text of the relevant speech, see Jadhav (ed), *Ambedkar Speaks,* Vol. III, pp. 131-34.
Also, in Proceedings of the RTC (1930-31), The Plenary Session (General Review), 19 January 1931, pp. 438-41; BAWS, Vol. 2, pp. 596-99. All quotes in this section are from the same intervention.

limited must necessarily make the future Government of India a government of the masses by the Classes."

Then launching a straight attack on the British Rule about the "deadlock" in respect of the distribution of seats as between the majority and the various minority communities, Dr Ambedkar argued that the "deadlock" was "largely due to the mischief done in the past…" He alleged that the "British government set different values on different communities according to the political use they made of them and gave to many communities an extraordinary share of political power by denying it to the Depressed Classes…." And in this regard, "the most aggrieved community", he said, was the Depressed Classes.

Dr Ambedkar expressed his frustration, "I was hoping that this Conference would proceed on the principle that what is wrongly settled is never settled, and give to the Depressed Classes their rightful quota of seats … But this has not happened …"

Dr Ambedkar lamented that the claims of the Depressed Classes "have just been heard, not even been adjudged…" He expressed his grave concern that the claims of the Depressed Classes for representation may be "whittled down to satisfy the ever-increasing scramble by other communities who are manoeuvring not so much for protection as for power."

He reminded the British Government that the British Parliament has always claimed that they are "the trustees of the Depressed Classes" and they would regard it as the greatest betrayal if they were "left to the mercy of those who have taken no interest in our welfare and whose prosperity and greatness are founded on our ruination and degradation."

Dr Ambedkar added that he was not afraid of being called "a communalist" by the nationalists and patriots of India. "A patriot and a nationalist in India is one who sees with open eyes his fellowmen treated as being less than men. But this humanity does not rise in protest," he said. He pointed out that he did not "belong to that Class of patriots", but belonged to "that Class which takes its stand on democracy and which seeks to destroy monopoly in every shape and form."

Dr Ambedkar brought his hard-hitting speech to a fitting passionate conclusion. He said:

> Our aim is to realize in practice our ideal of one man, one value in all walks of life—political, economic and social. It is because a representative government is one means to that end that the Depressed Classes attach to it a great value … You may tell me that the Depressed Classes have your sympathy. For a stricken people what is wanted is something more concrete, something more defined. You may despise me for being unduly apprehensive. My reply is it is better to be despised for too anxious apprehensions rather than be ruined by too confident a security.

***

At the First Round Table Conference, Dr Ambedkar emerged as a staunch nationalist. He forcefully argued that Independence from the British Rule was a precondition for creating an egalitarian, Caste-free society. This vision of nationalism, like that of Mahatma Phule, Periyar and other leaders of the anti-Caste movement, focused on building the nation as a democracy, not merely a transfer of power to Indians. The Indian society that Dr Ambedkar envisioned was democratic and Republican, incorporating the trinity of liberty, equality and fraternity.[7]

Outside the formal proceedings of the Round Table Conference, Dr Ambedkar gave interviews to the foreign press, contributed

---

7 In her book *Ambedkar: Towards an Enlightened India* (Delhi: Penguin, 2004), p. 39, Gail Omvedt, makes a similar observation.

articles to foreign journals and addressed several small gatherings including those of the Members of the British Parliament. Dr Ambedkar made the fullest use of the opportunity to bring the abominable plight of the Depressed Classes in India to the notice of the thought leaders in the Western world.

## CHAPTER EIGHT

# Confrontation at the Round Table Conference

In the meantime, the political situation in India was changing rapidly.

On 26 January 1931, Viceroy Lord Irwin released all Congress leaders, including Gandhiji, from jail. After detailed negotiations, a pact was reached between the two according to which Gandhiji withdrew the Civil Disobedience Movement and the boycott on the Round Table Conference (RTC). He promised to participate in the Second Session of the RTC, scheduled in September 1931.

The names of the delegates for the Second Session of the RTC were announced. Dr Ambedkar, who had already made his distinctive mark in the First Session of the RTC (in November 1930), was not only selected for the Second Session, but was also placed on the Federal Structure Committee, which was going to play a critical role in drafting the new Constitution for India.

Within days after the announcement of the Second RTC, Gandhiji wrote to Dr Ambedkar and sought a meeting with him in person. This historic meeting took place on 14 August 1931 at Mani Bhavan in Mumbai, just a day before Dr Ambedkar was scheduled to leave for London to participate in the Second RTC. Gandhiji along with Pandit Madan Mohan Malaviya, Sarojini Naidu and others were also going to sail for England for the same Conference shortly thereafter.

The historic face-off between the two leaders was a downright disaster.[1]

The Second Session of the RTC was scheduled to commence on 7 September 1931 and it was in this Session that Dr Ambedkar was going to come to a head-on collision with Gandhiji.

When the Second Session of the RTC began, nobody could have imagined the acrimonious and bitter debate that ensued between Mahatma Gandhi (who was attending the Conference for the first time as the representative of the Indian National Congress) and Dr Ambedkar.

## Confrontation in the Federal Structure Committee

Participating in the deliberations of the Federal Structure Committee, Dr Ambedkar extensively dealt with the issues such as the composition of Federal Legislature, representation of native (Princely) States and representation of other "Special Interests". The running theme of all of his assertions, all along, was consistently emphasizing an all-inclusiveness of democracy through direct elections.

Among other things, Dr Ambedkar said:[2] "Unless the Indian citizen is made to feel that it is he who can make or unmake the

---

1 As detailed in the Prologue.

2 All quotes in this chapter, unless specified otherwise, are from Indian Round Table Conference, 2 Session, 1931: Proceedings of the Federal Structure Committee and the Minorities Committee, London, 1931-32. Most of these quotes are readily available in Keer, *Dr Ambedkar: Life and Mission*, pp. 172-92. They are also available in Dr Ambedkar, *What Congress and Gandhi Have Done to the Untouchables*, pp. 61-79.

government, we shall never be able to succeed in establishing the true foundations of a responsible government in India..."[3]

Dr Ambedkar went on to add that citizens "must be allowed to see the effect of their election upon the government of the country and upon their welfare. I can, under no circumstances, consent to a system which will not provide for direct election to the Lower Chamber of the Federal Assembly."

Regarding the all-important issue of "minorities" Dr Ambedkar said, "The minorities in India are not only anxious to have their interests and their communities represented in the various Legislatures, but they are also insistent...that they shall get a certain minimum quantum of representation..." In this regard, Dr Ambedkar suggested that the model of the then Austrian Constitution could be suitably adapted to give a certain minimum representation to the minorities in India.

In the same Republican spirit, while referring to the Indian Princely States, Dr Ambedkar emphatically argued, "no concession can be made, no scheme can be adopted, if ultimately it is found... [it] ....is going to compromise the system of responsibility or... whittle [it] down..."

Before concluding, Dr Ambedkar referred to representation of special interests and made it abundantly clear that he did not "want the Depressed Classes to be treated as a special interest...but as a separate community for political purposes in the same way as the Mohammedans...in the Provincial Legislative Councils as well as in both Houses of the Central Legislature."

This was an extremely important strategic statement which was going to lead to an unprecedented political turmoil in the country.

***

---

3 Dr Ambedkar's commitment to Republicanism keeps surfacing, time and again.

In his first speech in the Federal Structure Committee of the RTC (on 15 September 1931) Mahatma Gandhi argued that the Congress represents all Indian interests and Classes, including the Muslims and the Depressed Classes; the latter because removal of Untouchability was a facet of the political platform of the Congress. And, since he was the sole representative of the Congress, it followed that he was the sole representative of the Indian nation as well.

Speaking in the same Committee the next day, Gandhiji made a specific reference to the problem of special representation for different communities and said that the "Congress had reconciled itself to special treatment of the Hindu-Muslim-Sikh tangle. There are sound historical reasons for it, but the Congress will not extend that doctrine in any shape or form…" He then clarified his position: "The interests of Untouchables are as dear to the Congress as the interests of any other body or of any other individual throughout the length and the breadth of India. Therefore, I would strongly resist any further special representation."[4]

Dr Ambedkar did not take on Gandhiji on this subject because it was going to come up before the Minorities Committee scheduled to meet on 28 September. Before that, a meeting was arranged between Gandhiji and Dr Ambedkar by Gandhiji's son Devdas (on 26 September 1931). The second one-on-one meeting between Gandhiji and Dr Ambedkar also turned out to be a damp squib.

In spite of the scepticism about the outcome of the meeting, Dr Ambedkar patiently elaborated his position for nearly three hours, while Gandhiji listened quietly, spinning. Gandhiji's unwillingness to respond explicitly disturbed Dr Ambedkar very much. Later, he described Gandhiji's behaviour as *Chanakya Niti*—an attempt to

---

4 Both quotes in the paragraph are from Keer, *Dr Ambedkar: Life and Mission*, p. 173.

gauge the position of an irreconcilable opponent without disclosing his own response.

***

Speaking to the Minorities Committee on 1 October 1931, Gandhiji called for its adjournment on the grounds that no compromise could be reached in his meetings with the Minority leaders of various groups. Gandhiji suggested that informal consultations would solve the "Communal Problem", for which he needed more time.

It was in the Minorities Committee Meeting after a week (8 October 1931) that Gandhiji and Dr Ambedkar faced each other and all hell broke loose.

In his speech, Gandhiji admitted failure of his informal negotiations with Muslims, Sikhs and other leaders to sort out the "Communal Problem". He moved for an adjournment of the meeting *sine die*.

In the course of his speech, Gandhiji, however, blamed the failure on the composition of the Indian delegation on the grounds that "they were almost all not the elected representatives of the parties or groups whom they were presumed to represent …"[5]

Dr Ambedkar's reply was sharp and hard-hitting.[6] He said, "What disturbs me is that instead of confining himself to his proposition that the Minorities Committee should adjourn sine die," Mr Gandhi started casting aspersions upon the Delegates that they "were nominees of the Government, and that they did not represent the views of their respective communities for whom they stood… ."

Dr Ambedkar added emphatically:

---

5 Keer, *Dr Ambedkar: Life and Mission,* p. 176.

6 Ibid., p. 177.

> Speaking for myself, I have not the slightest doubt that even if the Depressed Classes of India were given the chance of electing their representatives to this Conference, I would, all the same, find a place here ... Whether I am a nominee or not, I fully represent the claims of my community. Let no man be under any mistaken impression as regards that.

At this point, Dr Ambedkar's tone became acerbic. He said, "The Mahatma has been always claiming that the Congress stands for the Depressed Classes... . I can only say that it is one of the many false claims which irresponsible people keep on making... ."

Dr Ambedkar then read out aloud a telegram from a Depressed Classes Union in the United Provinces, a resolution declaring its non-confidence in the Congress movement.

Dr Ambedkar clarified that the Depressed Classes were not unduly anxious about the transfer of power under the then prevailing circumstances. However, if the British Government wanted to transfer the power, it should be "accompanied by such conditions...that the power shall not fall into the hands of a clique... . The solution shall be such that the power shall be shared by all communities in their respective proportions."

***

Before the last meeting of the Minorities Committee, leading representatives of the Muslims, the Depressed Classes and other minorities submitted a Memorandum, stating the general principles and special claims of the Muslims, the Depressed Classes, Christians, Anglo-Indians and Europeans.

This Minorities Pact enraged Mahatma Gandhi and in the last meeting, he said:[7] "I can understand the claims advanced by other minorities, but the claims advanced on behalf of the Untouchables

---

7 Ibid., p. 189.

that to me is the 'unkindest cut of all'.... I claim that if there was a referendum of the Untouchables I would get their vote, and I would top the poll."

During his uncharacteristically strongly worded speech, Gandhiji said that he had regard for Dr Ambedkar's capabilities and for his desire to see the Untouchables uplifted, but maintained that Dr Ambedkar's "bitter experiences in life had warped his judgement".

In the same speech, Gandhiji firmly asserted:

> ...I do not mind Untouchables, if they so desire, being converted to Islam or Christianity. I should tolerate that, but I cannot possibly tolerate what is in store for Hinduism if there are two divisions set forth in the villages.... I want to say with all emphasis that I can command that if I was the only person to resist this thing (i.e., divisions within Hinduism), I would resist it with my life.[8]

As fate would have it, his words proved to be prophetic; a few months later, he did resist it with his life!

***

After this acrimonious exchange, Dr Ambedkar wrote a letter from London to *The Times of India* (12 October) in which he made a serious allegation against Gandhiji. He wrote:[9] "We are, however, reliably informed that in carrying his negotiations with our Muslim friends, Mr Gandhi demanded that as one of the conditions for his accepting their 14 points, they should oppose the claims of the Depressed Classes and the smaller minorities."

---

8 Ibid., p. 189.

9 Ibid., p. 178.

Proceeding further in his direct attack on Gandhiji, Dr Ambedkar wrote:

> To say in public that I will agree if all others agree and then set out to work in private to prevent others from so agreeing by buying off those who are willing to agree, is, in our opinion, a piece of conduct unbecoming a Mahatma and to be expected only from an inveterate opponent of the Depressed Classes. Mr Gandhi is not only not playing the part of a friend of the Depressed Classes, but he is not even playing the part of an honest foe.

At one point Gandhiji had reportedly said: "Dr Ambedkar commands my sympathies in all he says. He needs the gentlest treatment." On another occasion, Gandhiji said: "He has a right to spit upon me, as every Untouchable has, and I would keep on smiling if he did so." Gandhiji's "resolutely smiling face was not a mask. It was a measure of the man. But when [he] confronted Dr Ambedkar at the Second Round Table Conference, [his] smile faded."[10]

Both Gandhiji and Dr Ambedkar departed deeply wounded. Gandhiji described it as "the most humiliating day of my life", while Dr Ambedkar reportedly later remarked acerbically: "Unfortunately, the Congress chose Mr Gandhi as its representative. A worse person could not have been chosen to guide India's destiny. As a unifying force, he was a failure. Mr Gandhi presents himself as a man of humility. But his behaviour at the Round Table Conference showed that … Mr Gandhi could be very petty-minded."[11]

The Second Round Table Conference ended in a stalemate. It created a lot of bitterness between Gandhiji and Dr Ambedkar.

---

10 Lelyveld, *Great Soul*, p. 214-15.

11 B.R. Ambedkar, *What Congress and Gandhi Have Done to the Untouchables* (Bombay: Thacker & Co, 1945), p. 55.

When Dr Ambedkar was leaving for the First Round Table Conference (which Gandhiji had boycotted), Gandhiji's followers had protested against him with black flags. In turn, when Gandhiji returned from London after attending the Second Round Table Conference, hundreds of Dr Ambedkar's followers assembled at the marine terminal in Mumbai to protest against the "uncharitable" stance taken by him.

The cheers from Gandhiji's followers were drowned in the slogan-shouting of activists from the Depressed Classes. In fact, the battle of slogan-mongering soon turned physical. Stones and bottles started flying, and several people were injured.

## In the Aftermath of Confrontation

Almost 15 years after the confrontation with Mahatma Gandhi in the Second Round Table Conference, Dr Ambedkar wrote in his book *What Congress and Gandhi Have Done to the Untouchables* that even Gandhiji's friends could not understand his attitude towards the Untouchables. Admitting the Muslims and the Sikhs as separate minorities for providing the political safeguards but not extending the same recognition to the Untouchables "came to them as a surprise and a puzzle. Whenever they asked for an explanation, Mr Gandhi did nothing except to get angry. Mr Gandhi himself could not give a logical and consistent defence of his opposition to the Untouchables."[12]

According to Dr Ambedkar, inside the RTC, Gandhiji's "defence was that the Hindus had seriously taken up the cause of the Untouchables and that therefore there was no reason to give them political safeguards". On the other hand, outside the RTC, Gandhiji presented "totally different reasons". He argued: "What

12 Ambedkar, *What Congress and Gandhi Have Done to the Untouchables*. pp. 70-71. All other quotes in this section are from the same source.

is needed is the destruction of 'Untouchability'." To accomplish this objective, Gandhiji proposed, instead of separate electorates, that the so-called Upper Castes engage in "penance for having neglected the 'Untouchables' for ages. This penance could be fulfilled through proactive social reform and by making the lot of the 'Untouchables' more bearable through acts of service."

Before the Second Session of the Round Table Conference was adjourned, the delegate members of the Minorities Committee had accepted the proposal of the British Prime Minister to submit a signed requisition authorizing him to arbitrate and give his decision on the "Communal Problem". Most delegates did it including Gandhiji. On the other hand, Dr Ambedkar wrote:[13] "I did not make any such requisition. I felt that the demands of the Untouchables were so reasonable that no arbitration was necessary."

## Announcement of the Communal Award

Gandhiji was in the Yeravada jail when the Communal Award was announced by the British Prime Minister (16 August 1932).

Well before the announcement of the Communal Award, Gandhiji wrote a letter to Sir Samuel Hoare (the then Secretary of State for India)[14] which reminded him that Gandhiji, at the end of his speech at the Second RTC, had said that he would "resist with [his] life the grant of separate electorates to the Depressed Classes. This was not said in the heat of the moment nor by way of rhetoric."

Noting that "any moment His Majesty's Government may declare their decision" Gandhiji firmly stated: "... I know that

13 Ibid., p.74.

14 Ibid., p. 78.

separate electorate is neither a penance nor any remedy for the crushing degradation… [the Untouchables] have groaned under. I, therefore, respectfully inform His Majesty's Government that in the event of their decision creating separate electorate for the Depressed Classes, I must fast unto death…."

After giving a warning to Sir Samuel Hoare, Gandhiji was under the impression that his threat to fast unto death was sufficient to scare the British Government and prevent them from accepting the claim of the Untouchables for separate electoral representation.

No wonder, when the British Prime Minister Ramsay MacDonald finally announced the Communal Award (16 August 1932) granting separate electorates for Untouchables and giving them 78 seats in the Legislature, it came to Gandhiji as a bombshell.

Earlier, when the Communal Deadlock was found to be difficult to resolve at the Round Table Conference, Gandhiji had committed in writing that the final decision given by the Prime Minister would be acceptable to him. Yet, when the Communal Award actually provided for separate electorates for Untouchables, Gandhiji refused to accept the verdict and announced an indefinite fast unto death, if separate electorates for the Depressed Classes were not abolished. Gandhiji commenced his "fast unto death" on 20 September 1932.

## CHAPTER NINE

# Truce with Gandhiji: The Poona Pact

As expected, Gandhiji's announcement of "fast unto death" threw the whole country into a state of an unprecedented turmoil. As soon as Gandhiji announced that he was beginning his "fast unto death" in opposition to the Communal Award, he was flooded with messages of support from all over India. The *Mahatma* by then had acquired a sort of saintliness. His discourses were appealing to the majority including many Untouchables.

Public appeals were made to Gandhiji, prayers were offered and Government issued statements to the Press. Leaders such as Dr Rajendra Prasad went to the extreme of stating that Hinduism was on its trial. There was a lot of confusion and nervousness among the Caste Hindus because the life of *Mahatma* was at stake.[1]

Pandit Madan Mohan Malaviya announced his intention to hold a Conference on behalf of the Hindu Mahasabha in Mumbai on 19 September 1932 to break the deadlock. The title

---

1 The detailed account here is based on the two original biographies of Dr Ambedkar—by Dhananjay Keer (English, first published in 1954) and C.B. Khairmode (Marathi, 12 volumes, reprints 1984-2008).

of the announcement of the meeting—"Conference of Hindu and Untouchable Leaders"—was an oxymoron: while Gandhiji refused to consider the Untouchables as outside Hinduism, for majority, in their heart of hearts, the title of "Hindus" was reserved only for the Upper Castes...[2] In order to save the life of the *Mahatma* it was necessary to modify the British Premier's Communal Award and, for that, in turn, it was necessary to get the approval of Dr Ambedkar who had defended and acquired those rights for the Depressed Classes. Naturally, all eyes turned to Dr Ambedkar.

Ironically, the political leaders and the Press that had refrained till then from recognizing Dr Ambedkar as the undisputed leader of the Depressed Classes, were now compelled by the evolving circumstances to recognize his leadership as well as spokesmanship for the Depressed Classes. He now became the centre of attention of the whole country.

Dr Ambedkar was of course fully aware of the significance and magnitude of the crisis that had arisen out of Gandhiji's "fast unto death". Gandhiji, in fact, had launched his most patent weapon at Dr Ambedkar.

On the eve of the Conference of the Hindu leaders, Dr Ambedkar issued a Statement to the Press in which he said:[3] "I am willing to consider everything, though I am not willing to allow the rights of the Depressed Classes to be curtailed in any way." What is the use of holding a "Conference in a vacuum or discussing things without any specific data?"

Dr Ambedkar pointed out in an interview that Gandhiji could have discussed his proposal with the British Premier. As Gandhiji did not put forth any proposal himself, he alone was to blame.

---

2 Jaffrelot, *Dr Ambedkar and Untouchability*, p. 65.

3 Keer, *Dr Ambedkar: Life and Mission,* p. 206.

Not surprisingly, a vicious campaign was launched against Dr Ambedkar. He was again called a monster, a traitor and a British stooge. But Dr Ambedkar remained calm and collected. He issued another statement on the eve of the Conference. "It would have been justifiable," he observed *If Mr Gandhi had resorted to this extreme step for obtaining Independence for the country* [emphasis added] …

In the same statement, Dr Ambedkar pointed out: "It is also a painful surprise that Mr Gandhi should have singled out special representation for the Depressed Classes in the Communal Award as an excuse for his self-immolation … Separate electorates are granted not only to the Depressed Classes but to the Indian Christians…as well as to the Mohammedans and the Sikhs."[4]

Dr Ambedkar asked: "If separate electorates to the Mohammedans and Sikhs do not split up the nation, why would the Hindu society be split up if the Depressed Classes were given separate electorates?" Concluding this statement, Dr Ambedkar said in a caustic tone: "The Mahatma is not an immortal person, nor the Congress…. There have been many Mahatmas in India whose sole object was to remove Untouchability and to elevate and absorb the Depressed Classes, but every one of them has failed in his mission. Mahatmas have come and Mahatmas have gone. But the Untouchables have remained as Untouchables."[5]

* * *

As announced, the Conference of the Hindu leaders was held on 19 September 1932 amidst this charged atmosphere. Dr Ambedkar was seated next to the President's Chair. Among those present were several dignitaries, including Sir Chimanlal Setalvad, Seth Walchand Hirachand, Dr Rajendra Prasad, Kamala Nehru, Tej

4 Ibid, p. 207.

5 Ibid, pp. 207-08.

Bahadur Sapru and others. Seth Walchand Hirachand suggested to Pandit Malaviya—the Chair—that he should call upon Dr Ambedkar to speak first.

As the opening speaker, Dr Ambedkar said that the Conference was going to serve no useful purpose unless "we know what Gandhiji has to say. Gandhiji ought to have proposed some alternative scheme before going on the fast unto death. Unless Gandhiji puts forward some new scheme, any efforts towards the settlement are going to be futile."

The Conference was adjourned when Dr Ambedkar refused to give up the Communcal Award.

***

The Hindu Mahasabha Conference took place at noon the next day. Dr Ambedkar, indicating to the Conference that he was placed on the horns of a dilemma, said:[6]

> It has fallen to my lot to be the villain of the piece. But I tell you I shall not deter from my pious duty, and betray the just and legitimate interests of my people even if you hang me on the nearest lamp post in the street. You better appeal to Gandhi to postpone his fast about a week and then seek for the solution of the problem.

This again came as a great shock to the Conference. On recovering, some prominent Members of the Conference led by Sir Tej Bahadur Sapru evolved a Scheme of Primary and Secondary Elections for the reserved seats. According to the proposed Scheme, the Depressed Classes themselves were to select for every seat a panel of not less than three candidates and then out of those three chosen candidates one was to be elected by the joint electorate

6 Ibid, p. 209.

of the Caste Hindus and the Depressed Classes. Dr Ambedkar accepted the proposal but demanded many more concessions for giving up the Communal Award, including a much larger number of seats than those offered. The Congress leaders examined those suggestions. Thereafter, Barrister Jayakar, Sapru, Rajagopalachari and Dr Rajendra Prasad left for Pune by the midnight train to meet Gandhiji.

On the early morning of Wednesday, 21 September, they met Gandhiji in the Yerawada Jail. Gandhiji said he would consider the proposal and let them know. Sapru then telephoned Dr Ambedkar requesting him to come over to Pune immediately.

***

On Thursday morning (22 September), Gandhiji had a talk with Dr Rajendra Prasad and Rajagopalachari and said the Primary and Secondary Election system should be applied to all seats alike. This was communicated to Dr Ambedkar, who demanded "concrete" proposals.

On the same day evening, Dr Ambedkar, accompanied by Jayakar, Birla and Rajagopalachari, went to meet Gandhiji in the jail. Gandhiji was lying on a white iron cot while Sardar Patel and Sarojini Naidu sat near Gandhiji.

When Dr Ambedkar approached the cot, there was a pin-drop silence loaded with expectations. Gandhiji was weak. He lay in his bed. The talk began.[7]

Sapru narrated to Gandhiji the whole story. Then in a soft voice, Dr Ambedkar said, "Mahatmaji, you have been very unfair to us."

"It is always my lot to appear to be unfair," replied Gandhiji. "I cannot help it."

7 The conversation here is reproduced from Keer (p.213) and corroborated by Khairmode.

Then Dr Ambedkar explained the prevailing situation and his own viewpoints. The sober yet earnest tone of Dr Ambedkar had the desired effect on Gandhiji. He replied: "You have my fullest sympathy. I am with you, Doctor, in most of the things you say. But you say you are interested in my life."

"Yes Mahatmaji, in the hope that if you would devote solely to the cause of my people, you would become our hero too," replied Dr Ambedkar.

Gandhiji said:

> Well, then, if it is so, then you know what you have got to do to save it. Do it and save my life. I know you do not want to forgo what your people have been granted by the Award. I accept your panel system, but you should remove one anomaly from it. You should apply the panel system to all the seats. *You are Untouchable by birth, and I am by adoption. We must be one and indivisible. I am prepared to give my life to avert the disruption of the Hindu community… [emphasis added]*

Dr Ambedkar accepted Gandhiji's suggestion. The interview ended, and the leaders from both sides started discussion for sorting out the relevant details. After several hours of discussion, two contentious issues still could not be settled. One was how long should the system of Primary Election continue and the second was regarding when should the referendum be taken.

Dr Ambedkar said that the system of Primary Election should be terminated at the end of 10 years, and insisted that the question of reserved seats should be settled by a referendum of the Depressed Classes at the end of further 15 years thereafter (i.e., after 25 years). The Congress leaders disagreed. In the meantime, news came in that Gandhiji's health had taken a serious turn, and he was fast losing strength. Gandhiji's son, Devdas Gandhi, with tears in his eyes, reported to the Conference that "Father was sinking".

The matter was referred to Gandhiji. Dr Ambedkar, with some leading leaders, met Gandhiji in the jail at nine o'clock that night. While Gandhiji approved of the idea of referendum, he said it should take place after five years. Gandhiji was hardly able to speak. His voice had now sunk to a whisper. Nevertheless Dr Ambedkar was not prepared to give in.

***

> At that stage, Mr M.C. Rajah, another leader of the Untouchables from Madras, who was in the Conference, said to Dr Ambedkar:[8]
>
> For thousands of years, we had been treated as Untouchables, downtrodden, insulted, despised. The Mahatma is staking his life for our sake, and if he dies, for the next thousands of years we shall be where we have been, if not worse. There will be such a strong feeling against us that we brought about his death, that…the whole Hindu community and the whole civilized community will kick us downstairs further still. I am not going to stand by you any longer…

That brought Dr Ambedkar around. He said, "I am willing to compromise".

***

On Saturday morning (24 September), negotiations resumed. The question of the total number of seats was decided by granting 148 seats to the Depressed Classes in the Provincial Assemblies, and it was also decided that 10 per cent of the seats of the Hindus from British India in the Central Assembly should be given to the

---

8 Quoted by Jaffrelot (p. 66) from B.R. Nanda, *In Gandhi's Footsteps: The Life and Times of Jamnalal Bajaj* (Delhi: Oxford University Press, 1990) p. 198.

Depressed Classes. However, there was no agreement on the issue of referendum. Again, the matter was referred to Gandhiji.

Gandhiji indicated to Dr Ambedkar that his reasoning was irrefutable, yet a mere statutory guarantee would not eradicate the underlying issue. He urged Dr Ambedkar to "give a last chance to Hinduism to make voluntary reparation for its sinful past". Gandhiji proposed that there should be a referendum, but insisted it should not be deferred for more than five years. "In five years or in my lifetime,"[9] said Gandhiji in a tone of decisiveness.

Upon returning to the discussion after an hour, the leaders decided to make the agreement without attaching the condition of a referendum to it. Gandhiji blessed it and gave his consent.

In no time, the agreement was drafted amidst an atmosphere of cordiality. It was signed on the evening on Saturday (24 September 1932), earning its place in history as the "Poona Pact". Dr Ambedkar signed on behalf of the Depressed Classes, while Pandit Malaviya signed on behalf of the Caste Hindus. Other notable signatories included Jayakar, Sapru, G.D. Birla, Rajagopalachari, and Dr Rajendra Prasad, among others.

The contents of the Pact were cabled to the British Cabinet and to the Viceroy, and a hard copy was handed over to the Secretary of the Bombay Governor. Next morning, the leaders returned to Mumbai to formally approve the pact.[10]

A meeting was held in Mumbai where Pandit Malaviya declared that "no one should be regarded as Untouchable by reason of his birth, and appealed to Hindus to make the idea of the Untouchability disappear from the land". Mathuradas Vasanji moved the resolution ratifying the Pact and Sapru supported it. With a wholesome tribute to Dr Ambedkar, Sapru congratulated him on his courageous fight for the cause which he represented

9 Keer, *Dr Ambedkar: Life and Mission*, p. 214.

10 Ibid, p. 215.

and added that Dr Ambedkar promised to be a great fighter in the future life of the country. [11]

When Dr Ambedkar rose to speak, a thunderous applause greeted him. Dr Ambedkar said that what happened the previous day was beyond his dream. After tremendous struggle and confusion, they had finally found the solution, he said. No man was ever placed in such a dilemma as he was. *There was the life of the greatest man of India to be saved, and on the other side the interests of the downtrodden community were to be safeguarded [emphasis added]*

"My only regret is," he added, "why did not Mahatmaji take this attitude at the Round Table Conference? If he had shown the same consideration to my point of view then, it would not have been necessary for him to go through this ordeal."[12]

Finally, Dr Ambedkar earnestly appealed to the Caste Hindus to abide by the Pact and that they should look upon the document as sacrosanct.

In the meantime, evening prayers were said in the Yerawada prison yard. Someone then handed over to Gandhiji a glass of orange juice, and he broke his fast amidst a gathering of around 200 disciples and admirers, which included poet Rabindranath Tagore, Sarojini Naidu, Sardar Patel and Swarup Rani Nehru among others.

***

The Poona Pact resonated throughout the country and had repercussions throughout the world. Dr Ambedkar emerged as the undisputed leader of the Depressed Classes.

---

11 Pyarelal, *The Epic Fast* (Ahmedabad: Mohanlal Maganlal Bhatt, 1932), p. 186.

12 Keer, *Dr Ambedkar: Life and Mission*, p. 215.

Under the Poona Pact, both sides had something to lose. The Caste Hindus were compelled to grant 148 seats to the Depressed Classes instead of 71. But the Caste Hindus did get the right to elect the representatives of the Depressed Classes.

"Dr Ambedkar became the only Indian politician whom Gandhiji challenged by resorting to a fast. Strategically, Gandhiji did this precisely because he knew that Dr Ambedkar would not respond by resorting to violence.... Dr Ambedkar was a lawyer who never turned the law to its advantage and he even adopted the *Satyagraha* as his *modus operandi* in Mahad in 1927."[13] It was believed widely that in 1932 Gandhiji "gambled" on Dr Ambedkar's self-restraint and won.[14]

The Poona Pact shaped India's electoral system and the electoral method by which Reserved Constituencies were defined. It has been argued that Gandhiji "skewed the electoral method, which made the election of Reserved candidate dependent upon the dominant Caste vote. This rendered them subservient to the interests of dominant social forces, defeating the very purpose for which such representation was secured."[15]

As a result, the Poona Pact in effect laid the foundation for Dr Ambedkar's defeats in elections. Not only did he lose heavily in the Assembly elections 1942 onwards but he could also not win the two Lok Sabha elections that he personally contested, in 1952 and again in 1954.

---

13 Jaffrelot, *Dr Ambedkar and Untouchability,* p. 65.

14 Upendra Baxi, as quoted by Jaffrelot, p. 65.

15 Raja Sekhar Vundru, "The Other Father", *Outlook*, 20 August 2012.

CHAPTER TEN

# Failure of Gandhi–Ambedkar Joint Efforts

The Poona Pact was signed on 24 September 1932. The very next day (i.e., 25 September 1932), in a public meeting of Gandhiji's followers held in Mumbai, a resolution was passed which, going well beyond the support to the Poona Pact, explicitly stated, *inter alia*:[1] "...henceforth, amongst Hindus, no one shall be regarded as an Untouchable by reason of his birth, and that [they]...will have the same right as other Hindus in regard to the use of public wells, public schools, public roads, and all other public institutions."

It was also resolved that "it shall be the duty of all Hindu leaders to secure, by every legitimate and peaceful means, an early removal of all social disabilities now imposed by custom upon the so-called Untouchable Classes...."

In the following week, on 30 September 1932, another public meeting of Hindus was held under the Chairmanship of Pandit Madan Mohan Malaviya, to form an All-India Anti-Untouchability

---

1 Dr Ambedkar, *What Congress and Gandhi Have Done to the Untouchables*, p. 103.

League with headquarters in Delhi and branches in different Provinces. Shri G.D. Birla (a prominent industrialist who had been financing many of Gandhiji's favourite projects) was chosen as the President while Shri Amritlal Thakkar (*alias* Thakkar Bappa) was chosen as the General Secretary. This project was inspired by Gandhiji who later renamed the League as the *Harijan Sevak Sangh* (i.e., a Society of those engaged in the service of the Untouchables).[2]

In order to provide funds for the work of the *Sangh,* Gandhiji launched an All-India tour from 7 November 1933 to 29 July 1934. The purpose of the tour was to generate sympathy among the Hindus for the cause of the Untouchables as well as to collect funds. Gandhiji did most of the tour on foot and collected Rs 8 lakh. With this amount and donations from Gandhiji's wealthy friends, the *Sangh* started its work.

Earlier, in February 1933, Gandhiji had started a new weekly newspaper titled *Harijan* (which literally meant "Children of God"). Agitations by the Untouchables had become one of Gandhiji's main concerns. "Untouchability Abolition Week" was launched by Gandhiji in September-October 1933.

Initially, these ongoing developments mollified Dr Ambedkar's hostility towards Gandhiji. Dr Ambedkar actually began to appreciate Gandhiji's public pronouncements concerning Untouchables. He indicated to his colleagues that there was a gradual convergence with his own position on certain issues. But he regretted that Gandhiji still refused to endorse inter-Caste marriage and inter-Caste dining.

In one of the letters to his colleagues, Dr Ambedkar indicated, in a rather Gandhian manner: "The Touchables and Untouchables cannot be held together by law, certainly not by any electoral law

---

2 Ibid., p. 126.

substituting joint electorate for separate electorates. The only thing that can hold together is love." In another letter, he even quoted Tolstoy, one of Gandhiji's main sources of inspiration, "Only those who love can serve".[3]

Subsequently, however, the viewpoints and agendas of Gandhiji and Dr Ambedkar became increasingly irreconcilable as can be seen from the critical assessment offered by Dr Ambedkar many years later in 1945 in his book, *What Congress and Gandhi Have Done to the Untouchables*.[4]

Dr Ambedkar's critique of Mahatma Gandhi may be discussed under two subheads:

A. The Temple Entry Movement

B. Activities of *Harijan Sevak Sangh*

## A. The Temple Entry Movement

The resolution (of 25 September 1932, in the aftermath of the Poona Pact) was followed by intense efforts among Hindus to open Temples to the Untouchables. Dr Ambedkar recounts week after week,[5] Gandhiji's mouthpiece *Harijan* featured a long list of temples, wells, and schools that had been opened to the Untouchables, which was prominently displayed in a special column titled "Week to Week" on the front page.

Whenever the trustees of temples were seemingly unwilling to open their temples to the Untouchables, the Hindus actually started *Satyagraha* against them to persuade or force them to do so. The *Satyagraha* by Mr Kelappan for entry of the Untouchables in the famous Guruvayur temple was a part of this campaign.

---

3 See Jaffrelot, *Dr Ambedkar and Untouchability,* p. 68.

4 For summary, see Jadhav (ed), *Ambedkar Writes*, Vol. I, pp. 293-309.

5 Ambedkar, *What Gandhi and Congress have Done to the Untouchables*, p. 103.

Simultaneously, several Hindu legislators came forward with Bills calling for the trustees to open the temples to the Untouchables provided that a referendum showed that the majority of the Hindu worshippers voted in favour. Gandhiji also joined this agitation, which was described by Dr Ambedkar as a "great surprise" in view of the fact that before 1932, Gandhiji was opposed to allowing Untouchables to enter the Hindu temples.

In this regard, Dr Ambedkar contemplated three reasons as to why Gandhiji took this "somersault":[6] First, it could be "an honest act of change of heart." Secondly, the object could be "to destroy the basis of the claim of the Untouchables for political rights." Thirdly, it could be because Gandhiji saw a distinct "possibility of adding to his name and fame and rushed to make the most of it, as is his habit to do. The second or the third explanation may be nearer the truth ..."

Dr Ambedkar reports that Gandhiji, in fact, had asked him to lend support to the Temple Entry Movement. Dr Ambedkar declined and issued a press statement instead, explaining the reasons thereof.

Dr Ambedkar's Statement[7] on Temple Entry Bill (dated 14 February 1933) unequivocally asserted that "the Depressed Classes cannot possibly give their support" to the prevailing draft of the Temple Entry Bill.

The Statement reasoned that the Bill is based on an ordinary principle of "Majority rule", which "cannot hasten the day of temple-entry". More importantly, "the Bill does not regard Untouchability in temples as a sinful custom". It regards "Untouchability merely as a social evil...." The Bill does not deem Untouchability to be illegal. "Its binding force is taken away, only if a majority decides to do so. Sin and immorality cannot become

6 Ibid., p. 107.

7 Ibid., pp. 108-12.

tolerable because a majority is addicted to them or because the majority chooses to practise them."

Dr Ambedkar then added one more argument against the Bill: self-respect. He reminded that "Hindus never begged for admission in those places from which the Europeans in their arrogance had excluded them." ["Dogs and Indians" not allowed, he quoted.] He asked, "Why should an Untouchable beg for admission in a place from which he has been excluded by the arrogance of the Hindus?"[8]

The Statement added:

> ...the Depressed Class man...is prepared to say to the Hindus, "to open or not to open your temples is a question for you to consider and not for me to agitate. If you think, it is bad manners not to respect the sacredness of human personality, open your temples and be a gentleman. If you rather be a Hindu than be gentleman, then shut the doors and damn yourself for I don't care to come...

Here, Dr Ambedkar made one of the early assertions regarding his discontent with regard to the Hindu religion when he stated:[9]

> ...the Hindu religion does not recognize the principle of equality of social status; on the other hand, it fosters inequality by insisting upon grading people as *Brahmins*, *Kshatriyas*, *Vaishyas* and *Shudras*...The doctrine of Chaturvarna is the root cause of all inequality and also the parent of the Caste System and Untouchability, which are merely forms of inequality. Unless it is done not only will the Depressed Classes reject Temple Entry, they will also reject the Hindu faith".

---

8 Ibid., p. 110. All quotes in this paragraph are from the same source.

9 Ibid., p. 111.

After an enthusiastic start in opening temples and wells to eradicate Untouchability, the momentum gradually fizzled out. As stated by Dr Ambedkar,[10] the reports in the "Week to Week" columns of the *Harijan* dwindled, became infrequent, and eventually vanished. He accused that a "large part of the news that appeared in the 'Week to Week' columns was fabricated, and was nothing but a lying propaganda engineered by Congressmen to deceive the world that the Hindus were committed to fight Untouchability."

Dr Ambedkar explained how the Temple Entry Movement was a strange game of political acrobatics.[11] Gandhiji began "as an opponent of Temple Entry". When the Untouchables demanded political rights, Gandhiji changed his position and became a "supporter of Temple Entry". Later, in order to preserve political power in the hands of the Congress, Gandhiji gave up Temple Entry. "Is this sincerity? Does this show conviction? Was the 'agony of the soul' which Mr Gandhi spoke of [anything] more than a phrase?" asked Dr Ambedkar.

## B. Activities of *Harijan Sevak Sangh*

Dr Ambedkar, in his critique of Gandhiji, also made a critical appraisal of the *Harijan Sevak Sangh*, established in 1932. According to Dr Ambedkar, this organization was "held out as a glorious testimony to the agony of Mr Gandhi's soul for the condition of the Untouchables, and to the passion he feels for their elevation".

In fact, many Americans were specially invited and were "shown … round as an unrivalled piece of social work that is being done by Mr Gandhi for the welfare of the Untouchables".[12]

---

10 Ibid., pp. 114-15.

11 Ibid., p. 125.

12 Ibid., p. 129. Both quotes.

Dr Ambedkar highlighted that in reality, the "*Sangh* has been carrying on a very poor existence,... with a budget of only Rs 3 for 500 Untouchables!"[13] This was worse than pittance.

***

Dr Ambedkar bared his heart out as to why he chose to sever his ties with the *Sangh*. He wrote:[14] "After the Poona Pact, I proceeded in a spirit of forget and forgive. I accepted the bona fides of Mr Gandhi...It was in that spirit that I accepted a place on the Central Board of the *Sangh*, and was looking forward to play my part in its activities..."

In the meantime, Dr Ambedkar had to go to London to participate in the Third Session of the RTC. Under the circumstances, he wrote a letter to the Secretary of the *Sangh*.

Dr Ambedkar argued in the letter that the task of uplifting the Depressed Classes could be based on two distinctly different and mutually exclusive premises:[15]

(i) If an individual is "suffering from want and misery it is because he must be vicious and sinful". Following this approach, efforts would have to be focused on making "the individual a better and virtuous individual".

(ii) The fate of the individual "is governed by his environment and the circumstances he is obliged to live under, and if an individual is suffering from want and misery it is because his environment is not propitious".

Dr Ambedkar argued in favour of the latter. In the same letter, he reasoned: "The former may raise a few stray individuals above

---

13 Ibid., p. 131.

14 Ibid., p. 133.

15 Ibid., p. 134.

the level of the Class to which they belong. It cannot lift the Class as a whole," and accordingly, advised the Board of the Sangh "to concentrate all its energies on a programme that will effect a change in the social environment of the Depressed Classes."

More specifically, Dr Ambedkar presented some "concrete proposals" for the League:

### *(1) A Campaign to Secure Civil Rights*

Undertake a nationwide campaign "to secure to the Depressed Classes the enjoyment of their civic rights such as taking water from the village wells, entry in village schools…" He argued that "such a programme if carried into villages will bring about the necessary social revolution in the Hindu Society, without which it will never be possible for the Depressed Classes to get equal social status."

### *(2) Equality of Opportunity*

Bring about "equality of opportunity for the Depressed Classes. Much of the misery and poverty of the Depressed Classes is due to the absence of equality of opportunity which in its turn is due to Untouchability".

### *(3) Social Intercourse*

Make efforts to "dissolve that nausea, which the Touchables feel towards the Untouchables, …the best way of achieving it is to establish closer contact between the two" including "the admission of the Depressed Classes to the houses of the Caste Hindus as guests or servants…"

Dr Ambedkar's letter was not even acknowledged. Evidently, all his proposals were disregarded. To his shocking disbelief, while Dr Ambedkar was away, the League had issued a statement (3

November 1932), barely two months after its establishment, which declared, *inter alia*:[16]

> … it is desirable to make it clear that while the League will work by persuasion among the Caste Hindus to remove every vestige of Untouchability, the main line of work will be constructive, such as the uplift of Depressed Classes educationally, economically and socially, which itself will go a great way to remove Untouchability … And it is for such work mainly that the League has been established. *Social reforms like the abolition of the Caste System and inter-dining are kept outside the scope of the League* [emphasis added].

Dr Ambedkar was appalled at this "complete departure from the original aims of the organization". He maintained that this "change in the aims and objects could not have been brought about without the knowledge and consent of Mr Gandhi".

Under the circumstances, Dr Ambedkar had no choice but to disassociate himself from the League. Later, Dr Ambedkar explained this volte-face by Gandhiji:[17] "Removal of Untouchability as a platform was very good, but as a programme of action it was bound to have made Mr Gandhi very unpopular with the Hindus…" Gandhiji, therefore, "preferred the programme of constructive work which had all advantages and no disadvantages…" Moreover, "the programme of constructive work had the possibility of being converted into a plan to kill Untouchables by kindness. This as a matter of fact has happened."

This line of argument by Dr Ambedkar has resonated in the writings of several later scholars. Jaffrelot, for example, has argued that Gandhiji's "soft-pedalling the issue of Untouchables needs

16 Ibid., p. 141.

17 Ibid., p. 141.

to be seen in light of the growing hostility of orthodox Hindus to his policy."[18] Orthodox Hindus viewed Gandhi as moving too fast. On the other hand, for Dr Ambedkar, Gandhiji was going far too slowly. Dr Ambedkar was "deeply disappointed and dismayed" by Gandhiji's actions.

According to Jaffrelot,[19] in the ultimate analysis, "the struggle between Gandhi and Ambedkar ended with the former's victory: while the social *status quo* was not totally preserved, the politicization of Untouchables by means of a separate electorate had been defused. Gandhi's signal success was the Poona Pact, which was to have serious consequences..."

* * *

While Dr Ambedkar had succeeded in awakening the downtrodden masses and uniting them, there was a brief period following the Poona Pact of 1932 when the movement was seemingly losing some of its momentum. To be sure, there were a few agitations and occasional public meetings, but the earlier intensity was somehow missing. Dr Ambedkar's both mass movement initiatives—at the Chavdar Lake at Mahad and at the Kala Ram Temple in Nashik—were stuck in litigations. Dr Ambedkar was fighting the legal suits but the cases were dragging on.[20] The failure of Gandhi-Ambedkar joint efforts destroyed whatever little hope Dr Ambedkar had in Mahatma Gandhi.

---

18 See Jaffrelot, *Dr Ambedkar and Untouchability*, pp. 70-71.

19 Ibid., p. 71.

20 Much later, in March 1937, the Mumbai High Court settled the long-drawn Mahad case, allowing Untouchables to draw water from the Chavdar Lake.

# CHAPTER ELEVEN

# Announcement of Conversion: Gandhi–Ambedkar Rift Widens

In the aftermath of the tumultuous events of 1932, Dr Ambedkar met with a major tragedy in his personal life. The health of his wife, Ramabai, had been failing for some time. His only surviving son, Yashwant, was suffering from rheumatism. Dr Ambedkar often said that one day he would earn enough money to send his wife and son for specialized treatment in London. Unfortunately, before he could do that, Ramabai passed away on 26 May 1935.[1] Ramabai (Rama *Mata* as she is now referred to) had gone through all the ups and downs of life together with Dr Ambedkar during the early part of his struggle. Her early death at the age of only 40 years was a big blow to Babasaheb. He fell into despair. After the death of Ramabai, Dr Ambedkar who was in his mid-forties became very lonely.

1 Keer, *Dr Ambedkar: Life and Mission.*

## Announcement of Conversion

On 13 October 1935, Dr Ambedkar presided over a major conference in Yeola in Nashik district of today's Maharashtra. The Conference was attended by about 10,000 Untouchables from all over the Bombay Province and representatives from the Hyderabad State and the Central Provinces.

In his hard-hitting speech lasting over an hour and a half, Dr Ambedkar recounted the plight of the Depressed Classes in all spheres—economic, social, educational and political—and pointed out the immense sacrifices made by them. He explained how their struggle to secure even preliminary rights had not yielded the desired outcomes and there was no change in the attitude of the Touchables. It gave him a very painful realization that the time and money spent on and efforts made to achieve those objectives had proved utterly fruitless, he said.

Dr Ambedkar emphasized that the time for making a final decision to settle the matter had arrived. The disabilities they were labouring under and the indignities they had to put up with, he added, were the direct result of their being members of the Hindu religion.

Dr Ambedkar described to the huge gathering of his followers how the struggle over the past decade to secure equal human status within the Hindu society had miserably failed. For the first decade or so of his public life, Dr Ambedkar had chosen to reform the Hindu religion by fighting it from within. He had tried to create a legitimate place for the Depressed Classes in the Hindu society, but the Upper Castes had not budged.

Then came a stunning surprise. Dr Ambedkar said he was contemplating a change of religion.[2] "Would it not be better to give

2 Marathi Speech. For English Summary, read Jadhav (ed), *Ambedkar Speaks*, Vol. II, pp. 274-77. An English report is also available in *The Bombay Chronicle*, 16 October 1935, reproduced in BAWS, Vol. 17(3), pp. 94-99.

up Hinduism and embrace another faith that would unreservedly give us an equal status?" he questioned. A hush descended the massive crowd. A moment later, he made his famous assertion: "Unfortunately, I was born a Hindu Untouchable—there was nothing I could do to prevent it. However, it is well within my power to refuse to live under ignoble and humiliating conditions. I solemnly assure you that *I will not die a Hindu* [emphasis added]."

Dr Ambedkar then announced a new strategy. He exhorted his followers to sever their connections with Hinduism and seek self-respect in another religion. However, he cautioned them to carefully select the new faith, and to ensure that equality of treatment, status and opportunities were guaranteed to them wholeheartedly.

Dr Ambedkar asked his followers to end the Kala Ram Temple *Satyagraha*, citing the futility demonstrated over the past five years in their attempts against the oppressive Caste Hindus who foiled their efforts. He encouraged them to conduct themselves in such a way in future that there would be no doubt to the outside world of their resolve to remain a separate community outside the Hindu fold, carving out for themselves a future worthy of free citizens.

Accordingly, after a detailed discussion, the Yeola Conference passed a Resolution instructing the Depressed Classes to stop the struggle which they had carried on for the past 10 years for raising the Untouchables to a status equal with that of the Caste Hindus. It further exhorted the Untouchables to stop frittering away their energies over fruitless attempts and to devote themselves to securing an honourable status, and an independent position on the basis of equality with the other sections of the Indian society.

***

Dr Ambedkar's announcement to renounce the Hindu religion and to embrace some other religion got world-wide publicity. The announcement sent shock waves throughout the country. Some called it a bluff and a political stunt. On the other hand, those who knew the strength of Dr Ambedkar's character could not doubt his determination. Some went to the extent of calling him a messiah; others felt it was a suicidal step. All eyes were on Gandhiji for his reaction, which came in almost immediately.

## Gandhiji's Reaction

When interviewed by a representative of the print media, Gandhiji indicated[3] that both Dr Ambedkar's speech and the resolution passed by the Conference were "unfortunate events". He said that he could "understand the anger of a high-souled and highly educated person like Dr Ambedkar over atrocities such as were committed in Kavitha[4] and other villages".

But he added: "...religion is not like a house or cloak which can be changed at will. It is more an integral part of one's self than of one's body. Religion is the tie that binds one to one's creator and whilst the body perishes, as it has to, religion persists even after death."

Gandhiji made an appeal saying: "If Dr Ambedkar has any faith in God, I would urge him to assuage his wrath and reconsider his position and examine his ancestral religion on its own merits and not through the weakness of its unfaithful followers."

Gandhiji did not stop at giving this advice to Dr Ambedkar; he also made a political statement: "I am convinced, change of faith by him, and those who passed the resolution would not serve the cause

3 Keer, *Dr Ambedkar: Life and Mission*.

4 Kavitha is a village in Anand district of Gujarat. In 1935, when Untouchables in the village "dared" to ask for their children to be admitted to the local school, the so-called Upper Castes were enraged and they imposed a complete social boycott on them.

which they have at heart; for millions of unsophisticated illiterate *Harijans* would not listen to him especially when it is remembered that their lives for good or evil are intertwined with those of Caste Hindus."

When Gandhiji's comment on Dr Ambedkar's announcement of conversion was shown to him, his immediate response was "… Hindu religion is not good for the Depressed Classes. Inequality is the very basis of it, and its ethics is such that the Depressed Classes can never acquire their full manhood".[5]

Dr Ambedkar agreed with Gandhiji that religion was necessary, but he did not agree that man should continue to profess his ancestral religion if he finds that the religion is repugnant to his notions of the sort of religion he needs.

He emphasized that Kavitha did not represent an isolated incident but rather formed the foundational basis of the system found in the ancestral religion of the Hindus.

Dr Ambedkar's detailed rebuttal to Gandhiji on the issue of conversion was to come about eight months later.

***

Gandhiji had predicted that millions of illiterate and unsophisticated Untouchables would not renounce their faith, because they were concerned with day-to-day survival rather than what he called, Dr Ambedkar's "attention-seeking stunts". Gandhiji's predictions, however, failed to convince other religious minorities such as Muslims, Christians and Sikhs. They looked at it as a great opportunity to convert the Untouchables *en masse* and strengthen their own faiths. Dr Ambedkar's house was flooded with letters and telegrams. While most of them eloquently attempted to convince him why their religion was the best choice as an alternative, some

5 Keer, *Dr Ambedkar: Life and Mission*, p. 257.

in fact hinted at tangible rewards. On the other hand, a few letters sent by some extremists were reportedly written in blood.

***

From time to time, Dr Ambedkar reviewed the progress of the mass movement led by him. The first such evaluation took place after a decade in social life. In a public meeting in Nagpur (on 4 May 1936), Dr Ambedkar explained to his followers that "what could not happen over hundreds of years has finally occurred in the last ten years".

On the issue of conversion, Dr Ambedkar questioned:[6] "If Hindus are not ready to remain under the British rule despite a Dominion Status that is being offered then why should we remain under the rule of Hindus?" He observed that just as another tree cannot grow under any tree, "…there cannot be our growth under this decaying tree of Hinduism. We must, therefore, change our religion."

***

## Dr Ambedkar's Detailed Rebuttal to Gandhiji

Dr Ambedkar presented his detailed rebuttal to Gandhiji in his essay "*Mukti Kaun Pathe?* (Which Way to Emancipation)". In that essay, Dr Ambedkar extensively dealt with reasons why Untouchables could no longer remain within the fold of Hinduism.[7]

---

6 Marathi Speech (17 May 1936). For English Summary, see Jadhav (ed), *Ambedkar Speaks*, Vol. I, p. 38. The original speech is available in BAWS, Vol. 18(1), pp. 473-74.

7 Marathi Speech (31 May 1936). For full English Summary, see Jadhav (ed), *Ambedkar Speaks*, Vol. I, p. 177. Full English translation is available in BAWS, Vol. 17 (3), pp. 115-47. All quotes in this section are from the same source.

Raising the question about "the nature of real religion" and the "ultimate goal of the society", Dr Ambedkar pointed out that modern social philosophers provided three answers: "to achieve happiness for the individual, the development of the inherent qualities and energies of man, and to help him develop himself or the creation of an ideal society".

Dr Ambedkar argued that the "ideas of the Hindu religion… are very different from all these concepts...." The Hindu religion is constituted on the basis of Class and there is no place for an individual. "The Hindu religion does not teach how one individual should behave with another individual."

Dr Ambedkar emphasized that individual welfare and societal progress should be the real aim of religion. He refused to "accept a religion in which one Class alone has the right to gain knowledge; another has a right to use arms; the third one to trade; and the fourth, only to serve. Everyone needs knowledge. Everybody needs arms. Everyone wants money".

According to Dr Ambedkar,

> The religion which has the intention to educate only a few and keep the rest in darkness is not a religion but a conspiracy to keep people in mental slavery. A religion which permits one person to bear arms, and prohibits another from doing the same is not religion but a craftiness to keep the latter in perpetual slavery. A religion which opens the path to acquisition of property for some, and compels others to depend on these few even for the daily necessities of life is not a religion but sheer self-aggrandizement. This is what is called the *Chaturvarna* in Hinduism.

Dr Ambedkar argued that the essential purpose of a religion is to uplift an individual. This requires "sympathy, equality and liberty"—all the three are denied to the Depressed Classes. He said: "Hindus have no sense of brotherhood towards you. You are treated worse than foreigners," and added: "Untouchability is nothing but concrete inequality. Such a living example of inequality is to be found nowhere."

Dr Ambedkar went on to say: "Some people say that Untouchability is a stigma on the Hindu religion.... No Hindu believes that the Hindu religion is a stigma. The majority of Hindus, however, believe that you are a stigma; that you are impure."

Asking as to how the Depressed Classes have been brought to their abominable condition, he said: "you have been thrust into this condition because you have continued to be Hindus". This has not happened to those who became Muslims or Christians.

Maintaining that the teachings of humanity and mutual respect "are completely wanting in the Hindu religion", Dr Ambedkar questioned: "What is the use of such a religion in which the man's sense of humanity is not respected? And what is the good of clinging to it?"

Dr Ambedkar alleged that the Hindus are "hypocrites", pointing out how their "utterances and acts are poles apart.... They speak like saints and act as butchers. They ... believe that God is omnipresent, but treat men worse than animals; ...[they] feed ants with sugar, but kill men by prohibiting them from drinking water...."

Pointing out that the Hindus consider the Depressed Classes as "the lowest of the low", Dr Ambedkar cautioned them: "If you have to get rid of these shameful conditions, if you have to cleanse this stigma and make this precious life graceful, there is only one way, and that is to discard Hindu religion and Hindu Society."

Dr Ambedkar made his followers ask themselves whether they were free in the Hindu religion and then pointed out that in "Hinduism, conscience, reason and thoughts have neither any importance nor any scope ... so long as you are a part of the Hindu religion, you cannot expect to have freedom of thought".

Dr Ambedkar argued emphatically that "…the whole of the Hindu religion is the creation of High-Caste Hindus for the welfare and prosperity of the high Castes … Hinduism has marred your progress from two sides. It has sucked your mental freedom and made you slaves … If you want freedom, you must change your religion …"

According to Dr Ambedkar, equality could be achieved either by remaining in the Hindu fold or by conversion to another religion. "If equality is to be achieved by remaining within the Hindu fold…, *Chaturvarna* must be abolished and the Brahminic religion must be uprooted. Is this possible?…," he asked.

On the other hand, he argued that "the path of Conversion is much easier.… Conversion is the only right path of freedom which ultimately leads to equality… Conversion is not the path of escapism; [or]…cowardice; it is the path of wisdom…. Conversion is the only way to eternal bliss…."

While concluding, Dr Ambedkar clarified: "For myself, I have already taken a decision. My Conversion is for sure…. The Hindu religion does not appeal to my reason [nor] to my self-respect."

He reminded his followers that "man is not for religion; religion is for man". In his indomitable style, in the hard-hitting grand finale, he exhorted his followers to think: "Why do you remain in that religion which does not treat you as human beings? …which does not allow you to be educated? …which prohibits you from entering a temple? …which prohibits you from taking water? …which obstructs you from getting a job? …which insults you at every step?"

Dr Ambedkar then forcefully added:

> … A religion which does not recognize a man as a human being is not a religion but a disease. A religion which allows the touch of animals but prohibits the touch of human beings is not a

> religion but a mockery. A religion which precludes one Class from education, and forbids it to accumulate wealth or to bear arms is not a religion but a mockery of the life of human being. A religion that compels the illiterate to be illiterate, and the poor to be poor is not a religion but a punishment.

***

After Dr Ambedkar's enlightening speech, the Conference adopted a Resolution that they were prepared to change their religion *en masse*, and, as a preliminary step towards the change of religion, urged the *Mahar* community to refrain thereafter from worshipping Hindu deities, to stop observing Hindu festivals and to stop visiting Hindu places of worship.[8]

The rift between Gandhiji and Dr Ambedkar was seemingly ever-widening.

8 Keer, *Dr Ambedkar: Life and Mission*, p. 275.

## CHAPTER TWELVE

# Gandhi–Ambedkar Debate on the Caste System

After the debate on Hindu religion and conversion, the next round of vigorous intellectual tussle between Mahatma Gandhi and Dr Ambedkar came about the Caste System in India. It all began with the publication of Dr Ambedkar's brilliant book *Annihilation of Caste.*[1] Actually, the book is based on a speech prepared for the 1936 Annual Conference of the *Jat-Pat-Todak Mandal* of Lahore. The speech, however, was not delivered.[2]

## Annihilation of Castes[3]

Dr Ambedkar, at the very outset, makes an important distinction between social reform of the Hindu Family and that of the

1 First published in May 1936. All quotes in this chapter, unless specified otherwise, are from the original source.

2 The Conference was cancelled by the Reception Committee because they thought that the views expressed in the speech would be unbearable to the participants in the Conference.

3 For full summary, see Jadhav (ed), *Ambedkar Writes*, pp. 209-68.

reconstruction of the Hindu Society. The former relates to widow remarriage, child marriage, etc., while the latter refers to the abolition of the Caste System. The battle between the Indian National Congress (INC) and its social wing, called Social Conference, was actually centred around family reform rather than broader social reforms covering the "break-up of the Caste System". According to Dr Ambedkar, the "break-up of the Caste System was never put in as an issue by the reformers ..."

## Castes and Division of Labour

Dr Ambedkar launched a frontal attack on the Caste System. The Caste System is defended on the ground that it is nothing but division of labour, and since "division of labour is a necessary feature of every civilized society ... (it is) argued that there is nothing wrong in the Caste System."

Dr Ambedkar's counter argument was on the following lines:

(1) Caste System is *not* merely a division of labour. Superimposed on it is a division of labourers. "Civilized society undoubtedly needs division of labour. But in no civilized society is division of labour accompanied by this unnatural division of labourers into watertight compartments ..."

(2) The division of labour underlying the Caste System "is not spontaneous; it is not based on natural aptitudes ... it involves an attempt to appoint tasks to individuals in advance—selected *not* on the basis of trained original capacities, but on that of the social status of the parents".

- This division of labour is *not* "based on choice. Individual sentiment, individual preference has no place in it". Rather, it is based on the maxim of predestination. "As an economic organization, Caste is, therefore, a harmful institution", since "it involves the subordination of man's natural powers and inclinations to the exigencies of social rules".

## Castes and Racial Purity

To others who defended the Caste System on the grounds of preservation of purity of race and blood, Dr Ambedkar pointed out that the "Caste System came into being long *after* the different races of India had commingled in blood and culture. The Caste System does *not* demarcate racial division. *Caste System is a social division of the people of the same race*"[4] [emphasis added].

## Caste Consciousness

Dr Ambedkar maintained that the Hindu Society is nothing but a "collection of Castes" which, "do not even form a federation". According to him, "each Caste endeavours to segregate itself and to distinguish itself from other Castes"... In every Hindu mind there exists only the "consciousness of his Caste". That is why "the Hindus cannot be said to form a society or a nation". Given the conspicuous absence of "common activity", Hindus have been prevented "from becoming a society with a unified life and a consciousness of its own being".

Dr Ambedkar rounded up his argument by pointing out:

---

4 Interestingly, this view has been vindicated recently on the basis of DNA research. See Tony Joseph, *Early Indians: The Story of Our Ancestors and Where We Came From* (New Delhi: Juggernaut Books, 2018), A more detailed discussion of this point is also presented in the Epilogue of this book.

> The Hindus … are not merely an assortment of Castes, but are so many warring groups, each living for itself and for its selfish ideal. The existence of Caste and Caste Consciousness … has prevented solidarity … The Higher-Caste Hindus have deliberately prevented the lower Castes who are within the pale of Hinduism from rising to the cultural level of the higher Castes.

## Why Hinduism is Stagnated?

Raising the question as to why the Hindu religion has not been expanding, Dr Ambedkar explained that "Caste is inconsistent with conversion". In the Hindu Society, he said, "there is no place for a convert." In other words, it is "the Caste which has prevented the Hindus from expanding and from absorbing other religious communities. So long as Caste remains, there will be no *Sanghathan*; and so long as there is no *Sanghathan* the Hindu will remain weak and meek …"

Regarding the uniqueness of the Caste System, Dr Ambedkar made several scathing observations. He reasoned: "A Caste has an unquestioned right to excommunicate any man who is guilty of breaking the rules of the Caste; and…excommunication involves a complete cessation of social intercourse, …[therefore] as a form of punishment there is really little to choose between excommunication and death…."

According to Dr Ambedkar, that is the reason why the individual Hindus generally have had no courage to break the barriers of Caste. Indeed, he argues, "Caste in the hands of the orthodox has been a powerful weapon for persecuting the reformers and for killing all reform."

## Caste and Ethics

Turning then to the effect of Caste on the ethics of the Hindus, Dr Ambedkar asserted:

> Caste has made public opinion impossible. A Hindu's public is his Caste. His responsibility is only to his Caste. His loyalty is restricted only to his Caste. Virtue has become Caste-ridden, and morality has become Caste-bound. There is no sympathy for the deserving. There is sympathy, but not for men of other Castes. There is charity to the needy … but it begins with the Caste and ends with the Caste …

Unlike Sikhs and Muslims, in Hindus there is no "social cement" which makes them *bhais* [i.e., brother]. Indeed, "one Hindu does not regard another Hindu as his *Bhai*…"

In sum, Dr Ambedkar argued that Hindus do not have the capacity to appreciate merits in a man apart from his Caste. "My Caste-man, right or wrong,"…, "good or bad". For Hindus, it "is not a case of standing by virtue and not standing by vice. It is a case of standing or not standing by the Caste."

## A Vision for Ideal Society

Dr Ambedkar then presented his vision of ideal society. He said, "… my ideal would be a society based on Liberty, Equality and Fraternity; and why not?"

He argued that fraternity among the people is "only another name for democracy. Democracy is not merely a form of Government. It is essentially an attitude of respect and reverence towards fellowmen".

As to liberty, he asked: "Why not allow a person the liberty to benefit from an effective and competent use of a person's powers?

…. liberty to choose one's profession?... to object to this kind of liberty is to perpetuate slavery."

In respect of equality, he emphasized, "… Equality may be a fiction, nonetheless one must accept it as a governing principle …"

## Why No Social Revolution under Hinduism?

Dr Ambedkar proceeded then to offer his own assessment of the evolution of the Hindu Society. He reasoned: "The three Classes, *Brahmins*, *Kshatriyas* and *Vaishyas*, although not very happy in their mutual relationship, managed to work by compromise. The *Brahmin* flattered the *Kshatriya*, and both let the *Vaishya* live in order to be able to live upon him. But the three agreed to beat down the *Shudra*."

The *Shudra,* Dr Ambedkar said:

> ….was not allowed to acquire wealth, lest he should be independent of the three [higher] *Varnas*. He was prohibited from acquiring knowledge, lest he should keep a steady vigil regarding his interests. He was prohibited from bearing arms, lest he should have the means to rebel against their authority. That this is how the *Shudras* were treated … is evidenced by the laws of Manu.

Social revolutions did not take place in India because "the lower Classes of Hindus have been completely disabled for direct action on account of this wretched Caste System …"

Dr Ambedkar elaborated on this important point by arguing that the "Caste System in India denied the masses access to three instruments of emancipation—namely physical (military service), political, and moral (education)". He contended that in Indian history, the Maurya Empire was the only period characterized by "freedom, greatness and glory. At all other times, the country suffered from defeat and darkness". According to him, during this era, the Caste System was completely eradicated, and when "the *Shudras*, who constituted the majority of the population, came into their own and became the rulers of the country. The period of defeat and darkness is the period when the Caste System flourished".

Referring to the defenders of the Caste System on the grounds that the Hindus after all have survived for centuries, Dr Ambedkar's response was sharp. He argued:

> The question is not whether a community lives or dies; the question is on what plane it lives. There are different modes of survival. But not all are equally honourable … To fight in a battle and to live in glory is one mode. To beat a retreat, to surrender and to live the life of captive is also a mode of survival. What we must consider is what the quality of their survival is.

## Abolishing the Castes

Dr Ambedkar forcefully maintained that no progress could be achieved unless the social order based on the Caste is changed. For abolishing the Caste, he argued: "The real remedy is intermarriage. Fusion of blood can alone create the feeling of being kith and kin, and unless this feeling of kinship, of being kindred, becomes paramount, the separatist feeling—the feeling of being aliens—created by Caste will not vanish … Nothing else will serve as the solvent of Caste."

Dr Ambedkar clarified, however, that the most fundamental remedy is to destroy the people's belief in the sanctity of the *Shastras*. He said that the Hindus follow Caste "not because they are inhuman or wrong-headed", but because they are "deeply religious". Accordingly, the "enemy to grapple with is not the people who observe Caste, but the *Shastras* which teach them this religion of Caste ..."

Dr Ambedkar pointed out that reformers "including Mahatma Gandhi, do not seem to realize that the acts of the people are merely the results of their beliefs inculcated in their minds by the *Shastras*, and that people will not change their conduct until they cease to believe in the sanctity of the *Shastras*...."

Recounting the stand taken by Buddha and Guru Nanak, Dr Ambedkar emphatically argued: "You must not only discard the *Shastras*, you must deny their authority, as did Buddha and Nanak."

This line of reasoning led Dr Ambedkar to reach a shocking conclusion: "Caste is sacred. Caste has a divine basis. The annihilation of Caste therefore calls for the destruction of the sacredness and divinity with which Caste has become invested. In the last analysis, this means you must destroy the authority of the *Shastras* and the *Vedas*."

## Why Caste System Has Survived?

Dr Ambedkar asserted that it is not possible to have a "general mobilization of Hindus for an attack on the Caste System". For this, he articulated three reasons:

First, the annihilation of the Caste System would ultimately result in the destruction of "the power and prestige of the Brahmin Caste" and therefore it would be unreasonable to expect them to lead such a movement. The Brahmins form the "intellectual class" of the Hindus, and when they are opposed to the reform of Caste, the chances of success of such reform "appear ... very, very remote".

Secondly, "each Caste takes its pride and its consolation in the fact that in the scale of Castes it is above some other Caste ... All are slaves of the Caste System. But all the slaves are not equal in status".

Thirdly, Castes form "a graded system of sovereignties, high and low, ... if a general dissolution came, some of them stand to lose more of their prestige and power than others do".

Dr Ambedkar wondered aloud: *"How are you going to break up Caste if people are not free to consider whether it accords with reason"* as *well as "morality"?*

Recognising that the "wall built around Caste is impregnable" and that "it would take ages before a breach is made", Dr Ambedkar arrived at the most contentious conclusion. He said that if one wants to destroy the Caste System, "...then you have got to apply the dynamite to the *Vedas* and the *Shastras*, which deny any part to reason; to the *Vedas* and *Shastras*, which deny any part to morality. You must destroy the religion of the *Shrutis* and the *Smritis*. Nothing else will avail. This is my considered view of the matter".[5]

## Way Forward

Finally, in the spirit of creative destruction, Dr Ambedkar proposed:

> You must give a new doctrinal basis to your Religion—a basis that will be in consonance with Liberty, Equality and Fraternity; in short, with Democracy. This means a complete change in the fundamental notions of life. It means a complete change in the values of life. It means a complete change in outlook and in attitude towards men and things.[6]

***

---

5 This thought of applying dynamite to the *Vedas* and *Shastras* became the most controversial issue leading to the cancellation of the Conference organized by the *Jat-Pat Todak Mandal* of Lahore.

6 This is exactly what Dr Ambedkar did many years later while drafting and piloting the Constitution of India.

## Gandhiji's Critique

Soon after the publication of "Annihilation of Castes", Mahatma Gandhi responded by way of two articles:

(i) "Dr Ambedkar's Indictment" (*Harijan*, 18 July 1936); and

(ii) "*Varna versus* Caste" (*Harijan*, 15 August 1936)

Dr Ambedkar reprinted the two articles in the Second Edition of his book (1937) as Appendix I and also presented his own views in reply to Gandhiji's two articles as Appendix II titled "A Reply to the Mahatma".

Dr Ambedkar's motivation in writing his reply has been articulated in the Preface to the Second Edition. Dr Ambedkar contended that he was responding to Gandhiji.

> … not because what he has said is so weighty as to deserve a reply, but because to many a Hindu he is an oracle, so great that when he opens his lips it is expected that the argument must close and no dog must bark. But the world owes much to rebels who would dare to argue in the face of the pontiff and insist that he is not infallible.

## Dr Ambedkar's "Reply" to the Mahatma

In his rebuttal, Dr Ambedkar, at the outset, expressed surprise at Gandhiji's accusation of "a desire to seek publicity". Even if it were true, questioned Dr Ambedkar, "who could cast a stone at me? Surely not those who, like the Mahatma, live in glass houses."

The sum and substance of Dr Ambedkar's argument was that "the Mahatma has entirely missed the issues raised … [and] the questions raised by the Mahatma are absolutely beside the point and show that the main argument of the speech was lost upon him."

Dr Ambedkar then proceeded to demolish Gandhiji's criticism, piece by piece. First, to Gandhiji's contention that "the texts cited" are "not authentic", Dr Ambedkar clarified that the texts cited were all taken from the writings of the late Mr Bal Gangadhar Tilak who was a "recognized authority on the Sanskrit language and on the Hindu *Shastras*".

To Gandhiji's point that "*Shastras* should be interpreted not by the learned but the saints and that, as the saints have understood them, the *Shastras* do not support Caste and Untouchability", Dr Ambedkar's response was that the "masses do not make any distinction between texts which are genuine and texts which are interpolations" … Masses have believed what they have been told i.e., that the "*Shastras* do enjoin as a religious duty the observance of Caste and Untouchability".

Dr Ambedkar then wrote about the saints and their contribution. He observed that howsoever "elevating their teaching maybe" they have been "lamentably ineffective". Pointing out that the "saints have never … carried on a campaign against Caste and Untouchability", Dr Ambedkar argued that they "did not preach that all men were equal. They preached that all men were equal, in the eyes of God—a very different and a very innocuous proposition which nobody can find difficult to preach or dangerous to believe in."

Dr Ambedkar, accordingly, contented that "it can be a matter of no consolation that there were saints or that there is a Mahatma who understands the *Shastras* differently from the learned few or ignorant many. That the masses hold a different view of the *Shastras* is a fact which should and must be reckoned with." How to address that issue "except by denouncing the authority of the *Shastras*…. is a question which the Mahatma has not considered."

As to the argument made by Gandhiji that "a religion professed by Chaitanya, Jnyandeo, Tukaram, Tiruvalluvar, Ramkrishna Paramahansa, etc. cannot be devoid of merit … and that a religion has to be judged not by its worst specimens but by the best it might have produced", Dr Ambedkar said, "I agree with every word of this statement. But I do not quite understand what the Mahatma wishes to prove thereby … The question still remains—why the worst number so many and the best so few?"

Dr Ambedkar pointed out that he had argued that "a society based on *Varna* or Caste is a society which is based on a wrong relationship. I had hoped that the Mahatma would attempt to demolish my argument. But instead of doing that he has merely reiterated his belief in *Chaturvarna* without disclosing the ground on which it is based."

Wondering why does Gandhiji "cling to the theory of every one following his or her ancestral calling", Dr Ambedkar asked in an acerbic tone: "Does the Mahatma practise what he preaches?" He wrote:

> The Mahatma is a *Bania* by birth. His ancestors had abandoned trading in favour of ministership which is a calling of the Brahmins. In his own life, before he became a Mahatma, when occasion came for him to choose his career, he preferred law to scales. On abandoning law, he became half saint and half politician. He has never touched trading which is his ancestral calling….

Dr Ambedkar then raised a barrage of sharp questions:

> When can a calling be deemed to have become an ancestral calling so as to make it binding on a man? …Must a man live by his ancestral calling even if he finds it to be immoral? If

> everyone must pursue his ancestral calling then it must follow that a man must continue to be a pimp because his grandfather was a pimp, and a woman must continue to be a prostitute because her grandmother was a prostitute. Is the Mahatma prepared to accept the logical conclusion of his doctrine?

Dr Ambedkar emphatically argued that Gandhiji's "ideal of following one's ancestral calling is not only an impossible and impractical ideal, but it is also morally an indefensible ideal".

Given that there was a time when Gandhiji had condemned inter-dining, inter-drinking and inter-marrying, Dr Ambedkar felt that some "might think that the Mahatma has made much progress inasmuch as he now only believes in *Varna* and does not believe in Caste".

Dr Ambedkar appreciated that Gandhiji has now "repudiated this sanctimonious nonsense and admitted that Caste is harmful both to spiritual and national growth", but made a rather uncharitable remark that "maybe, his son's marriage outside his Caste has had something to do with this change of view".

Thinking aloud, Dr Ambedkar asked whether the Mahatma has really progressed: "What is the difference between Caste and *Varna* as understood by the Mahatma? I find none." According to Dr Ambedkar, "the essence of the Vedic conception of *Varna* is the pursuit of a calling which is appropriate to one's natural aptitude". However, as defined by the Mahatma, "*Varna* becomes merely a different name for Caste for the simple reason that it is the same in essence—namely, pursuit of ancestral calling. Far from making progress the Mahatma has suffered retrogression."

According to Dr Ambedkar, Gandhiji's "view of *Varna* not only makes nonsense of the Vedic *Varna* but also makes it an abominable thing. *Varna* and Caste are two very different concepts. *Varna* is based on the principle of each according to his worth, while Caste is based on the principle of each according to his birth. The two are as distinct as chalk is from cheese".

Raising the question whether Gandhiji "the Saint failed to sense the truth" or whether "the politician stands in the way of the Saint", Dr Ambedkar postulates:

> The source of confusion is the double role which the Mahatma wants to play—of a Mahatma and a Politician. As a Mahatma he may be trying to spiritualize Politics. Whether he has succeeded in it or not, Politics have certainly commercialized him ... The reason why the Mahatma is always supporting Caste and *Varna* is because he is afraid that if he opposed them, he will lose his place in politics.

While concluding his rebuttal of Gandhiji, Dr Ambedkar wrote that the Hindu Society is "in need of a moral regeneration which it is dangerous to postpone. And ... who can determine and control this moral regeneration? Obviously, only those who have undergone an intellectual regeneration ..."

According to Dr Ambedkar, Gandhiji was incapable of doing so because the "Mahatma appears not to believe in thinking ..." and insofar as he "does think, to me he really appears to be prostituting his intelligence, to find reasons supporting this archaic social structure of the Hindus. He is the most influential apologist of it and, therefore, the worst enemy of the Hindus."

CHAPTER THIRTEEN

# Gandhi–Ambedkar: A Falling-Out

The next round of the conflict between Mahatma Gandhi and Dr Ambedkar was triggered by the Provincial Elections (1937), outbreak of the Second World War (1939), and Gandhiji's Civil Disobedience Campaign (1942).

As envisaged by the Government of India Act, 1935, the first-ever Provincial Elections were held in February 1937. The Congress Party swept the polls. (This happened in spite of the fact that Mahatma Gandhi did not address a single election campaign meeting.) By July 1937, in seven out of the then 11 Provinces, exclusive Congress Ministries were formed. A little later, coalition governments were formed by the Congress in two more Provinces. Consequently, only Bengal and Punjab Provinces had non-Congress governments. Of the two, only Bengal Province was ruled by a coalition involving the Muslim League.

The Provincial Governments, mostly led by the Congress Party, ruled the Provinces within the narrow confines of the power entrusted to them under the Government of India Act, 1935.

## Dr Ambedkar's Entry into Electoral Politics

Looking at the rapidly changing political scenario, Dr Ambedkar quickly reoriented his strategy to position the Depressed Classes in the new institutional framework of the Government of India Act, 1935. In view of the proposed first-ever Provincial elections, Dr Ambedkar formed his first political party, called the Independent Labour Party (ILP).

In the first-ever elections to the Bombay Province Legislative Assembly, held in February 1937, the ILP had fielded 18 candidates - 12 on reserved seats and 6 on general seats. In addition, 14 candidates contested the election in the Central Provinces. The new party had posted a good performance. Fifteen of its candidates were elected in the Bombay Province, of which 12 were from the Depressed Classes. Dr Ambedkar himself was elected with a thumping majority and thus began his new inning as an elected Legislator in the Bombay Legislative Assembly.

## Dr Ambedkar's Political Strategy

When Gandhiji returned from South Africa in 1915 (age 45-46), he had started his political movement by organizing peasants and farmers—for example, the Champaran agitation in Bihar (1917) and the Kheda *Satyagraha* in Gujarat (1918).[1] Interestingly, Dr Ambedkar was also 45 years old when he formally entered politics in 1936. There is yet another similarity between the two. Dr Ambedkar also initially focused his attention on giving effective expression to the grievances of the rural poor and urban working class in the Bombay Provincial Assembly and outside, combining them with mass movements.

1 As discussed in detail in Chapter 6.

In respect of the rural poor, Dr Ambedkar's contribution really stands out in respect of the abolition of the *Khoti* System. *Khoti* was a peculiar system of land tenure that prevailed in pockets of the Konkan region of Maharashtra. *Khots* had the rights to land which was cultivated by farmers and, in return, *Khots* collected land revenue from them and passed on a part thereof to the Government. It was an oppressive system that had subjected a vast majority of the rural poor in the region to virtual serfdom. All farmers and their families coming under the system were treated by *Khots* as bonded labour, generation after generation.

As a part of his sustained efforts, on 17 September 1937, Dr Ambedkar introduced a historic Bill in the Bombay Legislative Assembly aimed at the abolition of the *Khoti* System.[2] It is noteworthy that Dr Ambedkar was one of the first Legislators in India to introduce a Bill for the abolition of the slavery of agricultural tenants.

Dr Ambedkar's political strategy became discernible in several of his public speeches in 1937 and 1938. Two of these speeches are especially noteworthy. First, while addressing a public rally at the culmination of a peasants' march to the Legislative Council in Mumbai, Dr Ambedkar exhorted the peasants and workers to think over the causes of their poverty and told them that they lay in the richness of the exploiters. The way out for them, he said, was to organize a labour front without any regard to Caste or Creed, and to elect to the Legislatures those who were their real representatives. If they did so, they would have shelter and clothing, and they who produced the food and wealth of the nation would not die of hunger.

---

2 For full summary of the debate, see Jadhav (ed), *Ambedkar Speaks*, Vol. I, pp. 372-73. Also see Jadhav, *Ambedkar: Awakening India's Social Conscience* (New Delhi: Konark Publishers, 2014), pp. 244-46.

The philosophical basis of Dr Ambedkar's political strategy was fully spelt out in his Presidential Address at the Conference of Untouchable Workers of the Great Indian Peninsula (GIP) Railway, Manmad (13 February 1938). He emphasized that political power is the only means of securing liberty and freedom from all obstacles.[3] He expressed his hope that "one day, not before very long, the Depressed Classes will become organized, will become conscious of the power they have got and will begin to put it to wise and effective use in order to secure their social emancipation ..."

Dr Ambedkar was highly critical of the Congress Party. He ridiculed the Congress Socialists who were aiming at bringing about Socialism by converting the Right wing of the Congress Party. He said: "That is the explanation they give for not going out of the Congress. A more pathetic case involving utter ignorance of human nature cannot be imagined ..."

Dr Ambedkar alleged that "...the Right wing of the Congress is merely using Imperialism as an excuse for preventing separate and independent organization of labour..."

He then appealed the gathering to join his political party, ILP, which, he said, is based upon "Class interests and Class consciousness".

The ILP was not welcomed by the Communists who viewed it as an unnecessary division of the labourers. In the Class struggle, they argued, the interests of the Depressed Classes and others were the same, and, therefore, there was no need for an "Independent Labour Party"; the labour movement could be organized under the same banner.

---

3 Marathi Speech. For full English summary, see Jadhav (ed), *Ambedkar Speaks,* Vol. III, pp. 174-86.

In response, Dr Ambedkar reasoned that the Communist leaders were fighting for the rights of workers but *never* for the human rights of workers from the Depressed Classes.

When Dr Ambedkar did not support the strikes called in the 1920s and in the first half of 1930s, the Communists had called him a traitor, an enemy of the labour. Subsequently, however, Dr Ambedkar wholeheartedly participated in the general strike against the Industrial Disputes Bill in 1938, which was introduced by the Congress-led Government in the Bombay Province Legislative Assembly. The reason behind Dr Ambedkar's opposition was that the Bill had aimed at restricting the right of the labourer to strike and making strike illegal.

In a hard-hitting speech in the Bombay Legislative Assembly (on 15 September 1938) on the Industrial Disputes Bill, Dr Ambedkar argued that the Bill was really aimed at passing "The Workers" Civil Liberties Suspension Act", under which the workers will never be able to strike. He said:[4] "When the Bill comes into operation and the labourer stands face to face with the Bill, he will say that this Bill is bad, bloody and a brutal Bill."

In conformity with his principled stand, Dr Ambedkar joined forces with others, including the Communist-led Unions and brought the strike against the Industrial Disputes Bill to a successful conclusion.

While addressing a massive rally of workers for condemning the Industrial Disputes Bill in Mumbai (in November 1938), Dr Ambedkar claimed[5] that after coming to power, the Congress Party passed "totally unjustified Bills with the power of brute majority", and in the face of opposition it gave up the "values

---

4 Bombay Legislative Assembly Debates, Vol. 4. Reproduced in BAWS, Vol. 2, pp. 201-32.

5 Marathi Speech. Details in BAWS, Vol. 18(2), pp. 227-29.

of truth and non-violence". He said that Congress leaders have gone back on their "avowed policy of protecting the interests of labour" and are now "creating a new law which slices the throats of workers".

Dr Ambedkar added sarcastically: "The entire responsibility of patriotism and protecting the nation's interest lies with Congress, by inheritance, they claim! 'Dr Ambedkar is Casteist' they argue! 'Dr Ambedkar is a traitor' they say, 'as he never went to a prison!'"

Dr Ambedkar questioned "how does a man become patriotic just by going to the prison". Admitting that he has never been to a prison, he said that the Congress leaders are "hypocrites" who "enjoy the luxuries of A-class (in the prison) and deceitfully lie to... followers. Today's Congressmen have endured the prison life for only the namesake."

Dr Ambedkar recalled his encounter with Gandhiji at the Round Table Conference, and said: "It is my open challenge to the followers of Mahatma Gandhi that they put together, side by side, in a book all speeches by myself and Gandhiji in the Round Table Conference ... and let people decide who is a real traitor! ..."

## Disagreement over the "Federation of India"

The Government of India Act, 1935, passed by British Parliament in August of that year, contained several significant provisions, including the establishment of a "Federation of India" comprising both British India and the "Princely States".

Following the 1937 Provincial General Elections, the then Viceroy Linlithgow started garnering support for the proposal of Federation of India. According to Dr Ambedkar, Gandhiji "seems to have been prepared to accept the Federation [of India] in whatever form" whereas he himself strongly opposed the idea as he felt the

Federation "would lead to chaos and worsen the situation."[6] While the debate regarding the Federation was at its peak, Dr Ambedkar delivered a public address (in January 1939) titled "What is the Goal of India's Political Evolution?"

Towards the end of this brilliant speech denouncing the proposed "Federation of India", in the concluding remarks Dr Ambedkar came really hard on Gandhiji. He said[7] that "we are standing today at the point of time where the old age ends and the new begins. The old age was the age of Ranade, Agarkar, Tilak, Gokhale … The new age is the age of Mr Gandhi and this generation is said to be Gandhi generation …"

According to Dr Ambedkar, leaders of the Gandhi age claimed that it was an "agitated and expectant age" while the Ranade age was not. Dr Ambedkar argued to the contrary. He said that "if the India of Ranade was less agitated it was more honest and if it was less expectant it was more enlightened…" In fact, Dr Ambedkar called the Gandhi age as the "dark age of India".

Dr Ambedkar said: "In the age of Ranade, the leaders struggled to modernize India. In the age of Gandhi, the leaders are making her a living specimen of antiquity. In the age of Ranade leaders depended upon experience as a corrective method of their thoughts and their deeds. The leaders of the present age depend upon their inner voice as their guide.…"

Finally, Dr Ambedkar concluded: "…The fate of an ignorant democracy which refuses to follow the way shown by learning and experience and chooses to grope in the dark paths of the mystics and the megalomaniacs is a sad thing to contemplate.…"

---

6 Report from *The Times of India* (15 February 1939), reproduced in BAWS, Vol. 17(3), p. 208.

7 Kale Memorial Lecture at the Gokhale Institute of Politics and Economics in Pune (29 January 1939). The lecture was published later in a book titled *Federation Versus Freedom*. Available at BAWS, Vol. 17(3), pp. 203-07.

## Disagreement over Joining the War Efforts

The Second World War broke out in September 1939. The British Government of India immediately proclaimed a state of war between India and the Nazi forces. This was done without consulting the Indian national leaders.

Initially, Gandhiji, by his own admission, "broke down" shedding tears as he pictured the destruction of the Houses of Parliament, Westminster Abbey and the heart of London. But Gandhiji's resolution promising support to the British war efforts by all available non-violent means was rejected by the Congress. Gandhiji himself called it a "conclusive defeat".[8]

The Congress Party was willing to help the forces of democracy against Fascism. However, an internal question arose within the Congress: how could an enslaved nation assist others in their fight for freedom?[9]

The Congress demanded that India must be declared free—or at least effective power be put in Indian hands—before it could actively participate in the War. The British Government refused to accede to this demand. In response, the Congress asked its Provincial Ministries to resign *en masse*.[10]

Dr Ambedkar lamented this stance of the Congress Party and issued a statement on behalf of the ILP pointing out that patriotism was not a monopoly of Congressmen, and, therefore, persons holding views divergent to the Congress had a perfectly legitimate right to exist and be recognized.[11]

---

8 Lelyveld, *Great Soul*, p. 285.

9 Bipan Chandra, *History of Modern India* (Hyderabad: Orient Black Swan, 2009), p. 321.

10 Ibid, p. 321.

11 Keer, *Ambedkar: Life and Mission*, p. 327.

Dr Ambedkar had no hesitation in supporting the war efforts. In the event of a forced choice between Imperialism and Fascism, Dr Ambedkar was decidedly in favour of the former, but with some fundamental reforms towards self-governance.

For Dr Ambedkar, an independence gained on the basis of Britain's defeat by the Fascists could never lead to any true equality in India. He disagreed with those who held that England's difficulty was India's opportunity. In the statement issued, Dr Ambedkar insisted that it was the duty of Britain to reassure India of the status the country would occupy in the British Empire after the War was over.

The issue of resignation by the elected Congress Ministry of the Bombay Province *en masse* was discussed and debated in the Provincial Assembly. On 25 October 1939, the Speaker proposed a resolution to that effect.

Dr Ambedkar's immediate response to the draft resolution was: "No. The question of resignation of the Ministry is a matter for the Party. It is not a matter for the House."[12]

Dr Ambedkar agreed that "without our will and without our consent we are dragged in this slaughter…", However, he raised concerns over the place for Untouchables in the country after the War was over.

Dr Ambedkar talked about what he called "political *Chaturvarna*" in India. He said: "…Whether we admit it or not, the political system of this country is reflective of…the *Chaturvarna*. In that system, …the *Kshatriya* must rule; that the Brahmin must advise; that the *Vaishya* must trade but the *Shudras* or the *Ati Shudras* must serve."

And he added, "I find in politics the position has changed to some extent. The *Vaishya* no longer trades. If he trades, he trades

12 For the full details, see Jadhav (ed), *Ambedkar Speaks*, Vol III, pp 210-227.

in politics only[13] (*Laughter*). One thing has, however, remained unalterable, and it is that the *Shudras* shall have no part in the governance of this country…."

Dr Ambedkar warned that he will not allow the Untouchables, who are *Shudras* socially, to become political *Shudras* as well. He said:

> We shall fight tooth and nail against politics being perverted for the purpose of establishing an oligarchy of a ruling Class. …I am not going to support a tyrannizing majority simply because it happens to speak in the name of the country. I am not going to support a Party because it happens to speak in the name of the country…

***

In October 1940, Mahatma Gandhi gave the call for a "limited *Satyagraha*" by a few selected individuals (Vinoba Bhave was the first one among 25,000 *Satyagrahis* jailed by 15 May 1941).

On 22 June 1941, Nazi Germany attacked the then Soviet Union. On 7 December the same year, Japan launched a surprise attack on the US fleet at Pearl Harbour. Japan quickly overran the Philippines, Indonesia, Malaya and Burma. Rangoon was occupied in March 1942 and the War was at India's doorsteps.

The British Government, shaken by the events, released the Congress leaders from jail. The Congress leaders deplored the Japanese aggression and reiterated their offer to cooperate with the British in the defence of India, provided that Britain transferred a substantial power to India immediately and promised complete Independence after the end of the War.

---

13 Here again, Dr Ambedkar is seen taking a dig at Mahatma Gandhi.

This time, the British, desperate as they were for India's cooperation, sent a new Mission to India—the Cripps Mission—to negotiate a political settlement in India.

## Cripps Mission (1942) and Thereafter

The British Government sent the Cripps Mission to India essentially to secure India's full cooperation and support to Britain's efforts in the World War II. The Mission attempted to negotiate an agreement with Mahatma Gandhi and Jinnah that would keep India loyal to the British War effort in exchange for a promise of full self-government after the War.

Sir Cripps spent three weeks in India. He met with leaders of the Sikhs, the Muslims, the Princes and the Depressed Classes. And he spoke extensively to the leaders of the Congress—Mahatma Gandhi, Jawaharlal Nehru and Maulana Azad, the then President of the Congress.

Negotiations between Cripps and the Congress leaders broke down. The Congress objected first to the provision for Dominion Status rather than full Independence; secondly to the representation of the Princely States in the proposed Constituent Assembly (not by the people of the States but by the nominees of the Rulers), and thirdly to the provision for the partition of India. The British Government, on its part, refused to accept the demand for the immediate transfer of effective power to the Indians and for a significant share in the responsibility for the defence of India. About the Cripps' offer of Dominion Status after the War, Gandhiji reportedly said it was a "post-dated cheque drawn on a failing bank".[14]

14 https://en.wikipedia.org, (accessed on 5 July 2020).

The failure of the Cripps Mission led to widespread discontent, which was exacerbated by war-time shortages and rising prices. With the Japanese forces moving closer to India, the spectre of a possible conquest of the country by another foreign power loomed large. With tensions rising country-wide, persistently during the period—April to August 1942—the Congress under the leadership of Gandhiji decided to take strong steps to compel the British Government to accept the Indian demand for the Independence.

The All India Congress Committee in its meeting in Mumbai (8 August 1942) passed the now famous "Quit India Resolution" which, *inter alia* called for "the immediate ending of the British rule in India" claiming that the "ending of British rule … is a vital and immediate issue on which depends the future of the War and the success of freedom and democracy."

While addressing the Congress delegates that evening in Mumbai (8 August 1942), the uncharacteristically militant Mahatma Gandhi, *inter alia,* said:

> I am not going to be satisfied with anything short of complete freedom…. Here is a *mantra*…You may imprint it on your hearts and let every breath of yours give expression to it. The *mantra* is: "Do or Die". We shall either free India or die in the attempt; we shall not live to see the perpetuation of our slavery….

The historic resolution had also announced the decision to launch a nationwide non-violent mass struggle under the leadership of Mahatma Gandhi.[15] However, before the proposed mass movement could take off, the British Government struck a hard blow. In the early hours of the next day (i.e., 9 August), the

---

15 Both quotes above are from Bipin Chandra, *History of Modern India*, pp. 322-23.

Congress was declared illegal and all prominent leaders including Gandhi were arrested and taken to undisclosed destinations.

People of India reacted sharply. With no leadership or legal organization to guide them, people, especially students, peasants and workers, spontaneously organized *hartals*, boycotted schools and colleges, staged strikes in factories and held demonstrations across the country.

The British Government of India, on its part, went all out to crush the uprise of the people. Demonstrators were *lathi*-charged and fired upon. Angered by the repeated firings, people revolted. They attacked the police stations, post offices, railway stations and put some Government buildings on fire. In many places, the rebels seized temporary control over towns, cities and villages.[16] Illustratively, in Satara district of the Bombay Presidency the revolutionaries set up "parallel governments".

Repression by the British Government knew no bounds. The press was completely muzzled. Reportedly, over 10,000 people died in police and military firing. India had not witnessed such intense repression since the first war of Independence in 1857.

While the Revolt of 1942 was suppressed by the British Government with an iron fist, "it demonstrated the depth that nationalist feeling had reached in the country and the great capacity for struggle and sacrifice that the people had developed".[17]

After the crushing of the Revolt of 1942, political activity on the Congress front slowed down considerably.

***

Protecting the interests of the Depressed Classes always remained Dr Ambedkar's top priority. In a statement issued earlier,

16 Ibid, pp. 324.

17 Ibid, pp. 324.

Dr Ambedkar had stated that the minorities problem would never be solved unless Gandhiji and Congress gave up their egoistic and insolent attitude towards persons and parties outside the Congress.[18] Having been disenchanted with Gandhiji and disillusioned by the Congress, Dr Ambedkar had started leaning towards close cooperation with the British Government, well before Gandhiji's "Quit India" movement was announced.

In early 1941, Dr Ambedkar pressed for an enlargement of recruitment of Untouchables in the army, which was granted. Notably, Dr Ambedkar also succeeded in the reinstatement of the *Mahar* Battalion, for which his father Ramji had made a representation decades earlier. In the same spirit, Dr Ambedkar also agreed to serve as a Member of the Defence Advisory Committee set up by the Viceroy of India.

A major turning point came on 2 July 1942, when Dr Ambedkar was appointed as the Labour Member (i.e., Minister) in the Viceroy's Executive Council of India. Dr Ambedkar became the first Untouchable and also the first mass leader in India to be appointed as a Member (Minister) in the Viceroy's Executive Council of the British Government of India (where, as it turned out later, he was instrumental in laying the foundations of industrial relations and labour welfare reforms in India).

Just about the time when Dr Ambedkar took over as a Cabinet Minister in the Viceroy's Executive Council (July 1942), Mahatma Gandhi announced the Civil Disobedience Campaign.

Dr Ambedkar, on the eve of his departure from Mumbai to Delhi (27 July 1942) gave an interview to the *Times of India* where he described Gandhiji's all-out open rebellion as both "irresponsible and insane, a bankruptcy of statesmanship". "It would be madness",

---

18 Keer, *Ambedkar: Life and Mission*, p. 327.

he said, "to weaken the law and order at a time when the barbarians were at the gates of India".[19]

Looking at the massive repression of the Revolt of 1942 by the British authorities and reported deaths of more than 10,000 innocent Indians in police and military firing, Dr Ambedkar's warning regrettably had turned out to be prophetic.

Gandhiji and Dr Ambedkar had a complete falling-out.

19 Ibid, p. 354.

CHAPTER FOURTEEN

# Gandhi–Ambedkar: The Discord Deepens

As mentioned in the last chapter, after the ruthless crushing of the Revolt of 1942, political activity on the Congress front slowed down considerably. On the other hand, the events of the period engendered a remarkable change for the Untouchables. The British were questioning Dr Ambedkar's legitimacy as a representative of the Scheduled Castes[1] (in the Viceroy's Executive Council), when he did not have a specific Scheduled Caste organization behind him. As a result, Dr Ambedkar decided to wind up the ILP.

A Conference of the Depressed Classes was called in Nagpur in July 1942. A new organization was formed at the Conference, named Scheduled Caste Federation (SCF). Unlike the ILP, the SCF took shape as a truly national party. Movements that had begun independently in various Provinces, especially in the

---

1 The expression "Scheduled Castes" for the former Untouchables or the Depressed Classes became operational following the Government of India Act of 1935, vide "The Government of India (Scheduled Castes) Order 1936" issued by the British Government on 30 April 1936.

North and North-Western India, were now coming together and asserting themselves. A consolidated movement was emerging as a united force at the national level, and Dr Ambedkar was their sole undisputed supreme leader.

## Ambedkar Calls Gandhiji a Successful Humbug

In response to an invitation from the Chairman of the Institute of Pacific Relations (India Chapter), Dr Ambedkar wrote a paper in August 1942 titled "Mr Gandhi and the Emancipation of the Untouchables of India".[2]

While concluding the paper, Dr Ambedkar alleged that Mr Gandhi was a "social Tory and political radical". Gandhiji "presents himself to the world as a liberal but his liberalism is only a very thin veneer. You scratch him and you will find that underneath his liberalism he is a blue-blooded Tory. He stands for the cursed Caste. ... He is a Tory by birth as well as by faith".

Asserting that Gandhiji is neither a revolutionary nor a democrat, Dr Ambedkar wrote that Gandhiji wanted the Caste System to "remain intact" and the Untouchables to "remain as Hindus", "not as partners" but only as "poor relations". Gandhiji was kind to the Untouchables, only because he wanted to kill their movement for political separation from Hindus.

According to Dr Ambedkar, the "*Harijan Sevak Sangh* is one of the many techniques which has enabled Mr Gandhi to be a successful humbug ... To leave democracy and freedom in such Tory hands would be the greatest mistake democrats could commit ..."

---

2 The Paper was presented in a Conference held in Quebec, Canada (in December 1942), by Dr Ambedkar's colleague N. Shivraj. The paper was published as a Monograph in September 1943. For details, see Jadhav (ed), Ambedkar Writes Vol II, pp. 231-58.

## Gandhi-Ambedkar: Disagreements Abound

In the aftermath of the Quit India Movement, during a debate on the "Situation in India" in the Central Legislative Assembly, Dr Ambedkar, serving as a Member of the Viceroy's Executive Council, criticised Gandhiji and the Congress for the "disorder" which, in his view, was causing greater harm to the Indian people (18 September 1942).[3]

Some critics of the British Government had argued that the Congress Party being a believer in non-violence would have prevented the violence from erupting, had the Congress leaders not been arrested. In his intervention, Dr Ambedkar resolutely demolished this argument. On the basis of the proceedings of the Congress Party meetings during the previous two-three years, Dr Ambedkar demonstrated that there was a "terrible landslide in the principle of non-violence as has been proclaimed by the Congress. The non-violence has been deeply buried … right under the very nose of the Congress—Mr Gandhi."

***

The Deccan Sabha of Pune invited Dr Ambedkar to deliver an Address on the 101st birth anniversary of the late Justice Mahadev Govind Ranade. Initially, he was reluctant to accept the invitation. However, he ultimately agreed, and delivered the Address in Pune on 18 January 1943.[4] The Address was published as a book titled *Ranade, Gandhi and Jinnah* in the same year.

In his Address, Dr Ambedkar compared Justice Ranade to two of the greatest "idols and heroes of the hour", i.e.,

---

3 For details, see Jadhav (ed), *Ambedkar Speaks,* Vol. III, pp. 257-62. All quotes in this section, are from the same intervention.

4 For details, see Jadhav (ed), *Ambedkar Writes*, Vol. I, pp. 214-30. All quotes in this section are from the said Address.

namely Mahatma Gandhi and Jinnah. While discussing the two leaders, in by contrast to Justice Ranade, Dr Ambedkar severely criticized their "colossal egotism", noting that, to them, "personal ascendancy is everything … They choose to stand on a pedestal of splendid isolation … They are very unhappy at, and impatient of, criticism, …" Dr Ambedkar observed that the two leaders "have developed a wonderful stagecraft, and arrange things in such a way that they are always in the limelight wherever they go. Each claims to be supreme … each claims infallibility for himself …"

Dr Ambedkar's blistering criticism of Gandhiji and Jinnah grew even sharper. He alleged that they have "made half their followers fools and the other half hypocrites". He further charged that, in establishing their supremacy, the two leaders had enlisted the support of "big business" and wealthy magnates. "For the first time in our country, money is taking the field as an organized power …," he added.

Dr Ambedkar went on to describe the state of Indian politics as "a byword for corruption … a kind of sewage system, intolerably unsavoury and unsanitary. To become a politician is like going to work in the drain".

He lamented, "Never has there been such a deplorable state of bankruptcy of statesmanship as one sees in these two leaders of India … Between them, Indian politics has become 'frozen'… and no political action is possible."

In contrast, Dr Ambedkar described Justice Ranade as a leader who was "most modest", without even a "tinge of egotism". He praised Justice Ranade for refusing to be satisfied with the praise of fools and for never hesitating to associating with his equals.

Taking a dig at Gandhiji, Dr Ambedkar said:

> [Justice Ranade] never claimed to be a mystic relying on the inner voice. He was a rationalist prepared to have his views

tested in the light of reason and experience. His greatness was natural. He needed no aid of the stage nor the technique of an assumed eccentricity.... Ranade was principally a social reformer. He was not a politician in the sense of one who trades in politics. But he has played an important part in the political advancement of India ....

As expected, the reviews harshly condemned Dr Ambedkar's Address. In the Preface of the book, Dr Ambedkar clarified that he was "not in the least perturbed by the Press's condemnation of his Address". He said, "No matter how 'filthy' the abuses which the Congress Press chooses to shower on me, I must do my duty."

Dr Ambedkar insisted:

...if I hate Mr Gandhi and Mr Jinnah—I dislike them, I do not hate them—it is because I love India more....

I have hopes that my countrymen will someday learn that the country is greater than the men, that the worship of Mr Gandhi or Mr Jinnah and service to India are two very different things and may even be contradictory of each other.

***

## "Gandhi and Jinnah Should Retire"

The "Quit India" movement (August 1942) had ended after several weeks of disorder and mob violence. Following this, Gandhiji began a 21-day fast on 10 February 1943. The fast shook the whole nation, and cries of "Release Gandhiji" echoed all over the country. There was intense pressure on the Indian Members of the Viceroy's Executive Council to resign. Most Members compiled, except for Dr Ambedkar (and Srivastava of Hindu *Mahasabha*).

In contrast, Dr Ambedkar delivered a speech in Mumbai (on 9 May 1943), in which he stated, "Gandhi and Jinnah should retire."[5]

Asserting that Mr Gandhi and the Congress High Command had displayed "utter political bankruptcy", Dr Ambedkar pleaded that Mr Gandhi should retire from active politics. He further added that Mr Jinnah, "who has taken up an impossible position", should also step down. He emphasized that unless both leaders quit the stage, it would be utterly hopeless to attempt any effort to lift Indian politics from its present quagmire. Only then, he argued, could Indian politics be expected to move in a direction that might genuinely contribute to the country's progress.

## Dr Ambedkar's Olive Branch to Gandhiji

Mahatma Gandhi was released on 6 May 1944 from the Aga Khan Palace in Pune, where he had been detained after the Quit India movement. In contrast, Jawaharlal Nehru, Vallabhbhai Patel and other Congress leaders remained imprisoned for another 13 months. During this period, Gandhiji devoted himself to bridging the widening chasm between the Congress and the Muslim League.

Recognizing Gandhiji's overtures to Jinnah, Dr Ambedkar was prompted to extend an offer of peace to Gandhiji. In a letter to Gandhiji, Dr Ambedkar observed that, in addition to resolving the Hindu-Muslim issue, it was equally essential to address the Hindu-Untouchable question if India's broader political goals were to be achieved. Dr Ambedkar assured Gandhiji that he was willing to draft a formula around which a settlement could be reached. In response to Dr Ambedkar's letter, Gandhiji wrote on 6 August

5 Marathi Speech in Mumbai (9 May 1943). English details available in BAWS, Vol. 17(3), pp. 300-02.

1944, reiterating that, for him, the issue of the Depressed Classes was primarily one of religious and social reform, not political. Expressing his appreciation for Dr Ambedkar's abilities, Gandhiji added that, while he would be glad to have him as a colleague and co-worker, "I know to my cost that you and I hold different views on this very important question."[6]

## Dr Ambedkar's Indictment of Gandhiji and Gandhism

Agitated by Gandhiji's recalcitrant attitude, Dr Ambedkar released a new book 10 months later (in June 1945), titled *What Congress and Gandhi Have Done to the Untouchables*. The book offered a scathing critique of both Gandhiji and the Congress. It primarily documents what Dr Ambedkar described as "the deeds of the Congress and Mr Gandhi from 1917 to date, in so far as they touch the problem of the Untouchables". Dr Ambedkar concluded the book with two emphatic chapters, the titles of which say it all.

(i) "Beware of Mr Gandhi!"

(ii) "Gandhism: The Doom of the Untouchables"

## A. "Beware of Mr Gandhi"

At the outset, Dr Ambedkar pointed out that during the first 21 years of his public life, from 1894 to 1915 in South Africa, Gandhiji "never thought of the Untouchables". After returning to India in 1915, when Gandhiji emerged as the pre-eminent leader of the Congress Party and was released from prison in 1924 on health grounds, he had the opportunity "to advance his anti-

6 Keer, *Dr Ambedkar: Life and Mission*, pp. 363–64.

Untouchability campaign". However, as Dr Ambedkar noted, "Mr Gandhi did not do it".

Dr Ambedkar pointed out that even after 1924 and up until 1930, "there was a complete blank. Mr Gandhi does not appear to have taken any active steps for the removal of Untouchability ..." In the meantime, in 1927, the Untouchables launched a *Satyagraha* movement to secure their rights to access water from public reservoirs and wells, as well as to enter public temples. According to Dr Ambedkar, instead of offering the expected full support to the *Satyagraha*, Gandhiji "condemned it in strong terms".

According to Dr Ambedkar, Gandhiji had "two novel weapons for redressing human wrongs": *Satyagraha* and fasting ... [He] claims exclusive credit for forging and perfecting them." However, Dr Ambedkar argued that Gandhiji never used the weapon of *Satyagraha* to press Hindus to open wells and temples to the Untouchables. The same holds true for fasting. Dr Ambedkar states: "... It is said that there have been altogether 21 fasts to the credit of Mr Gandhi ... In these 21 fasts, there is not one undertaken for the removal of Untouchability. Dr Ambedkar considered these to be very significant facts.[7]

During the Second Round Table Conference in 1931, Dr Ambedkar noted that Gandhiji had yet another opportunity to demonstrate his sympathy for the Untouchables by supporting their demand. Instead, Dr Ambedkar claimed, "Mr Gandhi used every means in his power to defeat them. He made a pact with the Muslims with a view to isolate the Untouchables. Failing to win the Musalmans to his side, he went on a fast unto death to compel the British Government to withdraw their decision for giving to the Untouchables the same political rights as given to the Muslims and other minority communities."

---

7 Mahad *Satyagraha* and the burning of *Manusmriti* have been discussed in Chapter 3 of this book.

Deviating from his earlier stance, in 1933, Gandhiji took up the Temple Entry Movement. According to Dr Ambedkar, Gandhiji took a vow that he would "fast unto death if the trustee of the Guruvayur Temple[8] did not throw it open to the Untouchables by a certain date". The Guruvayur Temple, however, remained closed to the Untouchables for years "but Mr Gandhi has not fulfilled his vow of going on fast".

In the same context, Gandhiji had reportedly threatened the British Government in 1932 "with dire consequences" should Mr Ranga Iyer be denied permission to introduce his Temple Entry Bill on behalf of the Congress Party. However, when fresh elections to the Central Legislature were announced, the Congress Party withdrew its support to the Bill. This prompted Dr Ambedkarto raise a pointed question: "If Mr Gandhiji was truly earnest and sincere about the Temple entry, why did he align himself with the Congress Party's decision to retract support? What was more important—ensuring Temple entry for the Untouchables or securing Electoral victory for the Congress?"

Dr Ambedkar expressed strong reservations regarding the fast undertaken by Gandhiji in Yerawada Jail, Pune, in 1932. "It was a foul and filthy act. The fast was not for the benefit of the Untouchables. It was against them and was the worst form of coercion against a helpless people to give up the Constitutional safeguards .... and agree to live on the mercy of the Hindus. It was a vile and wicked act. How can the Untouchables regard such a man as honest and sincere?"

Dr Ambedkar firmly asserted that "Mr Gandhi's anti-Untouchability campaign has failed beyond cavil," and offered

---

8 Guruvayur Temple, dedicated to Lord Vishnu, is one of the most important places of worship in Kerala.

two key reasons for this failure. First, he argued, "Mr Gandhi is regarded primarily as an apostle of *Swaraj*. His anti-Untouchability campaign is seen as a mere fad, if not a side-show. That is why Hindus respond to his political biddings, but not to his social or religious preaching." Second, Dr Ambedkar noted, "Mr Gandhi does not wish to antagonize the Hindus—even when such opposition may be necessary to advance his anti-Untouchability programme."

As an illustration of Gandhiji's mindset, Dr Ambedkar cited the Kavitha incident[9] in Ahmedabad district.

When the Untouchables of Kavitha were socially boycotted for having the audacity to demand school admission for their children, Gandhiji reportedly advised them: "There is no help like self-help. God helps those who help themselves. I hope that well-wishers of *Harijans* will help these poor families to vacate inhospitable Kavitha."

Dr Ambedkar lambasted Gandhiji's stance on the issue:

> Mr Gandhi advised the Untouchables of Kavitha to vacate. But why did he not advise Mr Thakkar [of *Harijan Sevak Sangh*] to prosecute the Hindus of Kavitha and help the Untouchables to vindicate their rights? Obviously, he would like to uplift the Untouchables if he can, but not by offending the Hindus. What good can such a man do to promote the cause of the Untouchables?

Dr Ambedkar therefore concluded: "That is why Mr Gandhi's whole programme for the removal of Untouchability is just words, words and words and why there is no action behind it."

---

9 The Kavitha incident has been cited earlier in Chapter 11.

## B. "Gandhism: The Doom of the Untouchables"

In this chapter, Dr Ambedkar has discussed Gandhism, its meaning, teachings and philosophy about social and economic problems.

### *Gandhiji's Economic Vision*

Pointing out that there is nothing new in Gandhiji's economic ideas, Dr Ambedkar wrote: "Gandhism is merely repeating the views of Rousseau, Ruskin, Tolstoy and their school." While admitting that machinery and modern civilization have produced many evils, Dr Ambedkar clarified that "the evils are not due to machinery and modern civilization. They are due to wrong social organization…" He argued that if machinery and civilization have failed to benefit everyone, the solution is not to condemn them outright, but rather to restructure society so that their advantages are not monopolized by a few, but are shared by all.

Dr Ambedkar contended that Gandhism might be better suited to a society that does *not* uphold democracy as its ideal. This, he argued, is because "under Gandhism, the common man must keep toiling ceaselessly for a pittance and remain a brute". In other words, he observed, "Gandhism, with its call of 'back to nature', implies a return to nakedness, squalor, poverty and ignorance for the vast mass of the people."

He also pooh-poohed Gandhiji's concept of "trusteeship" in his indomitable style, stating:

> The idea of trusteeship which Gandhism proposes as a panacea by which the moneyed classes will hold their properties in trust for the poor is the most ridiculous part of it. All that one can say about it is that if anybody else had propounded it, [he] would have been laughed at as a silly fool who had not known the hard realities of life….

## *Social Vision of Gandhism*

Dr Ambedkar forcefully argued that the social ideal of Gandhism is not compatible fundamentally incompatible with democracy. He asserted that both the Caste System and the doctrine of *Varna* are irreconcilable with democratic principles. democratic principles of the Caste System is the most insensible piece of rhetoric one can think of. Examine Mr Gandhi's arguments in support of Caste, and it will be found that every one of them is specious, if not puerile."[10]

About Gandhiji's view that the Caste System is a natural order of society, Dr Ambedkar's hard-hitting response was [this]:

> ...No one who knows anything about the *Manu Smriti* can say that the Caste System is a natural system... *Manu Smriti*... shows that the Caste System is a legal system maintained at the point of a bayonet. If it has survived it is due to (1) prevention of the masses from the possession of arms; (2) denying to the masses the right to education; and (3) depriving the masses of the right to property. The Caste System far from natural is really an imposition by the ruling classes upon the servile classes.

Dr Ambedkar argued that Gandhiji's shift "from the Caste System to the *Varna* System does not make the slightest difference to the charge that Gandhism is opposed to democracy".

Dr Ambedkar contended that no one would be "deceived by the occasional aberrations of Mr Gandhi in favour of democracy and against capitalism". He argued that Gandhism, far from being a revolutionary creed, is actually conservatism at its worst. In his view, "So far as India is concerned, it is a 'reactionary creed', one that calls for 'Return to Antiquity'. Gandhism aims at the resuscitation and reanimation of India's dread, dying past."

---

10 Gandhiji's view on Caste and *Varna* have been discussed earlier in Chapters 10 and 12.

To Dr Ambedkar, Gandhism is a "paradox" because it aims at the "destruction of the existing political structure of the country", while simultaneously "seeking to preserve a social structure that allows the hereditary domination of one Class over another". He argued that this results in the "perpetual domination of one Class by another".

According to Dr Ambedkar, there are two special features of Gandhism that are truly revealing. The first is its philosophy, which "helps those who have to retain what they possess, while preventing those who have not from getting what they rightfully deserve". The second is its ability to "delude people into accepting their misfortunes by presenting them as best of good fortunes".

Dr Ambedkar presented two illustrations of this peculiar phenomenon. First, while the *Shastras* prevented the *Shudras* from acquiring wealth (which incidentally Dr Ambedkar calls a "law of enforced poverty unknown in any other part of the world"), Gandhiji actually blesses the *Shudra* for his moral courage to give up property!

In the same spirit, while the *Shastras* ordain that "a scavenger's progeny shall live by scavenging", Gandhism in fact "seeks to perpetuate this system by praising scavenging as the noblest service to society!"

Dr Ambedkar then adds in his unique style:

> To preach that poverty is good for the *Shudra* and for none else, to preach that scavenging is good for the Untouchables and for none else and to make them accept these onerous impositions as voluntary purposes of life, … is an outrage and a cruel joke on the helpless classes which none but Mr Gandhi can perpetuate with equanimity and impunity …

According to Dr Ambedkar, this is, in fact, "the technique of Gandhism—to make wrongs done appear to the very victim as though they were his privileges. If there is an 'ism' which has made full use of religion as an opium to lull the people into false beliefs and false security, it is Gandhism."

Arguing that Gandhism offers no hope for Untouchables, Dr Ambedkar concluded his critique by asserting that, for the Untouchables, Hinduism is a "veritable chamber of horrors". The "iron law of Caste, the heartless law of *karma* and the senseless law of status by birth" are, to the Untouchables, "veritable instruments of torture which Hinduism has forged against the Untouchables."

According to Dr Ambedkar, these very instruments—"which have mutilated, blasted and blighted the life of the Untouchables"—remain intact and untarnished within the core of Gandhism. "How, then," he asked, "can the Untouchables say that Gandhism is a heaven and not a chamber of horrors ...?"

***

With the publication of the book, *What Congress and Gandhi Have Done to the Untouchables,* in June 1945, the discord between Mahatma Gandhi and Dr Ambedkar appeared to deepen beyond all bounds. A rapprochement between the two titans seemed virtually impossible—yet, remarkably, it did occur in the run-up to Independence.

# CHAPTER FIFTEEN

# Gandhi–Ambedkar: Détente, Finally

In July 1945, general elections were held in Britain wherein the Labour Party dislodged the Tories and came to power with Clement Attlee as the Prime Minister. In August 1945, Lord Wavell went to London for consultation, returned to India in mid-September 1945 and announced general elections in India.

## General Elections 1945-46

The general elections of 1945-46 were meant to serve two purposes: (a) renewal of the Provincial Assemblies, the first time since the Provincial elections of 1937; and (b) endowing the country with a Constituent Assembly.

For Dr Ambedkar, it was also the first election that his new political party—the Scheduled Caste Federation (SCF)—would contest as a representative of the Depressed Classes on an all-India scale.

The election campaigns started gathering momentum in October 1945. The Congress Party entered the electoral arena with the slogan "Quit India" whereas the Muslim League came up with the slogan "Pakistan or Perish". Both parties had abundant funding and electoral machinery. Unlike these two main political parties, the SCF led by Dr Ambedkar had neither.

Dr Ambedkar inaugurated his election campaign in Pune (2-4 October 1945). In his inaugural speech, Dr Ambedkar emphasized that the Scheduled Castes must get their share in the political power and that the then forthcoming election was the question of life and death for the Scheduled Castes. This extremely important speech delineated Dr Ambedkar's election strategy.

Referring to Gandhiji and the Congress, Dr Ambedkar remarked[1] that Congress means "defeat at every step". ... He recalled, "Initially, Mr Gandhi was very fierce. His people would disobey the law, disrupt civic life and willingly go to jail ... Mr Gandhi sort of gave a burning torch into the hands of his followers. And in 1921, they burnt down a police *chowki*. Mr Gandhi got frightened and abandoned those methods."

When the World War broke out in 1939, the Congress remained inactive for more than three years, and then, in August 1942, they passed a resolution "Quit India (*Chale Jao*)".

The resolution was passed late evening on 8 August 1942, and within hours all Congress leaders including Gandhiji were jailed. Others went on rampage throughout the country and destroyed public property. Dr Ambedkar questioned the consequences of this unrest, asking: "Whose property they have damaged? ...this entire loss was borne by the poor public of India ..."

Dr Ambedkar lamented: "Such is Mr Gandhi's style of politics. This is the politics of the defeated. The Congress people are the failed kids of politics."

---

1 Marathi Speech. For English Summary, see Jadhav (ed), *Ambedkar Speaks*, Vol. III, pp. 326-30.

Dr Ambedkar accused Gandhiji of introducing the Caste factor into Indian Politics. He observed that when the Congress Party was founded, its founders recognized the importance of unity and thus included people from all religious backgrounds. However, after Gandhiji took over the Congress in 1920, "[this] country has now come to such a difficult passé that the differences of Castes have assumed political importance..."

While concluding, Dr Ambedkar underscored the historic importance of the then forthcoming elections, especially about the proposed formation of the Constituent Assembly, after the election. He alerted his followers saying: "We should have our eyes on those provisions in the future Constitution."

***

The election results of March 1946 proved most disappointing for Dr Ambedkar. While the Congress swept the general constituencies and the Muslim League secured nearly all the Muslim seats, the SCF performed—winning only two seats in the Provincial Assemblies, one in Bengal and the other in the Central Provinces and Berar. This outcome was a major political setback for Dr Ambedkar.

The 1945-46 elections had a "devastating" impact on Dr Ambedkar's credibility with the British. With only two reserved seats out of 151, the SCF could no longer claim to represent the Untouchables.[2]

## British Cabinet Mission to India: Transfer of Power

On 15 March 1946, British Prime Minister Clement Attlee explicitly acknowledged India's right to attain full independence—

2 Jaffrelot, *Dr Ambedkar and Untouchability*, p. 90.

whether within or outside the British Commonwealth. He also emphasized that no minority would be permitted to place a veto on the advancement of the majority.

Following this historic announcement, a British Cabinet Mission arrived in India on 24 March 1946. Its purpose was to discuss and plan the transfer of power from the British Government to Indian leadership, thereby paving the way for India's long-awaited independence. The Mission consisted of three British Cabinet Ministers. Its primary objectives were:

(1) Hold preparatory discussions with elected representatives of British India and the Indian (Princely) States in order to secure agreement as to the method of framing the Constitution;

(2) Set up a Constituent Assembly; and

(3) Set up an Executive Council with the support of the main Indian parties.

The Mission held detailed discussions with representatives of the Indian National Congress and the All-India Muslim League—the two largest political parties at the time. Both parties explored the possibility of a power-sharing arrangement between Hindus and Muslims to avoid communal conflict and to determine whether British India should remain united or be divided. The Congress Party, led by Gandhiji and Jawaharlal Nehru, advocated for a strong Central government with more powers vis-à-vis the Provincial governments. In contrast, the All-India Muslim League, under the leadership of Jinnah, favoured maintaining a united India, but only if adequate political safeguards were provided for Muslims, including a "guarantee" of "parity" in the Legislatures.

Dr Ambedkar met with the Cabinet Mission on 5 April 1946 and presented a strong case for the Scheduled Castes. He submitted a detailed Memorandum to the Cabinet Mission, demanding the inclusion of several safeguards in the new Constitution, including separate electorates, adequate representation in the Central and Provincial Legislatures and Executives, in Public Services and on the Public Service Commissions, besides providing earmarked financial provisions for the Scheduled Castes.[3]

***

After initial dialogue, the Mission proposed its plan regarding the composition of the new government on 16 May 1946. The Plan to create a United Dominion of India as a loose confederation of Provinces came to be known as the "Plan of May 16".

The Plan of May 16 had envisaged a United India in line with aspirations of Congress and Muslim League. But that was where the consensus between the two parties ended. The Congress strongly disapproved the idea of having groupings of Muslim majority Provinces and that of Hindu majority Provinces with the intention of "balancing" each other at the Central Legislature. The Muslim League was not willing to accept any changes to this Plan. The "parity" that the Congress detested, in fact, formed the very basis of Muslim demands of "political safeguards" aimed at preventing absolute rule of Hindus over Muslims.

Reaching an impasse, the British proposed a second alternative: "Plan of June 16". This Plan sought to arrange for India to be divided into Hindu-majority India and a Muslim-majority India that would later be renamed Pakistan, since Congress had vehemently rejected "parity" at the Centre.

After announcing that there will be a Caretaker Government, the Cabinet Mission left for London leaving it to the Viceroy to work out the necessary details. This meant disbanding of

3 Keer, *Dr Ambedkar: Life and Mission*, p. 379.

the Viceroy's Executive Council of which Dr Ambedkar was a Minister-Member. Dr Ambedkar, like the other Members of the Executive Council, bade goodbye to the Viceroy, and returned to Mumbai.

## Dr Ambedkar: Uncertainty and Restlessness

With the announcement of a Caretaker Government replacing the Viceroy's Executive Council, political turmoil started gathering momentum. For Dr Ambedkar, this brief period was marked by extreme uncertainty and restlessness. A Caretaker Government was formed at the Centre on 19 June 1946. Dr Ambedkar was not included in the Cabinet of Ministers (Shri Jagjivan Ram—a Scheduled Caste leader from within the Congress fold was included instead, apparently at the behest of Mahatma Gandhi).

On 10 July 1946, Jawaharlal Nehru held a press conference in Mumbai declaring that the Congress had agreed only to participate in the Constituent Assembly and that it regards itself free to change or modify the Cabinet Mission Plan as deemed fit. The Congress ruled out the June 16 Plan, seeing it as the division of India into small States.

Dr Ambedkar and his political party, the SCF, launched a *Satyagraha* in Pune (July 1946), Nagpur (September 1946) and in a few other places demanding an explanation from the Congress leaders regarding the rights of the Scheduled Castes and their representation in the soon-to-be-free India. But with the routing of the SCF in the latest Provincial elections, the British started ignoring, indeed marginalizing, Dr Ambedkar. B.G. Kher, the Chief Minister of the Bombay Province, reacted sarcastically, saying: "One does not know whether their (i.e., Scheduled Castes) grievance is against the Cabinet Mission's failure to give them what they want, or against the defeat of Dr Ambedkar and his party in the recent election, or whether it is due to a general sense of frustration."[4]

In the same vein, even Gandhiji took a dig at Dr Ambedkar's agitation calling it a "parody of *Satyagraha* in the show staged by Ambedkar" and remarked that even if its means were non-violent, the cause was certainly vague.[5]

## The Interim Government

In the meantime, the Viceroy began organizing the transfer of power to a Congress–Muslim League coalition. However, Jinnah denounced the conditional given by the Congress and withdrew the League's support for both plans. Nevertheless, Congress leaders joined the newly formed Viceroy's Executive Council, the Interim Government, in September 1946, under the leadership of Jawaharlal Nehru. Congress-led governments were formed in most Provinces, while League-led governments took power in Bengal and Sind. The Constituent Assembly was instructed to begin drafting a new Constitution for India.

Jinnah and the League condemned the new government and vowed to agitate for Pakistan by any means possible. This led to a law and order crisis in Punjab and Bengal as well as in the major cities of Delhi, Mumbai and Calcutta. Earlier, on League-organized Direct Action Day (16 August 1946), over 5,000 people were reportedly killed across India in violent clashes involving Hindu, Sikh and Muslim mobs.

In an effort to end the disorder and rising bloodshed, Viceroy Wavell encouraged Nehru to invite the League to join the government. While most Congress leaders opposed aligning with

4 As quoted in Keer, *Dr Ambedkar: Life and Mission*, p. 382.

5 *Harijan*, 9 August 1946.

the party that was seen as responsible for organizing unrest, Nehru conceded in the hope of preserving communal peace.

Muslim League leaders joined the Interim Government on 26 October 1946 under the leadership of Liaquat Ali Khan, the future first Prime Minister of Pakistan, who became India's Finance Minister. Interestingly, the League included Jogendra Nath Mandal, who was a close colleague of Dr Ambedkar and a member of the Working Committee of the SCF, as Law Minister in the Interim Cabinet.

However, the Interim Cabinet did not function in harmony. League ministers held separate meetings, and both parties frequently vetoed major initiatives proposed by the other, demonstrating their deep ideological differences and political enmity. Furthermore, the Muslim League decided to boycott the Constituent Assembly.

## Dr Ambedkar: Making Peace with Congress

According to the Cabinet Mission's Plan, the British Government had envisaged the election of a Constituent Assembly without guaranteeing any representation for the Scheduled Castes. As members were being elected to the Constituent Assembly by Provincial Assemblies, Dr Ambedkar's SCF, lacking the required numbers, had little chance of securing a seat for him. Fortunately, Jogendra Nath Mandal,[6] an SCF leader from Bengal, intervened. In a surprising and strategic move, he secured the necessary support to have Dr Ambedkar elected to the Constituent Assembly from the Bengal Province on 19 July 1946.

---

6 After the Partition, Mandal went to Pakistan and became temporary Chairman of Pakistan's Constituent Assembly and later Pakistan's first Minister of Law and Labour.

Meanwhile, in the last week of October 1946, Dr Ambedkar travelled to London, where he met with British Prime Minister Attlee, Secretary of State for India Frederick Pethick-Lawrence, prominent British Conservative politician Winston Churchill and other leaders. Apparently, except Winston Churchill, none of them showed interest in raking up the "Communal Problem" at such a late stage. It appears Dr Ambedkar was advised to "try his luck at the Constituent Assembly".[7]

Confronted with British apathy and scorn from the Congress, a dejected Dr Ambedkar chose to sever ties with the British and pursue reconciliation with the Congress. This attempt to mend relations unfolded in the newly formed Constituent Assembly.

## Dr Ambedkar: Game-changing Speech in Constituent Assembly

Despite the Muslim League's boycott, the Constituent Assembly convened for the first time on 9 December 1946 and elected Dr Rajendra Prasad as its President. On 13 December, Jawaharlal Nehru laid the foundation of the Constituent Assembly's mission by moving a Resolution on the Declaration of Objectives. In a most memorable historic speech, Nehru declared the aim of establishing an Independent Sovereign Republic as India's national objective.

During the discussion on this critical Resolution, Dr M.R. Jayakar proposed an amendment, urging a postponement of its adoption until the Muslim League members joined the Constituent Assembly. He objected to the timing of the Nehru's Resolution, arguing that it would be more appropriate to adopt such a foundational declaration with the participation of all major

---

7 Keer, *Dr Ambedkar: Life and Mission*, p. 385.

political groups. Although Dr Jayakar's amendment was moved in good faith, it immensely irritated the Congress High Command.

Amidst this state of consternation, an unexpected development occurred: on 17 December 1946, Dr Ambedkar was invited by the President of the Constituent Assembly, Dr Rajendra Prasad, to speak. Dr Ambedkar grabbed the opportunity and rose to the occasion, literally, in more ways than one.

At the outset of his Address, he remarked[8] that the Resolution reminded him of the age-old Declaration of the Rights of Man, proclaimed by the French Constituent Assembly nearly 450 years ago. However, he pointed out a critical shortcoming in Nehru's Resolution: "While the Resolution enunciates certain rights, does not speak of remedies … rights are nothing unless remedies are provided whereby people can seek to obtain redress when rights are invaded." He further stated that he had "expected some provision whereby it would have been possible for the State to make economic, social and political justice a reality."

Turning to the all-important issue of national unity, Dr Ambedkar said that he was absolutely certain about the "future evolution and the ultimate shape of the social, political and economic structure of this great country". He admitted that the people of India were "divided politically, socially and economically", resembling a group of "warring camps". Yet he expressed firm optimism, declaring, "I am quite convinced that, given time and circumstances, nothing in the world will prevent this country from becoming one." Despite differences of caste and creed, he believed that "we shall in some form be a united people".

---

8 Constituent Assembly Debates (CAD), Vol. I, pp. 99-103. Also reproduced in BAWS, Vol. 13, pp. 7-23; and in Jadhav (ed), *Ambedkar Speaks*, Vol. II, pp. 447-53. All quotes in this section are from the same speech.

Striking a strategically reconciliatory note, Dr Ambedkar concluded, "I have no hesitation in saying that, notwithstanding the agitation of the Muslim League for the partition of India, some day enough light would dawn upon the Muslims themselves and they too will begin to think that a United India is better even for them."

Referring to the ultimate goal of the country, Dr Ambedkar indicated: "Our difficulty is how to make the heterogeneous mass that we have today take a decision in common and march on the way which leads us to unity."

He then urged the Congress Party, "…in order to induce every party, every section in this country to take on to road (to unity) it would be an act of greatest statesmanship for the majority Party even to make a concession to the prejudices of people who are not prepared to march together…."

Dr Ambedkar then resorted to an emotional appeal. He said that leaving slogans and harsh words aside, let us bring "our opponents" in "so that they may willingly join with us on marching upon that road, which…if we walk long enough, must necessarily lead us to unity…. We should leave aside all legal considerations and make some attempt, whereby those who are not prepared to come will come."

Dr Ambedkar also earnestly pleaded for "a strong united Centre, much stronger than the Centre…created under the Government of India Act of 1935."

Actually, what Dr Ambedkar was saying was not materially different from what Dr Jayakar had said. But Dr Ambedkar put it in a totally different way, changing over from a "legalistic" style to a statesman-like manner. He said:

> I am not asking you to consider whether you have the right to pass this Resolution straightaway or not. It may be that you have the right to do so. The question I am asking is this. Is it prudent

> for you to do so? Is it wise for you to do so? ... The answer that I give is that it would not be prudent, it would not be wise.

Recommending yet another attempt at reconciliation between the Congress and the Muslim League, Dr Ambedkar said: "When deciding the destinies of nations, dignities of people, dignities of leaders and dignities of parties ought to count for nothing. The destiny of the country ought to count for everything...we must also consider what is going to happen with regard to the future, if we act precipitately...."

Dr Ambedkar said there are only three options for solving the "Communal problem": First, surrender by one party; secondly, a negotiated peace; and thirdly "open war".

At this point, he had given the debate an entirely new twist. He said that he has been "hearing from certain Members of the Constituent Assembly that they are prepared to go to war" and that he was "appalled" at the idea of "solving the political problems of this country by the method of war".

Quoting Edmund Burke[9] who had said on conciliation with the US: "... the use of force alone is but temporary. It may subdue for a moment; but it does not remove the necessity of subduing again; and a nation is not governed which is perpetually to be conquered.... A further objection to force is that you impair the object by your very endeavours to preserve it."

Dr Ambedkar added that if any attempt is made to solve the Hindu-Muslim problem by forcing the Muslims to surrender to the Constitution, possibly prepared without their consent, "this country would be involved in perpetually conquering them".

---

9 Edmund Burke speech, while moving his resolutions for conciliation with the British colonies (22 March 1775), Eighteenth Century Collections Online.

Dr Ambedkar concluded his speech by quoting Burke again, who had said that "it is easy to give power, it is difficult to give wisdom".

Passionately, he added: "Let us prove by our conduct that if this Assembly has arrogated to itself sovereign powers, it is prepared to exercise them with wisdom. That is the only way by which we can carry with us all sections of the country. There is no other way that can lead us to unity."

* * *

The speech drew the longest and the most enthusiastic applause. It was earnest, yet so statesman-like. To the surprise of many Congress leaders, it was notably free of bitterness. The entire Assembly listened in rapt attention, greeting Dr Ambedkar's words with resounding cheer, applause, and the thumping of desks.

This speech proved to be a game-changer. It significantly altered the attitude of Congress leaders, including Jawaharlal Nehru, towards Dr Ambedkar. His opposition to partition and support for a United government with a strong Centre was music to their ears. This was precisely the position the Congress leadership had long desired but apprehended that Dr Ambedkar would oppose. In that moment, Dr Ambedkar's strategic speech changed the course of his political trajectory.

***

On 29 April 1947, the Constituent Assembly announced: "Untouchability in any form is abolished and the imposition of any disability on that account shall be an offence." The world press hailed this event as the freedom for Untouchables. The *New York Times* mentioned: "The advance towards wiping out their ancient stigma has been matched in modern times only by our own abolition of slavery ..." The *New York Herald Tribune* described the event as one of the fresh and clean beams of light in the post-War world.[10]

All over the world, profuse praise was showered on Mahatma Gandhi for this great achievement of India. Curiously no foreign media mentioned, even in passing, the name of Dr Ambedkar—who, in reality, was the driving force behind this national accomplishment.

## The Independence of India

With the arrival of the new (and proclaimed final) Viceroy, Lord Mountbatten of Burma, in early 1947, Congress leaders increasingly voiced the view that the coalition between the Congress and the Muslim League was unworkable. This ultimately led to the proposal and subsequent acceptance of the partition of India.

On 3 June 1947, Lord Mountbatten announced the British Government's Plan for India's future. The Plan envisaged the partition of the country, resulting in the creation of two Central Governments and, accordingly, two Constituent Assemblies.

Gandhiji, who had earlier described the idea of Pakistan as a sin and a "patent untruth", and had solemnly urged its proponents to "vivisect me before you vivisect India", eventually changed his position. He reportedly "instructed" Jawaharlal Nehru (who had gone to Noakhali in East Bengal to consult Gandhiji) to reach "an accord with Jinnah", offering him "a universally acceptable and inoffensive formula for his Pakistan".[11] The following week,

10 Keer, *Dr Ambedkar: Life and Mission*, p. 393.

11 Dr Ambedkar was the one who wrote the first book on the "knotty" problem of Pakistan, titled *Pakistan or Partition of India,* published first in 1940. The second edition of Dr Ambedkar's book on Pakistan, titled *Thoughts on Pakistan* came in handy for both sides. In the Preface to the

Jawaharlal Nehru moved a Resolution in the All India Congress Committee, which was passed by a vote of 99-52.[12]

The British Parliament passed the Indian Independence Act on 15 July 1947, officially recognizing the Constituent Assembly as a sovereign body. With the partition of Bengal, several members, including Dr Ambedkar, lost their seats in India's Constituent Assembly. However, due to the changing attitude of the Congress leadership towards Dr Ambedkar, a new opportunity emerged. When Barrister M.R. Jayakar resigned[13] from his seat in the Assembly from the Bombay Province, Jawaharlal Nehru and Sardar Patel proposed Dr Ambedkar's name to fill the vacancy. Thus, in July 1947, Dr Ambedkar returned to the Constituent Assembly, this time with the support of the Congress.

On 15 August 1947, India became a free nation. Dr Ambedkar was inducted into the frist Cabinet of independent India as the Union Minister of Law. It is widely believed that his appointment came at the insistence of Gandhiji, who viewed Dr Ambedkar's inclusion as essential to the task of national reconstruction. While both Nehru and Patel were reportedly lukewarm about allocating a Ministerial berth to Dr Ambedkar, Gandhiji firmly supported the move.[14] This conjecture is further supported by a conversation

---

Second Edition, Dr Ambedkar states: "The fact that Mr Gandhi and Mr Jinnah in their recent talks cited the book as an authority on the subject which might be consulted with advantage bespeaks the worth of the book ..." For Summary of this book, see Jadhav (ed), *Ambedkar Writes*, Vol. I, pp.114-89.

12 Lelyveld, *Great Soul,* p. 310.

13 Barrister M.R. Jayakar then became the founder Vice Chancellor of Pune University.

14 S.M. Gaikwad, "Ambedkar and Indian Nationalism", *Economic and Political Weekly*, 7 March 1998.

between Gandhiji and two visiting foreigners,[15] wherein Gandhiji had reportedly expressed the wish that Dr Ambedkar should become a part of the first Government of Independent India.[16]

On 29 August 1947, Dr Ambedkar was appointed a Member of the Drafting Committee of the Indian Constitution, and was soon after chosen as its Chairman. As Independent India's first Union Minister of Law and the Chairman of the Drafting Committee, Dr Ambedkar assumed responsibilities that would give him a unique place in the foundation of modern India.

* * *

None of these developments could have occurred without the consent of Mahatma Gandhi. As the Supreme Commander of India's freedom struggle, Gandhiji was the *de facto* authority—the "remote control", some may say.

Against the backdrop of a series of conflicts, confrontations and often bitter war of words between the two great men, repeated time and again over the preceding 17 years, it came as a great surprise to everyone, including Dr Ambedkar, that Gandhi supported his inclusion in the first Cabinet of independent India.

It is not clear who, if any, "persuaded" Gandhiji to take such a momentous decision. Going by the scanty research available, it could not have been either Nehru or Patel, both of whom were reportedly lukewarm to the idea. Instead, it seems that the decision

15 M.S. Gore, *The Social Context of an Ideology* (New Delhi: Sage Publications, 1993), p. 180.

16 Yet another hypothesis is that Muriel Lester, International Organizing Secretary of the Fellowship of Reconciliation and a long-time friend of Gandhiji who hosted him in London during the Second RTC, insisted on Dr Ambedkar's inclusion in the Cabinet.

was Gandhiji's own, made independently and with far-reaching vision.

If that is indeed the case, it must be regarded as an overwhelmingly generous gesture on Gandhiji's part. It was Dr Ambedkar who had earlier stated in the Constituent Assembly, on 17 December 1946, that "when deciding the destinies of nations, dignities of people, dignities of leaders and dignities of parties ought to count for nothing. The destiny of the country ought to count for everything".

Mahatma Gandhi was actually doing it, setting a powerful example for others to emulate, one worthy of the title *Mahatma* (a great soul) and befitting his stature as the Father of the Nation.

# CHAPTER SIXTEEN

# What Congress and Nehru Have Done to Dr Ambedkar

In the preceding chapters, the conflicts and compromises between Mahatma Gandhi and the Congress Party on one hand, and Dr Ambedkar on the other, have been discussed in detail. But what happened after the ruthless assassination of Mahatma Gandhi in January 1948? How did Dr Ambedkar's relationship with the Congress Party in general and with the then Prime Minister Jawaharlal Nehru evolve thereafter? These crucial developments form the focus of this concluding chapter.

***

Dr Ambedkar joined the Congress-led government in independent India as the country's first Law Minister. However, even as he worked tirelessly on drafting the Constitution, moderating and steering discussions in the Constituent Assembly, Dr Ambedkar grew increasingly uncomfortable with the Congress Party.

A crisis arose in April 1948, barely three months after Gandhiji's assassination. While addressing the United Provinces Scheduled Caste Federation's Conference, Dr Ambedkar clarified that although he was part of the Central Government, he had not joined the Congress Party. He remarked that "the Congress Party was a burning house," and added that he "would not be surprised if it was completely destroyed in a couple of years".[1]

Sure enough, the speech caused an uproar. In a letter to one of his trusted lieutenants,[2] Dr Ambedkar reportedly wrote that a heated exchange had taken place between himself, Nehru and Sardar Patel, during which he had offered to resign. The issue, however, was soon defused when Dr Ambedkar issued a statement clarifying that his remarks had been misreported. In this statement, he emphasized that he had joined the Cabinet because he believed the cause of the Scheduled Castes would be better served from within the government.[3]

In his public speeches, Dr Ambedkar consistently underscored that political power was the key to all social progress and that the Scheduled Castes could secure their lifeline only by organizing themselves into a third political force capable of balancing power between the two dominant parties of the time, the Congress and the Socialists. Although the Congress Party made efforts to persuade Dr Ambedkar to join its fold, he steadfastly remained independent and continued to advocate for social reform and the advancement of human rights.

With Dr Ambedkar meticulously maintaining his separate identity and preserving his political base among the Scheduled Castes, relations between him and the Congress Party continued

---

1 English/Hindi Address to the Fifth Conference of United Provinces of SCF, Lucknow (24-25 April 1948). Reproduced in BAWS, Vol. 17(3), pp. 388-94.

2 Keer, *Dr Ambedkar: Life and Mission*, p. 405.

3 For details of the Statement, see Jadhav (ed), *Ambedkar Speaks*, Vol. III, pp. 358-60.

to deteriorate, eventually culminating in a head-on confrontation over the Hindu Code Bill.

## Controversy Over the Hindu Code Bill

The Hindu Code Bill, which Dr Ambedkar had hoped would emerge as one of the cornerstones of modern India, had a chequered history.

In 1941, the British Government decided to consolidate the Hindu personal laws into one Code and appointed a Hindu Law Committee under the chairmanship of B.N. Rau. The Committee issued a draft Hindu Code in August 1944, which was introduced in the [Central] Legislature in April 1947. However, due to the political upheaval caused by Independence and Partition, it could not be taken up for discussion at the time.

In 1948, Prime Minister Nehru entrusted the task of drafting the new Hindu Code to a sub-committee of the Constituent Assembly and appointed Dr Ambedkar as its Chairman.

In the revised Draft Hindu Code, Dr Ambedkar incorporated several essential principles: equality between men and women in matters of property and adoption, legal recognition exclusively for monogamous marriages and the elimination of Caste restrictions in civil marriages. He also included in the draft Code the requirement of concrete justification for filing a petition for divorce. Dr Ambedkar viewed the Hindu Code Bill as a crucial step towards the eventual realization of a Common Civil Code.[4]

The Hindu Code Bill was, without doubt, an unprecedented and comprehensive social reform effort championed by Dr Ambedkar in Parliament over nearly four years. What follows is a summary of the Bill, put together from various submissions and

4 Jadhav (ed), *Ambedkar Speaks,* Vol. II, p. 384.

presentations made by Dr Ambedkar in Parliament in his capacity as the Union Law Minister.[5]

According to Dr Ambedkar, the Bill aimed to codify the rules of Hindu Law, which were scattered across innumerable decisions of the High Courts and had created a bewildering patchwork for the common man—an issue that had the potential to give rise to extensive litigation. The Bill was set to bring clarity and uniformity by codifying laws related to several key areas, including the property rights of a deceased Hindu, the order of succession among various heirs, and the laws governing maintenance, marriage, divorce, adoption, minority, and guardianship.

### *A. Inheritance*

The Bill was aimed at the universalization of the law of inheritance. In the order of succession for a deceased Hindu, the Bill proposed several significant changes. The most important was that the widow, daughter, and the widow of a predeceased son were all granted the *same* rank as the son in matters of inheritance. In addition, the daughter was given half a share in her father's property.

### *B. Stridhan*[6]

So far as *stridhan* is concerned, the Draft Bill proposed two key changes. First, it consolidated the various categories of *stridhan* into a single unified category of property and laid down a uniform rule of succession. Second, the Bill sought to give the son also a right to inherit the *stridhan*.

---

5 For details, see Jadhav (ed), *Ambedkar Speaks*. Vol. II, pp. 355-61, and pp. 368-384.

6 *Stridhan* is the property that a woman obtains at the time of her marriage and thereafter. Unlike dowry, it is voluntary and involves no element of coercion.

In formulating the Bill and revising the rules of succession, it was proposed that the daughter would receive half the share in her father's property, while the son would similarly receive half the share in his mother's property. In this way, the Bill sought to establish a sense of equality between the son and the daughter.

### *C. Women's Estates*

Under the Hindu law, when a woman inherited property, she received only what was known as a "life estate". She could enjoy the income generated by the property but was not permitted to dispose of or manage the corpus of the property, except in cases of legal necessity. The Bill introduced a major change: it converted the limited estate into an absolute estate, thereby granting women the same absolute rights over inherited property as men.

### *D. Maintenance for Separated Women*

The Bill provided that a wife would be entitled to claim separate maintenance from her husband under the following conditions: (1) if he was suffering from a loathsome disease; (2) if he kept a concubine; (3) if he was guilty of cruelty; (4) if he had abandoned her for two years; (5) if he had converted to another religion; or (6) for any other cause that justified her decision to live separately.

### *E. Marriages*

Under the existing Hindu law, only "sacramental" marriage was recognized; "civil" marriage had no legal standing. The Bill proposed three major changes in this regard. First, while the existing law required the parties to belong to the same Caste or sub-Caste for a valid sacramental marriage, the Bill sought to dispense with this condition. Under the new provisions, a marriage would be considered valid regardless of the Caste or sub-Caste of the individuals involved. Second, whereas polygamy was permitted under the old law, the Bill prescribed monogamy as the legal norm.

Third, the sacramental nature of marriage under traditional Hindu law made it indissoluble, with no provision for divorce. The Draft Bill marked a significant departure by introducing provisions for the dissolution of marriage. Under the new Code, any party entering into marriage is granted three legal remedies to exit the marital relationship: (1) have the marriage declared null and void, (2) have the marriage declared invalid, or (3) have it dissolved.

### *F. Divorce*

Regarding the question of divorce, the Bill prescribed seven grounds on which divorce could be obtained: (1) desertion; (2) conversion to another religion; (3) keeping a concubine or becoming one; (4) incurably unsound mind; (5) virulent and incurable form of leprosy; (6) a communicable venereal disease; and (7) cruelty.

Undoubtedly, the Hindu Code Bill aimed at far-reaching and comprehensive social reform.

***

Dr Ambedkar presented the completely revised Hindu Code Bill to the Constituent Assembly in October 1948. The Bill sparked widespread and bitter controversy. Challenging long-standing customs that governed the private lives of Hindus led to a massive outcry in favour of protection of religious beliefs. The debate went on for nearly three years. While the Bill was still under discussion, orthodox groups denounced it as a threat to the sanctity of Hindu marriage, arguing that marriage and family were the bedrock of Hindu society and dissolving a marriage would ruin a society that had survived for millennia.

In October 1950, Dr Ambedkar circulated a booklet among the Members of Parliament, outlining the nature and scope of the changes made to the Hindu Code Bill brought out in the light of representations received from various Hindu organizations. He also delivered speeches across the country, seeking to build consensus around the revised Bill. But the controversy did not die down.

President Dr Rajendra Prasad, in his letter to Sardar Patel, expressed strong reservations against the Hindu Code Bill, alleging that its "new concepts and new ideas are not only foreign to the Hindu law but are susceptible to dividing every family".[7] Several Congress leaders apparently campaigned privately against the Bill on the grounds that the Members of the Provisional Parliament[8] did *not* have the mandate to address such far-reaching issues. Congress Party President Pattabhi Sitaramayya opposed the Bill on the grounds that it would alienate the Party's support base on the eve of the forthcoming first General Elections of Independent India.

Prime Minister Nehru, however, fully supported the Hindu Code Bill and had even declared that his Government would resign if the Bill was not passed by Parliament. This was despite the fact that Sardar Patel had expressed his stern opposition to the Bill and announced that it would not be taken up by Parliament at all.[9]

***

On 10 August 1951, Dr Ambedkar wrote to Prime Minister Nehru that his health was deteriorating, and that he was keen that the Bill be taken up in Parliament on priority. In response, the Prime Minister clarified that there was opposition to the Bill both inside the Government as well as outside. Nevertheless, it would be taken

---

7 Quoted in Jaffrelot, *Dr Ambedkar and Untouchability*, p. 116.

8 The Constituent Assembly itself was operating as the "Provisional Parliament" until the first General Elections were held in 1952.

9 A detailed account of this crisis is available in Keer, *Dr Ambedkar: Life and Mission*, p. 431.

up in Parliament at the beginning of September 1951. In order to contain and diffuse the Opposition, Prime Minister Nehru strategically divided the Code into four parts. It was decided that the Marriage and Divorce part of the Hindu Code Bill would be treated as a separate bill and would be taken up in Parliament on 17 September 1951.

The truncated Hindu Code in the form of Marriage and Divorce Bill was intensely debated in Parliament. The debate brought out the hostility that had accumulated amongst most traditionalist Congressmen. The orthodoxy from the Opposition also came forward to denounce the Bill. Notably, Syama Prasad Mukherjee said that the Hindu Code Bill "would shatter the magnificent structure of the Hindu culture and stultify a dynamic and catholic way of life that had wonderfully adapted itself to the changes for centuries."[10]

After four days of heated discussions, Dr Ambedkar made an earnest appeal on 20 September 1951. In response to the criticisms, he asserted that arguments about the invariance of Hindu society and its prolonged survival were irrelevant. Rather, the real question concerned the quality of what had endured. He argued that the proposed marriage system was not a blind imitation of the West but grounded in the values of liberty, equality and fraternity enshrined in the Constitution. In contrast, he reasoned, the "sacramental marriage of the traditionalists amounted to polygamy for the man and perpetual slavery for the woman".

The Bill failed to pass in Parliament. Prime Minister Jawaharlal Nehru, who had earlier committed to support it, never issued a whip and was either unable or unwilling to make the traditionally minded Congress MPs to fall into line. A little later, Dr Ambedkar attributed Pandit Nehru's backtracking to pressure from the

---

10 Ibid., p. 432.

Congress Party. He said in a statement: "I have never seen a case of chief whip so disloyal to the Prime Minister and the Prime Minister so loyal to a disloyal whip."[11]

There is a view that Jawaharlal Nehru feared that Congress MPs would reject the Bill *en masse*, and that President Dr Rajendra Prasad, who was firmly opposed to the Bill, might indeed follow through on his threat not to promulgate it into law.[12]

## Dr Ambedkar's Resignation as Cabinet Minister

Dejected and disgusted, Dr Ambedkar resigned from his position as a Cabinet Minister on 27 September 1951. In his resignation letter to the Prime Minister, he stated:

> For a long time, I have been thinking of resigning my seat from the Cabinet. The only thing that had held me back from giving effect to my intention was the hope that it would be possible to give effect to the Hindu Code Bill before the life of the present Parliament comes to an end. I even agreed to break up the Bill and restricted it to Marriage and Divorce in the fond hope that at least this much of our labour may bear fruit. But even that part of the Bill has been killed. I see no purpose in my continuing to be a Member of your Cabinet.

As a matter of courtesy to the Prime Minister and the Cabinet, Dr Ambedkar expressed his willingness to remain in office until the motions pending in his name were taken up. Jawaharlal Nehru agreed to accept his resignation effective from the last date of the ongoing Session.

---

11 Quoted in Reba Som, "Jawaharlal Nehru and the Hindu Code", *Modern Asian Studies*, 1994, pp. 185-87. Also quoted in Jaffrelot, *Dr Ambedkar and Untouchability*.

12 Jaffrelot, *Dr Ambedkar and Untouchability*, p. 117.

In a surprise move, Prime Minister Nehru requested an advance copy of Dr Ambedkar's parting speech. In response, on 4 October 1951, Dr Ambedkar informed the Prime Minister that he would provide an advance copy *if* he decided to prepare a written speech. He also informed Nehru that he had obtained the Deputy Speaker's permission to deliver his statement on 11 October 1951.

When Parliament convened on 11 October, Dr Ambedkar rose to speak at the assigned time. However, in an unexpected turn, the Deputy Speaker ruled that Dr Ambedkar could only be allowed to speak if he had submitted a copy of his statement to the Chair in advance. This ruling drew sharp criticism from several Members of Parliament, who accused the Deputy Speaker of engaging in pre-censorship and violating democratic and parliamentary norms. The (Deputy) Speaker defended his decision, stating that, as the custodian of the rights and privileges of Parliament, it was his duty to ensure that the statement did not contain anything irrelevant or libellous.[13]

Turning to Dr Ambedkar, the Deputy Speaker continued: "Hon'ble Minister ..." but before he could finish, Dr Ambedkar interjected sharply, asserting that he was no longer a Minister and that he refused to submit to such a dictate. He gathered his papers and stormed out of the House.

***

After the walkout, Dr Ambedkar distributed copies of his statement to newspaper reporters.[14] His statement outlined five key points of disagreement with the Union Cabinet:

---

13 Keer, *Dr Ambedkar: Life and Mission*, p. 435.

14 Full text of the Statement is reproduced in Das Bhagwan, *Thus Spoke Ambedkar: A Stake in the Nation,* Vol 1 (New Delhi: Navayana Publishers, 2011), pp. 117-30. Also available in Jadhav (ed), *Ambedkar Writes*, Vol. I, pp. 470-78.

(1) Despite Prime Minister Jawaharlal Nehru's promise to give him charge of the Planning Department upon his induction into the Cabinet, Dr Ambedkar was kept out of all Cabinet Committees;

(2) General indifference of the Congress Government towards the upliftment of the Scheduled Castes;

(3) Reluctance of the Government to implement a decisive and appropriate solution to the Kashmir issue;

(4) Inappropriate foreign policy of India which created more enemies than friends; and (most importantly),

(5) Pandit Nehru's lukewarm approach towards the Hindu Code Bill.

Dr Ambedkar categorically stated that, while he believed Prime Minister Nehru was sincere, he lacked the necessary determination and urgency to see the Hindu Code Bill through Parliament.

Beyond all these factors leading to the resignation, there was probably an unstated one too: Independent India's first General Elections were approaching and Dr Ambedkar wanted to fight them from his own political party. Nevertheless, it is highly significant that Dr Ambedkar chose to leave the Union Cabinet primarily on the issue of gender equality through the Hindu Code Bill.

The failure of the Hindu Code Bill perhaps made Dr Ambedkar realize that, although the Congress Party had approved the Constitutional framework of Parliamentary democracy, most Congressmen were still not prepared to support progressive, concrete reforms that challenged the social *status quo*. In other words, it was evident that the economic radicalism on display—such as a State-planned and largely State-owned economy—was not yet matched by corresponding social radicalism.

No wonder Dr Ambedkar concluded his statement by asserting that, in terms of significance, "the Hindu Code Bill was the greatest social reform measure ever undertaken in the Legislature in this country." He added that "...to leave inequality between Class and Class, between sex and sex, which is the soul of Hindu society, untouched and to go on passing legislation relating to economic problems, is to make a farce of our Constitution and to build a palace on a dung heap".[15]

★ ★ ★

The first-ever Parliamentary elections of the Indian Republic took place in January 1952. The results were most distressing for Dr Ambedkar. While the Congress Party secured a decisive victory, the SCF won only 2.3 per cent of the valid votes and just two seats in the Lok Sabha (one in the Bombay Presidency and another in Hyderabad).

Dr Ambedkar himself contested from Bombay City North, a two-member Constituency that was to elect both a general and a reserved category candidate. Despite it being considered his stronghold, he lost the Lok Sabha election to Congress candidate Narayan Kajrolkar (who was once a follower of Dr Ambedkar) by around 14,000 votes.

Despite this defeat, Dr Ambedkar was still hopeful of returning to Parliament. He asked his trusted colleagues to reach out to relevant persons and political parties about his interest in the Rajya Sabha. Accordingly, things were "arranged"[16] and Dr Ambedkar was elected to the Rajya Sabha in March 1952.

---

15 As explained by Omvedt in *Ambedkar* (2004), the word "Class" here refers to Caste, as was done frequently at the time. The quote is from Jadhav (ed), *Ambedkar Writes*, Vol. I, pp. 477-78.

16 Keer, *Dr Ambedkar: Life and Mission*, p. 441. It is not clear what those "arrangements" were; was the Congress' support involved? That seems

Still keen on entering the Lok Sabha, Dr Ambedkar contested another election in May 1954 (a by-election in Bhandara, Maharashtra) jointly with Ashok Mehta of the Socialist Party. However, electoral success continued to evade Dr Ambedkar. He narrowly lost the by-election by around 8400 votes to a relatively unknown Congressman called Bhaurao Borkar, described disparagingly as a "seventh class pass".[17]

This defeat was possibly the unkindest blow. The message from the Congress Party to Dr Ambedkar was loud and clear: "All your advanced degrees from the US and the UK do *not* really matter. We can use our brute majority and defeat you even by a faceless virtually illiterate Congressman."

From that point onwards, Dr Ambedkar became increasingly bitter towards the Congress Party, particularly towards Nehru. Dr Ambedkar had a face-to-face meeting with Nehru for the first time in 1939, when Nehru, then Chairman of the War Subcommittee of the Congress Party, visited Mumbai. At the time, Dr Ambedkar reportedly referred to him in private as a "fourth standard boy".[18] That disrespect had apparently now grown into deep disdain.

## Dr Ambedkar vs. Jawaharlal Nehru

Dr Ambedkar's resentment towards the then Prime Minister Jawaharlal Nehru became clearly evident during a discussion in the Rajya Sabha on the "Report of Commissioner for Scheduled

---

most likely, but it is not clear from the available records. According to some unconfirmed reports, Dr Ambedkar's second wife Dr Savita may have played an important role.

17 According to S. Anand, in spite of "reserved seats", "the first-past-post (FPTP) method ensures that those elected are inevitably pliable candidates propped up by parties with majoritarian interests." *Outlook*, 20 August 2012.

18 Keer, *Dr Ambedkar: Life and Mission*, p. 327.

Castes and Tribes for 1953".[19] Among other things, Dr Ambedkar remarked that one of the things which made him deeply sad was that "our Prime Minister has taken no interest in this matter at all. In fact, he seems to be not only apathetic but anti-Untouchable".

He referred to Nehru's biography, in which Nehru castigated Gandhiji "because Mr Gandhi was prepared to die for the purpose of doing away with separate electorates … to the Scheduled Castes" and said, "Why on earth is Mr Gandhi bothering with this trifling problem?"

Dr Ambedkar said, "I was shocked and surprised to hear the Prime Minister—rather Mr Nehru t hen in 1934—uttering these words. I thought that since the responsibility of the Government had fallen on his shoulder he may have changed his view … but I do not find any kind of a change in his mind …"

Dr Ambedkar also recalled that Prime Minister Nehru had publicly rebuked his Cabinet colleague Babu Jagjivan Ram for organizing a conference on the problems of Untouchables (Nagpur, 1952) saying:

> I do not recognize that there is such a problem as that of the Untouchables. There is a general problem of the economically poor and the problem of the Untouchables is a part of that problem. It will take its place and receive its attention along with the other problems. There is no occasion, no purpose in bestowing any special thought upon it….

Dr Ambedkar lamented: "…if the Prime Minister is prepared to throw such cold water…what enthusiasm can we expect from the rest of the [Congress] workers…."

***

19 Speech in Rajya Sabha (6 September 1954). Reproduced in BAWS, Vol. 15, pp. 925-43. All quotes in this section are from the same source.

Dr Ambedkar remained an unyielding critic of the Congress Party, and in turn, they either ignored or dishonoured him.

The climax of Dr Ambedkar's humiliation came in September 1956. On 14 September 1956, just one month before his historic conversion to Buddhism in Nagpur, Dr Ambedkar wrote a letter to Prime Minister Jawaharlal Nehru regarding his book titled *The Buddha and his Dhamma*.[20]

The letter included two copies of a printed booklet summarizing the contents of the book, which Dr Ambedkar had been working on for five years. He explained that the printing cost amounted to Rs 20,000, which was beyond his means, and that he was therefore seeking financial assistance. More specifically, Dr Ambedkar wrote:

> I wonder if the Government of India could purchase about 500 copies for distribution among the various libraries and among the many scholars whom it is inviting during the course of this year for the celebration of the Buddha's 2500 years' anniversary.
>
> I know your interest in Buddhism. That is why I am writing to you. I hope that you will render some help in this matter.

Prime Minister Jawaharlal Nehru responded to Dr Ambedkar's letter the very next day. Here is what he wrote in response:

> I rather doubt if it will be possible for us to buy a large number of copies of your book suggested by you. We had set aside a certain sum for publication on the occasion of the Buddha Jayanti. That sum has been exhausted and, in fact, exceeded … I am, however, sending your letter to Dr Radhakrishnan, the Chairman of the Buddha Jayanti Committee.

---

20 Both, the letter from Dr Ambedkar and Jawaharlal Nehru's response, are available in BAWS, Vol. 17(1), pp. 444-45.

*I might suggest that your book might be on sale in Delhi and elsewhere at the time of the Buddha Jayanti celebrations when many people will come from abroad. It might find a good sale then* [emphasis added].

Dr S. Radhakrishnan promptly called Dr Ambedkar to express his inability to assist in the matter.

***

This incident needs to be placed in proper perspective. Gautam Buddha's 2500th birth anniversary was being celebrated in his home country, India, with grand events planned throughout the year. To oversee the celebrations, a high-powered Committee was formed under the Chairmanship of Dr S. Radhakrishnan, the first Vice President of India.

By that time, Dr Ambedkar was not only a national leader but also a recognized authority on Comparative Religion, particularly Buddhism. Yet, he was excluded from the Committee, *persona non grata* that he was.

Dr Ambedkar was gravely unwell. Perhaps he sensed that he did not have much time left. It was this urgency that led him to hasten the mass conversion to Buddhism that he would soon lead.[21] Over the preceding five years, he had worked tirelessly on his *magnum opus* on Buddhism, completing it just in time. It was for the publication of this work that he sought financial assistance from Jawaharlal Nehru. In fact, such a gesture was entirely out of character for Dr Ambedkar. Yet, the circumstances appear to have compelled him to seek help for publishing the book—a request that was brusquely denied.[22]

---

21 On 14 October 1956, more than 7,00,000 people embraced Buddhism in Nagpur under Dr Ambedkar's leadership.

22 The book was published only posthumously in 1957.

Come to think of it, Rs 20,000 was *not* a large amount of money, even by 1956 standards. It is difficult to believe that the Prime Minister of India was genuinely unable to raise such a paltry sum.

As if turning down the request weren't enough, Nehru went a step further. He reportedly suggested that Dr Ambedkar, the Principal Architect of India's Constitution, could sell his book during the Buddha Jayanti celebrations, when "many people will come to Delhi from abroad"!

If this is not the height of meanness, one wonders what is.

***

After the *Nirvana* of Dr Ambedkar, tributes were paid in both Houses of Parliament. Here is what Prime Minister Jawaharlal Nehru said in Lok Sabha on 6 December 1956:[23]

> Dr Ambedkar ... played a very important part in the making of the Constitution of India,...
>
> He is often spoken of as *one* of the architects of our Constitution. There is no doubt that no one took greater care and trouble over Constitution making than Dr Ambedkar...
>
> But I imagine that the way he will be remembered most will be as a symbol of the revolt against all the oppressive features of Hindu society. *He used language sometimes which hurt people. He sometimes said things which were perhaps not wholly justified. But let us forget that* [emphasis added]. The main thing was that he rebelled against something against which all ought to rebel...
>
> Dr Ambedkar,...became prominent in his own way...I have no doubt that, whether we agree with him or not...that perseverance, that persistence and that...sometime *virulence of his opposition*...did keep the people's mind awake and did not

23 From Sudarshan Agarwal (ed.), *Dr B.R. Ambedkar: The Man and His Message* (Delhi: Prentice-Hall of India, 1991), pp. 208-09.

> allow them to become complacent about matters which could not be forgotten…, It is, … sad that such a prominent champion of the oppressed and depressed in India and one who took such an important part in our activities, has passed away ….

***

Anybody familiar with Nehru's eulogy on Gandhi's untimely death, particularly the iconic line "The light has gone out of our lives" would agree that he was capable of deeply moving, eloquent expression. It was a tribute straight from the heart, full of passion and charged with emotion.

In contrast, Nehru's eulogy for Dr Ambedkar came across as dry and perfunctory, more of a formal obligation than a sincere tribute. It seemed to come not from the heart, but from lingering hurt. Why else would Nehru choose to say, in an obituary speech: "He used language sometimes which hurt people. He sometimes said things which were perhaps not wholly justified," only to add, in a rather patronizing tone, "But let's forget that"?

Isn't it akin to someone mentioning in Gandhiji's obituary that "he was occupied in sexual intercourse in the next room at the precise moment his father breathed his last" or that "after his wife died, he he began the habit of sharing his bed with naked young women, 60 years his junior, to test *his* self-control", and then condescendingly add, "But let's forget that"?

If one truly wants others to forget something about the departed, why mention it at all in the first place, only to say, "let's forget it"? Does that not, in fact, amount to reminding people of it, lest they forget?

One wonders whether Nehru was offering a eulogy or exacting a final act of petty revenge against Dr Ambedkar!

***

The process of undermining Dr Ambedkar's monumental contribution to India continued unabated for decades after his *Nirvana* in 1956.

Traditionally, Indian textbooks are replete with stories of the life and times of Mahatma Gandhi and Jawaharlal Nehru. The pedagogical narrative rightly portrays Gandhiji and Nehru as national leaders, "in prose and poem, skit and song". Regrettably, Dr Ambedkar appears only marginally, if at all. And even when he mentioned, he is almost invariably referred to as the leader of the Untouchables—a Caste leader or champion of the downtrodden—but never as a national leader.

Dr Ambedkar was conferred with the Bharat Ratna posthumously on 31 March 1990, almost 34 years after his *Nirvana*, and only when a non-Congress Government, led by V.P. Singh, was in power. Why did this not happen earlier, during the decades-long rule of the Congress Party? It is not as though the Congress Party was averse to awarding the Bharat Ratna posthumously. Former Tamil Nadu Chief Minister M.G. Ramachandran, for instance, was awarded the honour after his death when Rajiv Gandhi was the Prime Minister (who himself was posthumously awarded the Bharat Ratna within a year of his untimely demise). Nehru received the award in 1955 while serving as Prime Minister, and Indira Gandhi likewise was accorded the great honour during her tenure in office.

The point here is *not* to question why others were awarded the Bharat Ratna; they undoubtedly deserved the honour. The real question is: why was Dr Ambedkar, one of India's most illustrious sons, *not* conferred this honour during the long years the Congress Party was in power?

The disdain the Congress Party has always shown towards Dr Ambedkar hardly needs further proof. Does it?

## Dr Ambedkar vs. Mahatma Gandhi

One cannot imagine how Gandhiji's relationship with Dr Ambedkar might have evolved had Gandhiji not been assassinated in 1948. But it is clear that Gandhiji had forgiven Dr Ambedkar well before his untimely death, perhaps because the world press gave him, rather than Dr Ambedkar, all the credit (April 1947) for abolishing Untouchability in India.[24] On the other hand, Dr Ambedkar never seemed to have forgiven Gandhiji for pressuring him to sign the "Poona Pact" of 1932, which he believed had irreparably damaged the political prospects of the Scheduled Castes and Tribes forever.

Dr Ambedkar's bitterness towards Gandhiji was expressed, quite unambiguously in an interview with the British Broadcasting Corporation (BBC) barely one year before his *Nirvana.* He said:[25]

> …I met Mr Gandhi in the capacity of an opponent, I have the feeling that I know him better than most other people because he had opened his fangs to me and I could see the inside of the man. [Those] who generally went there as devotees…only saw his external appearance which he had put up as a Mahatma. I saw him in his human capacity….
>
> …I must say at the outset that I feel quite surprised at the interest that the outside world, Western world particularly, seems to be taking in Mr Gandhi…. His memory is kept up…. If these artificial respirations were not given, I think Gandhi would have long been forgotten.

In response to a question about whether Gandhiji fundamentally changed anything, Dr Ambedkar said:

24 This has been elaborated in Chapter 15.

25 Recording available at https://www.youtube.com/watch?v=ZJs-BJoSzbo.

> Not at all. All the time he has engaged in double dealings. He conducted papers in two languages: *Harijan*[26*] and *Young India* in English, and *Din Bandhu* (or something like that) in Gujarati. If you read the two papers together, you can see how Mr Gandhi is deceiving the people. In the English paper, he poses himself as an opponent of the Caste system and Untouchability and as a democrat. If you read his Guajarati magazine, you can see him as the most orthodox man…supporting the Caste system, the *Varnashrama dharma* and all orthodox dogmas that have kept India down all through ages…. The people, especially the Western world, only read the English paper, where Mr Gandhi, in order to keep himself in the esteem of the Western people who believe in democracy, is advocating democratic ideals. You have to see what he actually talked to people in the vernacular papers …

Responding to a question about whether Gandhiji was an orthodox Hindu, Dr Ambedkar said: "Gandhi was absolutely an orthodox Hindu. He was never a reformer. He had no dynamics in him [to be one] … Beyond that, I don't think he has any real motive of uplift [of the Untouchables]. He was not like Garrison (William Lloyd Garrison) in the US who fought for the Negroes."

At one point in the interview, Dr Ambedkar offers his "measure of the man": "*He was just a politician, not a Mahatma. I refuse to call him Mahatma. I have never called him Mahatma. He does not deserve that title on the basis of morality…in my judgement, he was an episode in the history of India, never an epoch-maker* [emphasis added]."

26 Note: Harijan was earlier called Young India.

# Epilogue

## Gandhi–Ambedkar Conflict: An Ancient History Perspective

In a significant contribution, Tony Joseph[1] has given an extraordinary twist to the confrontation between Mahatma Gandhi and Dr Ambedkar.

His book *Early Indians*, obviously, is not on the theme of Gandhi-Ambedkar conflict. The book essentially brings together "path-breaking DNA research of recent years" as well as "archaeological and linguistic evidence" to throw fascinating light on the ancestry of modern Indians. Running into Gandhiji and Dr Ambedkar is only one of the many surprises that the book springs up.

The narrative developed in the said book seems to have the following building blocks:

1. Around the time Patanjali wrote *Mahabhasya* (roughly 150 BCE), the definition of *Aryavarta* roughly corresponds to the

---

1 Joseph, *Early Indians*.

North-Central region of India. Outside *Aryavarta* there was the Southwestern-Eastern region called Magadha.

2. In *Aryavarta*, the Brahmins had a prominent social position whereas in Magadha they did not.
3. *Aryavarta* had a "more rigid view of social hierarchy and opposition to mixing between different classes and races". On the other hand, Magadha's ideologies were "more open, freewheeling, progressive and anti-ritualistic".
4. The theory that incoming "Aryans" imposed the Caste system on the population when they arrived in the subcontinent has been proved wrong by genetic evidence.
5. Genetic evidence also shows that between 2200 BCE and 100 CE there was "extensive admixture" between the different Indian populations with the result that almost all Indians had acquired "First Indian, Harappan and Steppe ancestries" though, of course, to varying degrees.
6. The five or six centuries BCE and a couple of centuries into CE would rank as "one of the most creative and progressive periods" in the history of India. The first Indian empire, that of the Mauryas (322–180 BCE), flourished during this period. This period was marked by the emergence of Buddhism and Jainism as well as the composition of the Upanishads.
7. The racial inter-mixing came to an end sometime around 100 CE. Perhaps around that time, a new ideology which gained ground and those who were in power imposed on the society "new social restrictions and a new way of life". It was "social engineering on a scale never attempted before or after, and it succeeded wildly".

The book states: The genetic studies link "the sudden downing of the shutters on (racial) intermixing" to the beginning of the Caste system and goes on to raise a series of questions:

> Could the end of the Maurya Empire (180 BCE) have had anything to do with this change in ideology? Did the defeat of the Mauryas also presage the eventual disappearance of Buddhism from the subcontinent? Did the rapid expansion of the Maurya Empire into the heartland of *Aryavarta* between the fourth and second centuries BCE threaten the Brahmanical ideology, the supremacy of Brahmins and their special relationship with rulers, and could the orthodox (ritualistic) traditions of *Aryavarta* have defeated the anti-ritualistic ideologies of Magadha that had posed a challenge to it?

All these hypotheses in the said book seem to be eminently plausible.

As a matter of fact, Tony Joseph seems to have overlooked a crucial missing link that was provided by Dr Ambedkar himself in one of his two Anthropological books.[2]

In the year 185 BCE, the Buddhist Emperor Brihadratha of the Maurya dynasty was murdered by his Brahmin Commander-in-chief called Pushyamitra Sunga. According to Dr Ambedkar:[3] "It was an epoch-making event. Its significance cannot be measured by treating it simply as a change of dynasty. It was a political revolution as great as the French Revolution, if not greater. It was a bloody

2 Dr Ambedkar's two Anthropological books are: 1) *The Untouchables: Who Were They and Why They Became Untouchables* (1948) and 2) *Who Were the Shudras: How They Came to be the Fourth Varna in the Indo-Aryan Society* (1946). The missing link mentioned here is from the first one.

3 See Jadhav (ed), *Ambedkar Writes*, Vol. II, pp. 140-41.

revolution engineered by the Brahmins to overthrow the rule of the Buddhist Kings."

Dr Ambedkar argues that the *Manusmṛiti* must have come into being after this event in 185 BCE. Why? According to him, for at least two reasons:

> First of all, 'triumphant Brahmanism was needed to make *Chaturvarna* the law of the land, whose validity was denied by the Buddhists. It needed to make animal sacrifice, which was abolished by the Buddhists, legal.'
>
> Secondly, triumphant Brahmanism wanted a sacred text, infallible in its authority, to justify their transgressions. [No wonder] a striking feature of the *Manusmriti* is that it not only makes *Chaturvarna* the law of the land; not only it makes animal sacrifice legal but it goes to state when a Brahmin could justifiably resort to arms, and when he could justifiably kill the king....

According to Dr Ambedkar, it was "a complete departure," "a new thesis." Why should the *Manusmriti* do this? The only answer is that it had to strengthen the revolutionary deeds committed by Pushyamitra by propounding philosophic justification.

It is against this backdrop that one ought to look at the Epilogue of the book *Early Indians.* Among other things, it says:

> That Bhimrao Ambedkar chose Buddhism for himself and his followers when he wanted to challenge still existing inequities in the twentieth century shows how the historical threads of a difference of opinion ... have continued to this day. In this sense, the spectacular ideological confrontation between Mohandas Karamchand Gandhi and Bhimrao Ambedkar too can be seen as a contest between the best of the philosophy of life and society that the conservative *Aryavarta* had to offer and

the best of the rationality and progressivism that Magadha had to offer.

Underlying all this history, there is a steady unfolding of genetical, demographical and, of course, political developments in a continuum, after all…

# Afterword

## by Professor Kevin Brown

I first came to India as American Fulbright Scholar in December of 1996. My initial assignment was at the National Law School of India University in Bengaluru, Karnataka. On the second weekend of my assignment, Professor S. Japhet (who later beccame the Vice Chancellor of Bengaluru Central University) introduced me to the Dalit struggle by taking me to a rally of 80,000 Dalits at a soccer stadium in the coastal city of Mangalore. As I walked into the crowded stadium, the one sign immediately over the speaker's podium struck me, "We Shall Overcome". This was the slogan and title to one of the most revered songs of the Civil Rights Movement of the 1960s. As an African-American child growing up in the 1960s, I would sing that song with my black congregation at our Baptist Church every Sunday. Seeing the sign allowed me instantly to connect to the Dalit struggle in India.

Since that time, I have been a frequent visitor to India in order to interact with Dalit intellectuals, social activists, and political leaders, including leading 13 mostly African-American scholars on a 17-day trip through India in October of 2012 and a three-week trip with a different group of mostly African-American professors in June and July of 2015. Because of those trips and others, I have participated in over a dozen conferences, roundtable discussions and exchanges in India where the principal topic was comparing and contrasting the African-American experience with racial discrimination in the US, to the Dalit experience with caste discrimination based on untouchability in India. I have also spoken at major celebrations of the anniversary of the birth of Dr. Ambedkar in New Delhi, Mumbai, London, and Columbia University in New York City. Indeed, it turns out that if you adjust for the time difference between India and the United States, I was born on October 14, 1956, a date of obvious significance for Ambedkarites and Buddhists in India.

Since that weekend in December of 1996, my desire has been to further an alliance of African-Americans and Dalits. I believe that we can learn so much from each other's struggles. One of the major obstacles to African-Americans fully comprehending the struggles of Dalits in India, however, is the high esteem African-Americans have for who we call "Mahatma Gandhi". Virtually all students of the African-American racial struggle in the United States are familiar with the embrace by Reverend Martin Luther King, Jr. of Gandhi's advocacy of non-violence, "Satyagraha". King learned of Gandhi as a student at Crozer Theological Seminary in 1949, which he attended after graduating from Morehouse College at age 19. However, even before King arrived at Morehouse, Gandhi was already a revered figure in the African-American Community.

Since Africans walked off the first slave ship and into the Jamestown colony of Virginia in 1619, we have come face-to-face with attitudes, opinions, theories, customs, social practices and laws designed to restrict or confine our social, religious, political, economic, and educational rights and opportunities. The discriminatory practices and policies that African-Americans have faced in the US were "justified" by rationales generated by the dominant white community that started with their presumed superiority and our presumed inferiority. However, against the background of 400 years of racial domination, the descendants of the sons and daughters of the soil of Africa in the United States and those non-blacks sympathetic to our pursuit of racial equality formulated a counter discourse. This alternative pattern of understanding the black racial experience rejected the notion that there was something wrong with us that explained our degraded condition. Instead, we built our counter discourse upon the firm conviction that we were oppressed, not inferior. Thus, the central feature of the African-American counter discourse was, is, and, perhaps, always will be dedicated to the resistance of black people in the US to our racial subordination and the liberation of black people from racial oppression. As James Forman stated about the African American experience, "our basic history is one of resistance."

Professor Henry J Richardson, III, who has been called the "Father of Black International Tradition," noted that the African-American counter discourse always contained an international tradition. What the African-American Community knows, but seldom truly appreciates, is that once our international tradition shifted to an analogy of the condition of blacks in the US to a place other than Africa, it shifted to the Indian subcontinent. Drawing analogies between the liberation struggles of blacks in the US with those on the Indian subcontinent did not start with King borrowing from Gandhi. It started with abolitionists in the 1830s comparing African-American subordination to oppression on the Indian subcontinent resulting from the caste system.

Abolitionists, including Frederick Douglass, Robert Morris, William Lloyd Garrison, and Charles Sumner, used the caste analogy not only to critique slavery but also to highlight the discriminatory treatment that free blacks encountered in the North.

The comparison of the oppression of blacks to caste remained one of the primary ways for both the black and white communities in the US to think about race discrimination up to the end of the 19th Century and the early part of the 20th Century. The best examples of the use of the caste analogy by proponents of racial equality included the following:

- The attorneys representing the black schoolchild, Sarah Roberts. The case of *Roberts v Boston* was the first school desegregation case in US history. Sarah's father sought to enroll her in the white-only school closest to her home in the City of Boston in the 1840s. The attorneys for Sarah employed the caste analogy to argue that racially segregated schools violated the Constitution of the State of Massachusetts.
- The first federal anti-discrimination statute enacted by Congress was the Civil Rights Act of 1866. It was adopted one year after the end of the US Civil War and just four months after the ratification of the 13th Amendment, which abolished slavery. This Act was passed at the height of the time when commentators compared and contrasted the treatment of blacks to the Indian caste system. Thus, several Congressmen specifically referred to the caste system while advocating for the passage of the Act.
- The same Congress that enacted the Civil Rights Act of 1866, two months later passed the 14th Amendment to the US Constitution and sent it to the states for ratification. Many of the proponents for the ratification of the 14th Amendment, which was added in 1868, used the caste analogy. Section 1 of the Amendment made blacks citizens of the US and the state in which they resided. This Section also guaranteed to individuals due process of law, equal protection of the

laws, and forbid any state from making or enforcing any law that abridged the privileges or immunities of any citizen of the US. Many supporters of the 14th Amendment asserted that its purpose was to eradicate the functioning of caste in the US.

- Black activists invoked the caste analogy in their legal arguments on behalf of Homer Plessy in the infamous 1896 US Supreme Court case *Plessy v Ferguson*. This was the case in which the Court gave legal sanction to the doctrine of "separate but equal" that helped spawn Jim Crow legislation. Plessy lost the case in an 8 to 1 decision by the US Supreme Court. Yet, accepting the arguments of the plaintiffs, Justice Harlan wrote a separate opinion as the lone dissenter from the Court's decision. In what may very well be the most famous passage from any legal opinion in all of American history, Justice Harlan wrote "...in view of the constitution, in the eye of the law, there is in this country no superior, dominant, ruling class of citizens. ***There is no caste here.*** **Our constitution is color-blind, and neither knows nor tolerates classes among citizens"** (emphasis added).
- Even the most significant civil rights organization in the history of the US, the National Association for the Advancement of Colored People (NAACP), employed the caste analogy in its original charter adopted in 1911. Stating its core objectives, the NAACP stated: "To promote equality of rights and to eradicate caste or race prejudice among the citizens of the United States; . . ."

Throughout the 19th Century and into the early 20th Century, the caste-analogy would remain central to the argument that the treatment of blacks was illogical, immoral, unchristian-like, and unjust. While the caste analogy has continued in importance up to the present day, as the 19 century ended, blacks were focusing more attention on international issues in the aftermath of the Scramble for Africa in the 1880s and the Spanish-American War of 1898. African-Americans increasingly stressed an international perspective that viewed world affairs as mediated by the importance of the role of race and racism. This new black international perspective drew connections between the discrimination that African-Americans encountered domestically with that suffered by other people of colour because of the expansion of European and American imperialism. Because of this emerging point of view, African-Americans came increasingly to view their struggle against segregation and its various attendant components of disenfranchisement of black voters, legal segregation, job discrimination, and educational disparities, as a local struggle that was part of a global struggle of people of color against white supremacy.

The precipitating event for this new perspective was the 1905 military defeat of Russia by Japan. Although Japan won the decisive battle at sea, at the time, Russia had the largest army in the world. Within months of Japan's victory, legendary black intellectual W. E. B. Du Bois would enthusiastically write:

> [F]or the first time in a thousand years a great white nation has measured arms with a colored nation and has been found wanting. The Russo-Japanese war has marked an epoch. The magic of the word "white" is already broken and the Color Line in civilization has been crossed in modern times as it was in the great past. The awakening of the yellow races is certain. That the awakening of the brown and black races will follow in time, no unprejudiced student of history can doubt. Shall the awakening of these sleepy millions be in accordance with, and aided by, the great ideals of white civilization or in spite of them and against them? This is the problem of the Color Line.

In the aftermath of the Japanese victory over Russia, black commentators became more aware of the efforts of Indian Freedom Fighters pursuing independence from British colonial rule. Several important Indian nationalists came to the US, in part to educate the Black community about their struggle for independence, including Kumar Gohsal and Haridas Muzumdar. Indian intellectual and freedom fighter Lajpat Rai, known as the "Lion of the Punjab," deserves special attention. He visited the US in 1905 and again from December 1914 to December 1919. Touring the country, Rai made a point of studying the American racial situation. He became personally acquainted with Booker T. Washington, John Hope (the first African-descended president of Morehouse College and later Atlanta University), and Mary Ovington. As a member of Arya Samaj, Rai condemned untouchability and rejected caste based on birth. Rai also developed a close friendship with Du Bois, primarily based on the notion of analogizing Indian independence and black equality. Du Bois would even go on to dedicate to Rai his 1928 novel *Dark Princess*, which is an allegorical story about a Hindu princess who weds an African-American man to unite black and brown people. Up to the point of meeting Rai, Du Bois had not devoted much attention to the anti-colonial struggles on the Indian subcontinent.

For the Black Community, the struggle of the Indian Freedom Fighters fit nicely into the emerging concept of a global fight of people of color against white supremacy, or as Nico Slate calls it "color cosmopolitanism". Conditioned by its long use of the caste analogy, as renowned black historian, Gerald Horne put it, "The question of 'untouchables' was the hallmark of relations between Black America and India …." Ambedkar, however, was rarely mentioned by the Black Press. *Gandhi, Nehru and Ambedkar vs. Dr Ambedkar* is a terrific book because it fills the vacuum in the African-American understanding of the Dalit struggle that the lack of knowledge about Ambedkar and his leadership of the Dalit Community has created.

Most African-American leaders at the time believed that the Indian Freedom Fighters were seeking a dual victory, overcoming white supremacy and eradicating the curse of untouchability. For African-Americans, the dual victory made the cause of Indian independence an incredibly noble one. By supporting it, African-Americans were not only backing a fight against white supremacy, but also the eradication of one of the most extreme forms of oppression that the world has ever known. As a result, even black leaders who opposed each other, like the Jamaican Marcus Garvey and W. E. B. Du Bois, increasingly analogized the African-American struggle against white supremacy in the form of segregation to the struggle of the Indian independence movement against white supremacy in the form of British colonialism.

Gandhi became the focal point of the dual victory. The Black Press often pointed to Gandhi's commitment to abolish untouchability, and Gandhi communicated his point of view about the African-American Community to them through the Black Press. For example, Marcus Garvey's organization, the United Negro Improvement Association, which was the largest mass movement organization of the African-American Community ever, produced a magazine titled the *Negro World*. The *Negro World* published a brief statement by Gandhi on the front page of its May 31, 1924 edition. The first line of Gandhi's statement was "Removal of the curse of untouchability among Hindus." *The Crisis* magazine may be the most influential black magazine of all time. It is the official publication of the NAACP. However, it was under the editorial control of Du Bois, as its founding editor, from 1910 until 1934. In July 1929, *The Crisis* published a message from Gandhi entitled "To the American Negro". In the message he urged the 12 million Negroes not to be ashamed of being the grandchildren of slaves and that there was no dishonor in being slaves, the dishonor was in being slave owners. The Black Press also continued to point out how Gandhi abhorred the treatment of the untouchables. While the Black Press did not cover Dr. Ambedkar leading the temple entry agitation at the Kala Ram Temple at Nashik, it did cover the Gandhi led 240-mile Salt March that occurred at the same time.

Even the coverage by the Black Press of the Round Table Conferences highlighted Gandhi as the spokesperson for the Dalits. The British government held the first one from November 1930 to January 1931 and invited Dr. Ambedkar to attend to represent the Dalits. Ambedkar's participation at this Conference was one of the few times that *The Crisis* magazine mentioned him by name. In the January 31, 1931 edition, Du Bois wrote:

> There is the splendor of India in London. Prince and Untouchable, Muslim and Hindu, all standing shoulder to shoulder, when England counted upon disunion and mutual jealousies and hatreds to perpetuate her tyranny in India. That was a splendid speech of Mr. Ambedkar. He said when the British came to India 150 years ago, "We were in a loathsome condition. We could not draw water at the village wells; we could not enter a temple; we could not serve on the police force; we could not serve in the army." And what happened, he said. Nothing. We are just as badly off now as we were before the English came. It was precisely what the English planned. From no country which they dominate do they propose to remove the internal friction which helps to keep it in subjection. Magnificent India, to reveal to the world the inner rottenness of European imperialism. Such a country not only deserves to be free, it will be free.

In the above selection, Du Bois is making several points about Indian independence accepted by most black leaders who supported Gandhi and the independence struggle. First, Du Bois pointed out that for the Indian Freedom Fighters, uniting the different Indian factions who demand independence from the British rule furthered their struggle. Second, the British were no friends of the Dalits; after all, Ambedkar himself stated that their condition did not improve under British domination. Third, the British imperialist only wanted to use the Dalits to divide the Indian people into a number of factions that were in conflict with each other and, thus, weaken the Indian independence movement.

While there were dissenting views by black commentators, especially from George Schuyler, as the 1930s progressed, it was "not uncommon for African-American journals and newspapers to present Gandhi to their readers as one of the foremost sages and seers of human history". The Black Press compared Gandhi to the Buddha, Mohammed, and Jesus Christ and lauded his moral leadership in world affairs. William Pickens, who was a founding member of the Niagara Movement, which the NAACP later absorbed, and field secretary of the NAACP, wrote an article in the September 1931 issue of *The New York Amsterdam News* that was complimentary of Gandhi. In it, Pickens stated that Gandhi was "the greatest man of the world and the age". In his syndicated column of October 28, 1931, which was during the Second RTC, Du Bois praised how Gandhi conducted himself in London. Du Bois noted that Gandhi refused the social attention and great dinners that the British gentry normally showered on visitors whom they wish to impress. Instead, Gandhi chose to go to the poverty-stricken East End of London and stay in a simple settlement house.

Perhaps the place where Gandhi's positive reputation within the African-American Community became sealed was during the events that led to the Poona Pact. During the Second RTC,

Gandhi and Ambedkar clashed over who truly represented the Dalits. The African-American press, however, did not cover this dispute regarding who spoke for the Dalits. In light of the failure of the Second RTC to reach an agreement, on August 16, 1932, the British Prime Minister Ramsay MacDonald announced a plan for providing India with more self-government. The plan divided elected representatives into those selected from general voter rolls and those that separate communities would elect from voter rolls composed of only voters from their respective communities. Thus, the Prime Minister's plan also included communal awards for Dalits, Indian Christians, Anglo-Indians, and Europeans as well as to Muslims and Sikhs. And, Dalits would also be allowed to vote in the general election for those legislators determined by the general voters roll. Gandhi objected bitterly to the communal award for Dalits, but not the other groups. On September 18, 1932, Gandhi announced he was going on a hunger strike to death to prevent the communal awards for Dalits. Ambedkar was reluctant to give up this political power bestowed upon Dalits by the British. But the pressure put on Ambedkar, including threats and physical retaliation by caste Hindus against Dalits, forced Ambedkar to come to the Poona Pact compromise with Gandhi.

A sharp contrast exists between the views of many modern-day Dalit activists that follow Ambedkar regarding Gandhi's fast and how the Black Press in the US portrayed the fast. For example, the black-owned *Washington Tribune* stated, "The dramatic 'Fast Unto Death' undertaken by Gandhi on behalf of India's 'forgotten men', the 60,000,000 untouchables, came to an end Monday evening with the British and Indian governments approving settlement of the Hindu problem." Wendell P. Dabney, editor of the *Cincinnati Union,* said, "The starving Gandhi (sic) shows the world the greatness, grandeur, sincerity of his soul! Shows in all its pristine purity, a humanitarianism that has not flowered since Jesus died." In an article in the November 1932 issue of *The Crisis*, Du Bois stated the purpose of Gandhi's fast was to force His Majesty's government to reach an agreement with all Hindus of all castes that would lead to the termination of control by the British and would not strengthen the caste barriers in India.

In the aftermath of Gandhi's popularity, African-American leaders who came to India sought a very valuable audience with him. Such a visit added to their stature in the Black Community. The African-Americans who came to India were no ordinary leaders. In February 1936, Howard Thurman met with Gandhi. Thurman has been called "a teacher of teachers, a preacher of preachers, an activator of activists, and a mover of movers". He was a spiritual guide to legendary civil rights leaders of the 1960s and beyond such as James Farmer, Marion Wright Edelman, Bayard Rustin, and Jesse Jackson. At the time when Thurman visited India, he was a professor of religion at Howard University. Founded in Washington D.C. shortly after the Civil War, by the 1930s, Howard was the most prestigious historically black university in the country. Thurman was also a graduate of Morehouse College and would later have a joint appointment as a professor of religion and philosophy there and at Spellman Colleg, both of which are in Atlanta, Georgia. The Black Community also considers both Morehouse and Spellman, along with Howard, to be among the most respected historically black colleges in the country even today. These three universities are Yale, Harvard and Columbia.

Accompanying Thurman on his journey to India were his wife, Sue Bailey, who would become influential in her own right as the first editor of the National Council of Negro Women's *Aframerica Women's Journal*. The other two members of Thurman's group were Reverend Edward Carroll—the son of a Methodist minister, a graduate of Morgan State University, another historically black university, and the Yale Divinity School—and his wife, Phenola. Carroll would go on to become a Bishop of the United Methodist Church.

In late 1936, Gandhi hosted a visit with Channing Tobias and Benjamin Mays. Tobias eventually became the Chairman of the NAACP and an appointee of President Harry S. Truman to the President's Committee on Civil Rights. At the time that Mays met Gandhi, he was the Dean of the School of Religion at Howard University, a position later offered to and turned down by Martin Luther King Jr. Mays would go on to serve as the long-time President of Morehouse College from 1940 to 1967. During that time, Mays taught and mentored many influential civil rights leaders of the 1960s and beyond, including Julian Bond and Maynard Jackson. Mays was also one of King's mentors and would eventually give King's eulogy at his 1968 funeral.

Gandhi confirmed his commitment to eradicating untouchability to Thurman's group. They came away from their meetings with Gandhi very impressed. According to Homer Jack, the Thurmans were so enamored with Gandhi that they asked him to come to the United States "not for White America, but for the Negroes," pleading, "[W]e have many a problem that cries for solution, and we need you badly." Gandhi also confirmed his commitment to end untouchability with Mays and Tobias. According to Mays,

> Gandhi condemned caste as it was practiced and that he himself recognized no caste in his evaluation of people. Certainly, Gandhi condemned the hard, rigid lines that had developed among the various castes in India, where by one caste had no social concern for anyone outside its own group. Essentially, however, Mahatma Gandhi thought that caste was not an evil in itself. Caste does not give status, he believed, but the untouchable had no status and no rights which any caste man was bound to respect. All caste men could with impunity step on and spit upon the untouchable. So, Gandhi had cast his lot with the man farthest down, the untouchable.

The concern that African-American leaders had about the Indian independence struggle would continue to grow up to World War II. With the outbreak of hostilities in World War II, the support for Indian independence by leaders in the African-American Community intensified. For example, A. Phillip Randolph asserted that blacks should support Indian independence, because their struggle was connected to the black cause in the US. Executive Director of the NAACP, Walter White, sought to use the opportunity of the World War II to press American politicians to form an alliance with Indian Freedom Fighters. As White saw it, with America joining the Allies fighting against Hitler's Germany, the Allies were waging a war against white supremacy in the form of Aryan Supremacy, while the US practiced white supremacy in the form of segregation of blacks; and the British practiced Anglo supremacy in the form of colonialism in India. In order to address this hypocrisy, White envisioned an American mission sent by President Roosevelt to the British to help push for Indian independence. The mission would include an African-American representative. To start it off, Roosevelt would take a sweeping stand against discrimination based on race in the US. The members of the mission would urge the British to commit to Indian independence after the war as a way for the British to take a stand against Anglo Supremacy. White shared this plan with several prominent black leaders in the US, including Du Bois, Randolph, Roy Wilkens, and William Hastie, as well as eminent author Peal S. Buck and 1940 Republican Party presidential nominee Wendell Willkie. White sent a copy of his proposal to President Roosevelt. While unable to convince the Roosevelt administration to send such a delegation, White's plan reveals how committed African-American leaders were to the Indian Freedom Fighters.

More than 70 years have now elapsed since India's independence and its adoption of a Constitution that sought to abolish untouchability. For African-Americans, the US Supreme Court's 1954 decision in *Brown v Board of Education*, that struck down statutes segregating public school students and initiated the Desegregation Era in the US, occurred over 65 years ago. The passage of that time allows the African-American Community to reassess its relationship to oppression on the Indian subcontinent. To begin with, it is obvious that even though India obtained independence, it did not eliminate the oppression that Dalits encountered due to untouchability. Thus, the dual victory upon which the African-American relationship to the Indian independence struggle was based upon did not occur. Nor is an independent India engaged in a fight against white supremacy in ways that it was during the time of the British Raj. As a result, the basis of the connection between the African-American Community and India forged during early decades of the Twentieth Century no longer exists. No event dramatizes that reality for African-Americans more than the reception that President Donald Trump received during his state visit to India in February of 2020. He kicked off his travels to the second most populous country in the world with a massive enthusiastic rally attended by 100,000–125,000 people in the world's largest cricket stadium. Yet, Donald Trump is a very unpopular figure in the Black Community. One need only look to polling data from the 2016 Presidential election where Trump only received 8 percent of the black vote and the 2020 election where he only received 12 percent.

Now is an appropriate time for the African-American Community to revisit its historical embrace of the caste analogy and use it as a basis in which to foster closer ties with the Dalit Community's struggle against caste oppression. Under the caste analogy, the natural allies for blacks in the US are Dalits in India. I recognize that the first lesson of any transnational comparison of the struggle against racial oppression of blacks in the US with caste oppression based on untouchability in India is that all oppression is local. Oppression depends upon the history of a specified group in a particular locale at a given time. Thus, a solution to a given social problem that works at one time in one place within a given cultural context does not necessarily work somewhere else. No one can deny that the history and cultures of the United States are vastly different from those of India. Blacks in the US are struggling for liberation by responding to the unique circumstances and situations affecting them, while Dalits are doing the same in India. This means that experiences of discrimination, oppression, and subordination of African-Americans are qualitatively different from those of Dalits. Nevertheless, from my long association with the Dalit struggle, I can say with firm conviction that there are a number of very significant benefits that those committed to African-American liberation can derive from engaging in transnational comparisons and dialogues about the nature of these two different forms of oppression our peoples encounter. For Dalits it is the same. No doubt, some of the benefits of this alliance may occur to both groups, but due to the differences in the socially constructed nature of each group's oppression, it is critical to note that the benefits will be unique to each group. Indeed, it could very well mean that a strategy, policy, or approach that will advance the interest of African-Americans in the United States may harm the interest of Dalits in India. The reverse could also be true.

**Kevin Brown**
Mitchell S. Willoughby Distinguished Professor,
Joseph F. Rice School of Law, University of South Carolina;
Richard S. Melvin Professor Emeritus,
Indiana University Maurer School of Law
Bloomington, Indiana, USA

# References

Agarwal, Sudarshan, ed. *Dr B.R. Ambedkar: The Man and His Message. A Commemorative Volume*. Delhi: Prentice-Hall of India, 1991.

Ambedkar, Dr Babasaheb. *Writings and Speeches* (BAWS) Vol.1–22. Mumbai: Government of Maharashtra, 1979–2012.

Anand, S. "B.R. Ambedkar Greater than Nehru?" *Outlook,* 12 August 2012.

Burke, Edmund. *Reflections on the Revolution in France*. London: James Dodsley, 1790.

Chandra, Bipan. *History of Modern India*. Hyderabad: Orient Blackswan, 2009.

Constituent Assembly Debates: Vol. 1–12, New Delhi: Government of India, 1946–1950.

Das, Bhagwan. ed. *Thus Spoke Ambedkar* Vol. 1-3. Lucknow: Dalit Today Prakashan; New Delhi: Samyak Prakashan, 1969-79.

Desai, Mahadev. *The Diary of Mahadev Desai* Vol. 1. Mumbai: Navajivan Publishing House, 1953.

Durant, Will. *The Story of Philosophy*. New York: Simon & Schuster, 1926.

Gaikwad, S.M. "Ambedkar and Indian Nationalism". *Economic and Political Weekly* XXXIII, no. 10 (7 March 1998).

Gandhi, M.K. *An Autobiography or The Story of My Experiments with Truth*. Translated by Mahadev Desai. New Delhi: General Press, 1940.

Gandhi, Mahatma. "Dr Ambedkar's Indictment". *Harijan*, 18 July 1936.

———. "Varna Venus Caste". *Harijan*, 15 August 1936.

Gore, M.S. *The Social Context of an Ideology: Ambedkar's Political and Social Thought*. New Delhi: Sage Publications, 1993.

Guha, Ramachandra. *Gandhi Before India*. Gurugram: Penguin Random House, 2016.

Jadhav, Narendra, ed. *Ambedkar Speaks* Vol. 1–3. New Delhi: Konark Publishers, 2013a.

——— *Ambedkar Writes* Vol. 1–2. New Delhi: Konark Publishers, 2013b.

——— *Ambedkar: Awakening India's Social Conscience*. New Delhi: Konark Publishers, 2014.

——— *Ambedkar: An Economist Extraordinaire*. New Delhi: Konark Publishers, 2015.

——— "India and the United States: Caste, Race, and Economic Growth". Sixth Annual Patrick O'Meara International Lecture at Indiana University Bloomington, 14 November 2016.

Jaffrelot, Christophe. *Dr Ambedkar and Untouchability: Analyzing and Fighting Caste: Fighting the Indian Caste System*. London: Hurst and Company, 2000.

Joseph, Tony. *Early Indians: The Story of Our Ancestors and Where We Came From*. New Delhi: Juggernaut Books, 2018.

Kamble, B.C. *Samagra Ambedkar Charitra Khand* Vol.1–24 (Marathi). Pune: Sugava Prakashan, 1984–2008 (Reprint).

Khabde, D.T. PhD diss. Dr Babasaheb Ambedkar Marathwada University, 1985. https://shodhganga.inflibnet.ac.in

Khairmode, C.B. *Dr Bhimrao Ramji Ambedkar Chandra Granth* Vol.1–12 (Marathi). Pune: Sugava Prakashan, 1984–2008 (Reprint).

Keer, Dhananjay. *Dr Ambedkar: Life and Mission*. Bombay: Popular Prakashan, 1954.

Lancaster, Lane W. *Masters of Political Thought: Hegel to Dewey*, Vol. 3. London: George G. Harrap and Co Ltd, 1959.

Laski, H. *A Grammar of Politics*. London: George Allen and Unwin Ltd, 1925.

Lelyveld, Joseph, *Great Soul: Mahatma Gandhi and His Struggle With India*. Delhi: Harper Collins Publishers and the India Today Group, 2011.

McCutcheon, Richard. "The Impact of the Jallianwala Bagh Massacre on Gandhi". PhD diss. McMaster University, 1989. Available from http://hdl.handle.net/11375/11927

Mehta, M. "Gandhi and Ahmedabad, 1915-20". *Economic and Political Weekly* 40, no. 4 (22 January 2005).

Omvedt, Gail. *Ambedkar: Towards an Enlightened India*. Delhi: Penguin, 2004.

*Outlook*. Various articles. Special Independence Day Issue, 20 August 2012.

Power, P.F. "Gandhi in South Africa". *The Journal of Modern African Studies* 7, no. 3 (1969).

Prasad, R. *Satyagraha in Champaran*. Ahmedabad: Navajivan Publishing House, 1949.

Pyarelal. *The Epic Fast*. Ahmedabad: Mohanlal Maganlal Bhatt, 1932.

Rajasekhariah, A.M. *B.R. Ambedkar: The Politics of Emancipation*. Bombay: Sindhu Publications, 1971.

Rodrigues, Valerian, ed. *The Essential Writings of B.R. Ambedkar.* New Death: Oxford University Press, 2002.

Roy, B., ed. *Gandhi's Campaign Against Untouchability, 1933–34: An Account from the Raj's Secret Official Reports.* New Delhi: Gandhi Peace Foundation, 1996.

Sethi, Pravat Ranjan. "Gandhi and the Jallianwala Bagh Massacre and Beyond". *Mainstream Weekly* LVII, no. 18 (2019). https://www.mainstreamweekly.net/article8659.html (accessed on 22 July 2020).

Shanker, Rajkumari. *The Story of Gandhi*. Delhi: Children's Book Trust, 1969. https://www.mkgandhi.org/ebks/The%20Story%20of%20Gandhi.pdf

Shraff, Anne. *Mahatma Gandhi* (20th Century Biographies). California: Saddleback Educational Publishing, 2008.

Shourie, Arun. *Worshipping False Gods: Ambedkar, and the Facts Which Have Been Erased.* New Delhi: ASA Publications, 1997.

Som, Reba. "Jawaharlal Nehru and the Hindu Code: A Victory of Symbol over Substance?" *Modern Asian Studies* 28 no. 1 (February 1994): pp. 185–87.

Sorokin, Pitirim. *The Ways and Power of Love*. West Conshohocken, PA: Templeton Press. 2002.

Tendulkar, D.G. *Mahatma: Life of Mohandas Karamchand Gandhi.* Bombay: Vithalbhai K. Jhaveri, 1951.

Todd, A.M. *Mohandas Gandhi*. New York: Infobase Publishing. 2004.

Verma, Vidhu. "Colonialism and Liberation: Ambedkar's Quest for Distributive Justice". *Economic and Political Weekly* 34, no. 39 (25 September – 1 October 1999): pp. 2804–10.

Vundru, Raja Sekhar. "The Other Father". *Outlook,* 20 August 2012.

Weber, Thomas. *Gandhi as Disciple and Mentor*. New York: Cambridge University Press, 2004.

Zelliot, Eleanor. *From Untouchable to Dalit: Essays on the Ambedkar Movement.* New Delhi: Manohar, 1992.

# Index

# About the Author

**DR NARENDRA JADHAV** is a multi-faceted professional, renowned as an Economist, Educationist, Academic, Administrator and Author (in English, Marathi and Hindi). He has also taken on the roles of a web series producer and a podcaster.

Until April 2022, Dr Jadhav served as a Member of Parliament in the Rajya Sabha (nominated by the President of India). As an independent MP, Dr Jadhav carved out a distinct place for himself through his studious interventions in Parliament, setting new standards of excellence for nominated MPs.

Currently, Dr Jadhav is producing a comprehensive web series on the Indian Constitution, spanning nearly 60 hours, featuring insights from 35 MPs, 20 Judges (both from the Supreme Court and High Courts) and other top legal luminaries. He also hosts an audio-visual podcast series on Dr Ambedkar titled "Bhim Bhashya" on his YouTube channel "Dr Narendra Jadhav World".

Dr Jadhav serves as an Independent Director for five corporates, including two from the Tata Group, and Jain Irrigation Systems

Ltd. He is also a Member of the Governing Council/Advisory Council of several Universities. For the past eight years, Dr Jadhav has been serving as a Visiting Professor simultaneously at four universities, including Ashoka University.

With a PhD in Economics from Indiana University, USA, Dr Jadhav has had an illustrious career spanning nearly five decades in public service. Some of the distinguished positions he has held include: Member of the Planning Commission; Member of the National Advisory Council; Vice-Chancellor of Savitribai Phule Pune University; Adviser at the International Monetary Fund; Chief Economist at the Reserve Bank of India and Advisor to the central banks of Afghanistan and Ethiopia. Dr Jadhav also chaired the Advisory Committee on RBI History: Volume V (1977–2007).

Dr Narendra Jadhav is a prolific writer, having authored or edited 47 books: 23 in English, 15 in Marathi and 9 in Hindi. He has also contributed 34 official reports on various public policy issues and published around 200 research papers and articles. His family biography *Untouchables* (Simon and Schuster, USA) is an international bestseller, translated into 15 languages, including French, Spanish, Korean and Thai. Its Marathi original, *Aamcha Baap Aan Amhi,* achieved unprecedented success with 200 editions and earned a Sahitya Akademi Award for its Punjabi version.

A celebrated public figure, Dr Jadhav is the recipient of 75 national and international awards for his contribution to the fields of Economics, Education, Literature and Social Work. These include four Honorary D.Litt. degrees and the title of "Commander of the Order of Academic Palmes", conferred by the Government of France.